BETTER SURE THAN SORRY

AN EXPLORATION OF TRANSGENDER PSYCHOLOGY THAT AIMS TO REDUCE THE RISK OF GENDER TRANSITION REGRET

Dr. Raj Pathagoerer

ShieldCrest Publishing

ISBN: 978-1-913839-92-5

MMXXII

A CIP catalogue record for this book
is available from the British Library.

Published by
ShieldCrest Publishing,
Boston, Lincolnshire,
PE20 3BT England
Tel: +44 (0) 333 8000 890
www.shieldcrest.co.uk

ACKNOWLEDGEMENTS AND APPRECIATION

The phrase, "Better sure than sorry" was used by two important people in my life:

Firstly, by my father - it was one of his favourite forms of advice to me.

Secondly, by my most significant medical tutor who was remarkably fastidious and told me this cautionary phrase in relation to treating patients - particularly regarding drug doses and side effects and then doubly weighing up *the whole* of a medical situation before starting treatment.

Gratitude also to my late mentor in psychiatry. A most charming Indian gentleman of the old school whom I miss very much and with great sadness.

Of course, appreciation is given to my loved ones whom I neglected whilst writing.

The best teachers are the patients themselves. I am grateful to you for sharing extremely personal and delicate matters - I will of course never identify you. May you make the best of your personal, emotional and sexual lives no matter how you choose to express your gender identity and sexual orientation.

My fullest acknowledgement and gratitude to authors on transgender related subjects whose works I read in order to try and help the increasing number of transgender patients being seen in a clinical setting. Their concepts, insights and wisdom have been highly illuminating and helpful in both clinical practice and in providing much material for this book. Please see the bibliography at the rear of the book. The examples of the complex and deep psychosexual matters referred to in this book are from my former patients supplemented by those from the references in the bibliography.

Please can we all discuss this important matter for the benefit of anyone who feels that they might be transgender. This will also help psychological and medical staff to do their very best for their patients but at the same time to safeguard them.

Contents

A BOOK THAT WILL HOPEFULLY HELP TRANSGENDER AND CISGENDER PEOPLE COME TO A BETTER UNDERSTANDING OF EACH OTHER - *PLEASE DO NOT SKIP THIS CHAPTER*

The author spent his entire working life in medical practice. Having retired from his work in psychiatry and other areas, he now wishes to reflect on the human pain and suffering he has seen in the social, psychological and medical aspects of people's lives.

If transgender choices help someone to get the very best out of their life, this is clearly a very good thing. This book is an attempt to provide an understanding of transgender feelings to try to reduce the risk of gender transition regret - for the purposes of safeguarding. The author is also very aware of the importance of safeguarding the rights of LGBTQIA+ people.

When looking back on his life the author can admit to himself that the younger he was, the more prone he was to making mistakes in many aspects of his existence - what seemed to be a good life choice at the time sometimes turned out to be disastrous. He looks back regretfully on how he could have done many things much better. He also looks back with humility and remorse about how he could have related to people in much better ways. Sometimes it is only possible to improve oneself after gaining enough life experience - the author had to reach old age to learn from some of his personal mistakes. It is this personal experience that makes him plea for caution in relation to medical gender transition treatments for younger people. Who hasn't had the feeling of wanting and wanting and wanting something - but on getting it realised it wasn't what you really wanted? Please consider two examples at opposite ends of the scale. Many women with beautiful long hair keep thinking and thinking of having it cut really short - but only on doing so do they realise it's a

1

mistake. Tragically, there is a bridge in America, which is known as "suicide bridge". This is the Golden Gate Bridge in San Francisco - it has the second highest suicide rate in the world after the Nanjing Yangtze River Bridge in China. A number of people who jumped actually survived and many of them said that they had contemplated suicide for months and were sure about their decision - but once their feet left the bridge they regretted it. This was particularly the case for those who made an impulsive jump after a spur of the moment decision.

At present there is an unfortunate and uncomfortable "war" between those who are strongly pro-gender transition and those who are particularly sceptical about transgender matters. This is unpleasant for all concerned and helps no one. As a spokesperson said, "Transgender is here to stay" and it would be helpful if an understanding and an accommodation of everyone's viewpoints can be achieved - no matter what those viewpoints may be so that everyone can get along. We have one life on this Earth and we all need to make the best of it - we may not agree but we can take a look and understand and respect each other's point of view. We would be better off engaging in each other's humanity rather than focusing on our disagreements about gender theory - please!

This book was written by a retired doctor who regards himself as a Straight LGBTQIA+ Ally and was written with conciliation, cooperation and understanding between transgender and cisgender people in mind. It was hoped that providing an understanding of relevant mind processes would be helpful for all.

For example, if we can understand what goes on in the mind of an anxious or depressed person it can help us to understand them and the difficulties they face. Likewise, if we can understand the difficulties any minority group experiences we can also be more accommodating. In other words, we can all have a greater compassion for each other if we can appreciate another person's situation. To aid us in this respect some of the difficulties that transgender people might experience will be explored. Whether you are transgender or cisgender we're all in this world together, struggling through life - trying to make the best of it.

For some people full gender transition is the very best thing but if it's a mistake it can be the very worst choice.

The text of the book may be uncomfortable to read but this is sometimes unavoidable when writing about deep psychology, particularly if matters relate to someone's very identity and highly personal sexual matters. The author merely wished to provide a "lightbulb moment" understanding of what might going on in the mind of someone who is considering hormonal and surgical gender transition. It is surely better to think:

"Oh, no, doctor I have carefully considered what you have written, I think some of it is complete rubbish and uncomfortable to read but I have now fully explored a number of deep personal matters in the gender identity clinic with a psychotherapist. It is clearly right for me to undergo full hormonal and surgical gender transition having now lived as a transgender woman/man for a considerable time".

OR

"Ah, yes, doctor I see what you mean, that explains it, I wasn't born in a body of the wrong sex. I am now beginning to deal with a number of complex thoughts and feelings with the help of a psychotherapist".

These two examples illustrate how with care and careful decision making it can be possible to live life to the maximum potential, either via gender transition - or not.

Having fully considered what lies in the depths of the mind and become aware of treatment side effects there will be a smaller chance of looking back with bitter regret and self-remorse due to the permanent effects of hormonal and surgical gender transition treatments.

There was not the slightest intention in writing this book to try and coerce someone to change their point of view or decision regarding gender transition - merely to explore what might be their underlying mindset. It would in any case be a very naïve author who felt that they could change someone's wishes by means of a mere publication.

PLEASE CONSIDER SIX VITAL AND IMPORTANT POINTS

The author initially worked in general health care and was always pleased to see patients improving their health by means of a healthy lifestyle - a good diet and exercise but avoiding smoking, excess alcohol and drugs of abuse.

Having also worked in the mental health services, the author was delighted to learn of anyone who managed to improve their general mental wellbeing by means of psychotherapy, lifestyle changes and if necessary, with medication.

The author is naturally similarly pleased to hear of anyone who achieves contentment by means of hormonal and surgical gender transition. However, it is sometimes only in the much longer term that those who have undergone hormonal and surgical gender transition may come to experience gender transition regret for reasons that will be explored. The concept of transitioning from one sex to another is a highly controversial and complex area in which feelings run extremely high but this difficult subject will be covered in this book.

Those who are considering hormonal and surgical gender transition can understandably become reluctant to consider alternative viewpoints. Therefore, after reading just a few pages of this book they may regard it as a load of nonsense. The author respectfully requests the parents of a transgender child and any transgender person considering hormonal and surgical gender transition to continue reading to ensure they make the correct decision so that they can appropriately proceed to gender transition - or not.

Important Note Number 1:

THERE SHOULD BE NO DISCRIMINATION AGAINST THOSE IN THE LGBTQIA+ COMMUNITY - "LOVE IS LOVE" AFTER ALL.

Fortunately, due to the promotional activities of LGBTQIA+ groups there is now a wider acceptance and understanding of sexuality and relationships that are not "mainstream" or "cisheterosexual".

"Love is love" and it is all to the good if as many people as possible can enjoy their relationships to the maximum in the areas of emotional, romantic, sensual and sexual contact - whatever their gender identity or sexual orientation may be.

Please excuse the invented terminology but we could describe the current huge change in society as a "libero-diverse sexual revolution" and this is why as the spokesperson mentioned above said, "Transgender is here to stay". However, it must be remembered that transgender feelings have been present in humankind for millennia.

We don't have to think back very far to recall the terrible difficulties faced by lesbian and gay lovers but of course we should not overlook that there are still painful difficulties in many parts of society for such partners.

Important Note Number 2:

CERTAIN DESTINIES.

There are some people who by their very nature will always deeply feel that they are in the body of the wrong sex - that is just the way they are. They will not feel comfortable in themselves until they are able to live as the other sex.

The are *other* people, *particularly in the younger age group* who are struggling with uncomfortable feelings about themselves and the way they fit into the world. Certain personal factors about these young people together with the influence of transgender information in the Social Media may result in them concluding that they are transgender. This latter group will not actually be "living in the body of the wrong sex" and for them gender transition could be a terrible mistake.

Important Note Number 3:

HOW CAN AN AUTHOR AVOID CAUSING OFFENCE WHEN WRITING ABOUT TRANSGENDER MATTERS?

Transgender matters and the complexities of gender transition are difficult subjects to understand and discussion regarding such matters may quickly become tense and heated. The author has been in the company of pro-gender transition psychologists and medical practitioners *and* also those who take a very cautious viewpoint about gender transition. *Both* pro and cautious groups say that they have experienced hostility from the "other side".

It is very easy to unintentionally cause offence by using certain words and terminologies in relation to transgender subjects. A particular word can be offensive to some transgender people but not to others - this therefore presents a challenge to both those within the transgender population and those outside it.

In order to try and use terms that are acceptable to transgender people the Pink News LGBT Glossary will be quoted and its terminologies generally used in this book. If there is not a relevant term in the glossary the author's best attempt to use general terminology will be employed. The author again apologises for repeatedly referring to some highly personal psychosexual matters but without doing so it is very difficult to understand the processes in the mind that maybe related to transgender feelings in *some* people. Having said that, the type of sexual desires that the author is referring to can be readily seen in transgender Social Media sites, the Internet in general, in transgender porn and academic publications - and so the author isn't really referring to anything that isn't already "out there" in the Internet.

It is also necessary to refer to delicate matters relating to the psychology of family life. This takes the form of general observations and is not in any way meant to be critical.

There was no desire during writing this book to come across as pro or anti-gender transition but rather to emphasise that a decision regarding hormonal and surgical gender transition is one of those life choices that can seem right for some people but totally life destroying for others. To repeat, the book's position was intended to be "gender transition neutral" so to speak and to try and find a middle ground - although this is difficult. As the author hoped to encourage caution, there is an inevitable emphasis on the potential difficulties of gender transition. It is entirely possible to adopt an approach that supports anyone who wishes to live a transgender lifestyle but at the same time take a cautious viewpoint about hormonal and surgical gender transition - especially in children and young adults. This leads us to the next point.

Important Note Number 4:

MAXIMUM LEVELS OF CARE AND ASSESSMENT ARE REQUIRED TO REDUCE THE RISK OF MISTAKEN GENDER TRANSITION - PARTICULARLY IN CHILDREN AND YOUNG ADULTS WHERE THE RISK OF A MISTAKE IS GREATEST.

As in notes 2 and 3, the reason for writing this book about gender transition was to give a number of cautionary comments in order to try to prevent catastrophic and permanent harm, particularly to the younger members of society, which can result from premature or mistaken entry into gender transitioning treatment pathways. Some gender transition treatments can cause permanent infertility and other serious side effects. The mind and personality are quite immature until the mid twenties and even beyond - it is very doubtful that young people can realistically decide that they would never want to produce their biologically own children.

It is advisable to look deeper into gender transition before making a treatment decision by reading, researching, discussing, consulting, reflecting and exploring the mental wellbeing matters that may accompany or actually underlie the desire for gender transition in a young person. Much harm can come from rushing into mistaken gender transition in a young person. It is hoped that transgender groups will appreciate the author's desire as a medical person to take a safeguarding approach to try to reduce the risk of gender transition regret. To do this it is important to explore many difficult aspects of mind, body and treatment side effects.

Very young children have no realistic understanding of sex, gender and female to male or male to female sexual interaction. Teenagers are often much troubled by the physical, emotional and sexual insecurities of puberty. This begs a very important question. Should parents let their children make gender related life changing decisions given their *obviously* immature and muddled mindsets? Surely it is preferable to help young people through life's inevitable emotional roller coaster of growing up rather than let them take the path to gender transition as the believed "solution to all of their problems". Pursuing a transgender lifestyle can add so many additional social, psychological, medical and surgical complications to life but we must remember that for some mature people it can be of enormous benefit. It is therefore critically important to make the correct decision. If gender transition truly helps, that is extremely good news - but if it doesn't the results can be tragic.

There are some practitioners who take the view that better gender transition results can be obtained if transition is carried out at an early age. This point can be fully appreciated and understood as physically, the results can be better, but the profound difficulty is that the decision is more likely to be wrong at a younger age. This is therefore a "Catch 22" situation.

It is important to not avoid the moral duty of exploring the issue of gender transitioning treatments in order that regret can be avoided as a much as possible. To repeat, the author hopes to foster an understanding of the psychological background that can lead to the wish for gender transition in *some* people. This will hopefully help readers to better understand some complex sexual and non-sexually related psychological processes - whether these are happening within themselves or in someone they care for. He also hopes to inform readers about the potential difficulties and dangers of the gender transition processes and procedures - particularly for younger people.

Apologies once again for the exploration of some highly personal and sensitive mental processes and fantasies.

It is the author's hope that people can make the right choice whether it be to proceed to:

1. Gender transition or
2. Psychotherapy to understand and come to terms with inner mental conflicts about gender, sexual orientation and other deep psychological matters.

It is of course a personal right for a mature adult to embark upon on things that involve personal choice whether that be riding a 180mph motorcycle on a racetrack, having extreme tattoos or undergoing any form of major cosmetic surgery. It is all about balancing the risks of extreme highs against terrible lows.

Those who have undergone hormonal and surgical gender transition procedures and later try to detransition may find that they cannot truly regain the appearance and function of their sex that was identified and confirmed at birth. Depending on the degree of transition they may have lost their ability to produce their own children. Their sexual enjoyment may also have been permanently impaired. These consequences are not just a tragedy in the ordinary sense of the word but one that is also totally catastrophic.

Fortunately, many more people are satisfied with life after gender transition than suffer regret. The unfortunate reality is that the number of people suffering gender transition is on the increase - this is a sad statistical fact. All of those involved in the welfare of patients have a responsibility to help young people to be able to make the correct decision - surely nobody could disagree with this important safeguarding approach.

It is best to not lose sight of the fact that once breast and genital tissue have been surgically removed or cross-sex hormones have produced irreversible effects it is simply too late. It is impossible to go back and so please let's explore important note 5.

Important Note Number 5:

PLEASE LET'S HAVE FULLY OPEN DISCUSSION BETWEEN PRO-GENDER TRANSITION GROUPS, SOCIAL WORKERS, PSYCHOLOGISTS, MEDICAL PERSONNEL AND DETRANSITION GROUPS FOR THE FUTURE BENEFIT AND MUTUAL UNDERSTANDING OF ALL CONCERNED.

It is hoped to encourage deep discussion as to whether transgender feelings may *sometimes* be due to an underlying lack of mental wellbeing rather than necessarily "being born in the body of the wrong sex". Once dialogue starts, prejudice and misunderstanding can be reduced. Thus, discussion between those inside and outside of the transgender population can only be of benefit. There might be disagreement, but the important thing is that all can get on with their lives as suits them best - perhaps even by "agreeing to disagree" and to "live and let live".

Neither pro-gender transition spokespersons or gender transition sceptics are in a position to say that they are definitely 100% correct in their viewpoints as even with today's incredible advances in our understanding of science, biology, psychology and medicine there are still huge unknowns in the areas of genetics, sex and brain function. We just don't have all the necessary facts at our fingertips. Different writers will obviously have different opinions about transgender matters and no single book can cover all viewpoints.

Calm and measured discussion is the hallmark of a society that is motivated to best deal with a difficult subject and it is hoped that a more comfortable situation can be reached when discussing transgender matters. Strong protest can of course be an indication of the need for resistance to oppression that should quite rightly be heard - but the other side of the coin is that vehement protest can *sometimes* indicate a deep discomfort *within* the mind of the protesters.

Viewpoints about transgender matters vary widely even between transgender people. These viewpoints differ because all people are highly individual due to the fact that the development of their mindsets is a result of life stresses and personal sensitivities to those stresses that are absolutely unique to each person. Total agreement about any matter in life is very rare and this is why the author makes a plea for open speech and listening between all interested parties. It would be helpful to consider how, just like all feelings, transgender feelings are a result of the influence of:

1. Nature's biology.
2. Nurture.
3. Or in reality, a combination of the two.

There are many excellent and highly academic books on transgender matters but many of them are over 200k or 300k words. This book aims to be quicker to read in order to give an understanding of the mental processes that might underlie transgender feelings. This book was never intended to be a lengthy, academic or scientific publication. It was deliberately designed to be a briefer read for someone who is unsure of what is going on in a loved one's mind or in their own mind and wants a shorter overview of the pros and cons of gender transition. Having said that, at times the book repeats itself but this is to allow certain sections to stand alone or to emphasise an important matter. This book will hopefully provide a relatively brief resource for the parents, partners, lovers and healthcare professionals of those who are experiencing complex emotions about their gender. At times the book is easy to read and at other times more challenging. If a section is hard going, please just skip it and move on but perhaps return to it later.

It is felt that there is an absolute need for explorative psychotherapy to be undertaken prior to embarking on even the earliest stages of medical gender transition. This should not be regarded as an attempt to change someone's gender feelings or sexual orientation (sometimes known as "conversion therapy"). Poor mental wellbeing often coexists with transgender feelings and *it is only correct that decisions about gender transition are made in the best possible frame of mind.* The importance of this cannot be overemphasised but far too often it just doesn't happen.

Again, no apologies are made for the very frequent repetition of the need for sufficient psychological evaluation and treatment being undertaken before gender transition throughout this book.

It is clearly better that psychological assessment is carried out initially rather than psychotherapy being required after mistaken hormonal and surgical gender transition to help someone cope with their drastic error of choice. Some repetitions of other important points are made in the book and this is so that they are more likely to be read - as people often either just dip into a book or read only part of it.

Many people say that they, "Just know in their deepest mind" or "Feel 100% sure" that they are "Trapped in a body of the wrong sex". It seems as if "The problem is *with* the body" but please remember that every bodily feeling is actually experienced *in* the brain **and** *in* the body. Please consider for a moment that whilst our thoughts and feelings originate in the mind/brain, they are not just experienced in the mind/brain - they also experienced physically in the body. *Human experience **is** a total mind-body experience. Nothing can happen in the brain without something happening in the body and nothing can happen to the body without something happening in the brain.*

Some adolescents and young people who are struggling with puberty and other life stresses maybe consciously and *unconsciously* taking on a transgender identity as a way of psychologically hiding from themselves or reinventing their persona instead of coming to accept themselves as they are. It would be hoped that in the current increasingly libero-diverse times aided by the hard work of LGBTQIA+ groups that people can be more accepting of their own and other people's gender expression and sexual orientation.

This book was hoped to adopt a "middle of the road" approach to hormonal and surgical gender transition but perhaps the best and most useful future book would be written by a collaboration of people who take differing viewpoints. This book was only intended to criticise those people who are woefully mismanaging the United Kingdom's National Health Service and therefore delaying and impairing the treatment of patients. The book also does make some criticism of those who are preventing the fullest discussion about how best and most safely assist young people who are struggling with their gender identity. From a safeguarding point of view it would be most helpful if we can ensure that people who feel they are transgender can receive the best possible treatment but only if this is likely to be the correct thing for them in the long term. In order for people who take widely differing views to collaborate to write a follow-on book it would be necessary to enter some very contentious, confusing and controversial areas where there are many unknowns. It would not be easy, but it would be wonderful if it could be done.

Many people who have gone through gender transition gain an excellent degree of happiness and contentment having been prepared to enter the complex territory of long-term cross-sex hormones. They were also prepared to accept the potential risks of surgical complications or serious medication side effects and so let us please consider note number 6.

Important Note Number 6:

LIFE IS DIFFICULT ANYWAY - PLEASE BEWARE OF THE RISK OF MAKING IT MORE DIFFICULT.

Life is difficult for the vast, vast majority of people. It is difficult for women, and it is difficult for men but in very different ways. Have you ever thought that you would like a day to go really well for a change without too many snags? You will doubtless have noticed how rarely a whole day actually goes particularly well. Life *is* hard. Each sex may at times feel that it has a more difficult time than the other, but it is really pointless to make endless comparisons to try and work out who has it the worst. The important matter to consider is whether someone may be risking making their life even more difficult and complicated by living a transgender life with or without undergoing hormonal and surgical gender transition.

Undergoing gender transition results in a "new you" and this entails forming a new relationship with yourself. This new relationship with yourself can be just like any other new relationship. Many relationships tend to follow a similar pattern:

1. Starting with initial excitement and idealisation.
2. But then a better knowledge and insight into the situation comes about that ...
3. Can lead to a stage of disgruntlement and disappointment with the relationship once the stage of idealisation is over. It isn't as wonderful as it seemed once the initial gloss wore off.

If surgical gender transition turns out to be a mistake or there are surgical side effects, there may be a lifetime of bitter regret due to the life-changing and sex-identity destroying consequences.

Please balance the pros and cons.

The difficulties of living a transgender life include:

1. The obvious inconvenience of having to take hormones, dealing with any side effects and requiring repeated medical check-ups.
2. Attending to physical appearance. It can be much "harder work" to maintain cross-gender appearances than it is for cisgender people to maintain their appearance.
3. Each surgical gender transition procedure may not necessarily be a one-off process as surgical revision is sometimes required. Any form of surgery can go very

badly wrong even in the best hands. There is occasionally the risk of constantly wanting "just one more procedure". This is also seen in those who undergo general cosmetic plastic surgery procedures.

4. The expense of 1, 2 and 3 can be a problem if the treatments wished for are not funded by the National Health Service if living in the United Kingdom or if living elsewhere and a medical insurance company refuses to cover the cost. If a job is lost, affording continued treatment may not be possible.

5. One of the major difficulties faced by transgender people is that of not always feeling accepted in society and therefore not feeling socially comfortable. *The absolute majority of human existence is extremely gendered.* Just look at the incredibly different ways women and men dress and act - and have always done so. Women and men are constantly sizing up other people in very gendered ways - it is what humans have always done because the survival of the species depends on the interaction between females and males. These female to male and male to female observations occur in microseconds - human brains are programmed to do this and it is entirely automatic and instinctive. In other words, it is unavoidable, we can't help ourselves but do it. It is of course possible for transgender people to socially present themselves as the gender transitioned to in a very convincing way but not every transgender person can completely "pass". Cisgender people will usually (although not always) tend to realise that the transgender person in front of them is, in fact, transgender. This will often cause a completely involuntary or automatic confused feeling in spite of a cisgender person's desire to interact politely and appropriately. Even with increased contact and familiarity with people who have undergone full hormonal and surgical gender transition, cisgender people will possibly still feel somewhat consciously or *unconsciously* unsettled about transgender people as they don't fit in perfectly with the way that female to male

and male to female interaction is genetically and socially "programmed" into the brain. Quite rightly, there are laws and social guidelines in many countries designed to prevent discrimination, impoliteness and unsavoury treatment of people in the areas of sex and gender. These laws make cisgender people outwardly behave in suitably courteous ways but quite simply cannot change what goes on automatically in the depths of their minds. Humans are very perceptive to each other's inner thoughts and feelings and as a result, transgender people might easily pick up on the deeper conflicted emotions of cisgender people about transgender people. Transgender people may notice a "double-stare" given by cisgender people - this is because humans instinctively need to know the sex of the person they are interacting with, and they are merely doing an involuntary "double-check". It is of course very understandable that transgender groups ask for polite and accommodating treatment - and they should receive it, absolutely they should.

6. Often it is stated, particularly in relation to young people that undergoing gender transition is carried out to reduce the risk of suicide. Sadly, the statistics so far do not suggest any overall reduction in the incidence of suicide in the longer term. Many transgender people experience suicidal thoughts - far more than the average person. The reasons for this tragic situation will be touched upon later in the book. *A most important point to emphasise is that anyone experiencing self-harming or suicidal thoughts and feelings should urgently obtain support and assistance.*

7. Over time, there will be a number of people who have undergone gender transition who for medical reasons will no longer be able to continue to take their cross-sex hormones. If they have undergone gender transition surgery that has failed they may end up appearing as if really neither one sex or the other. There will be those who suffer permanent side effects from cross-gender

surgery ranging from incontinence to loss of sexual satisfaction. It could therefore be for reasons such as these that suicide rates might be worsened in the future as more and more people undergo transgender medical processes with all of the possible risks of such complications and problems.

Once again, the aim of this book is to provide an understanding and to request the fullest intellectual discussion regarding transgender matters. It is far too important a matter to allow discussion to become too difficult. Many academics who have with good conscience and motivation tried to raise transgender safeguarding concerns been harshly treated. It is acknowledged that transgender people have also been badly treated in society. It is sincerely hoped that this can be avoided in the future as much as possible.

Much pro-gender transition material has been put out into the Social Media and this has obviously helped those people whose lives can be improved by gender transition. However, some of the Social Media pronouncements become less convincing once properly assessed in slower time when it is realised that they are not always evidenced based and tend to sometimes take the view that "only" a transgender pathway is the way forward. This book aims to offer some balance by referring to some of the potential downsides of gender transition.

Please remember it is the moral duty of doctors to try and explain the nature of medical treatments to patients and to fully advise them of potential side effects. Gender transition is a difficult subject to write about and it is a relatively new psychological and medical specialty. It may also be a subject that is difficult to understand for those without a psychological, medical or relevant scientific background. This is precisely why this book was written by a retired medical practitioner who has seen much avoidable suffering in forty years of practice in many areas of medicine.

It may be difficult for the reader without the relevant background to "get their head round" certain aspects of gender identity theory and practice - for this reason the contents list has more detailed headings than would normally be used in order that the reader can easily find a topic that they need to re-read.

DEFINITIONS AND TERMINOLOGY USED IN RELATION TO TRANSGENDER MATTERS - THE PINK NEWS LGBT GLOSSARY

In order to discuss this difficult subject and to try and use acceptable terms it was considered important to provide some definitions and terminologies favoured by transgender people. Some relevant excerpts are now listed and were taken from the **Pink News LGBT Glossary** (please refer to www.pinknews.co.uk for more details if required):

AGENDER

A person who does not identify as having any gender - male, female or otherwise.

ASSIGNED SEX

The sex which a person is assigned at birth, which usually corresponds to the gender identity you were raised with or assumed to have. Preferred by many in the transgender community to terms like "genetic", "biological", or "birth" gender, which suggest that a trans person's gender identity is less valid than a cisgender person's.

ASEXUAL

A person who has limited or no sexual feelings or desires.

BIGENDER

A person who experiences exactly two genders. These gender identities can be experienced either simultaneously or not. The two identities can be male and female, but could also include non-binary identities.

BISEXUAL

A person who is romantically or sexually attracted to people of multiple genders. (Author's note: It is often regarded by many people that being bisexual means being attracted to both women and men but the Pink Dictionary refers to multiple genders. The book will defer to the Pink Dictionary's definition).

Cisgender or CIS

A person whose gender identity corresponds with their assigned sex. Contrasting with trans. (Author's note: The words cis and trans have a Latin origin. Cis means "this side of" and trans means "the other side of". The author will therefore refer to ciswomen, cismen, cisgender and so forth).

CROSS-DRESSING

Wearing clothes typically associated with another sex, for any reason.

DRAG or DRAG UP

Clothing that is more conventionally worn by another sex, especially women's clothes worn by a man.

FLUID

Sexual fluidity refers to a person changing their sexuality or sexual identity during their lifetime.

FTM or F2M

Sometimes considered offensive. An outdated term for transgender people who have transitioned from female to male.

GENDER CONFIRMATION SURGERY (PREVIOUSLY GENDER REASSIGNMENT SURGERY)

Surgery for changing a transgender person's physical appearance and function of their existing sexual characteristics to resemble that of their identified gender.

GENDER DYSPHORIA

The discomfort felt when a person's assigned sex does not match their gender identity. Also known as Gender Identity Disorder (previously known as transsexualism or transgenderism).

GENDER IDENTITY or GENDER

A person's internal sense of self as it relates to femininity or masculinity.

GENDER NON-CONFORMING or GNC

A person or act that defies traditional expectations of their gender or assigned sex.

GENDER RECOGNITION ACT 2004

A law that allows legal recognition of a new gender. A Gender Recognition Certificate is given as a result.

GENDER X

Refers to a gender other than female or male. In some countries X can be used on documents instead of F or M.

GENDERQUEER

An identity that does not feature the gender binary, involving combinations of femininity or masculinity.

GENDER FLUID

A person who does not identify themselves as having a fixed gender.

MEDICAL TRANSITION

The parts of a transgender person's transition that change their body. This can include hormonal and or surgical transitioning. Not a necessary requirement for a person to identify as trans.

MTF or M2F

Sometimes considered offensive. An outdated term for transgender people who have transitioned from male to female.

NON-BINARY

A person with a gender identity that is not exclusively female or male.

PANSEXUAL

A person who is not limited in sexual choice with regard to biological sex, gender or gender identity. Sometimes referred to as "hearts not parts".

PASSING (GENDER)

A transgender person's ability to be considered at a glance to be either a cisgender woman or a cisgender man.

PASSING (SEXUALITY) aka STRAIGHT PASSING

A gay or bisexual person who is considered by some at a glance to be heterosexual.

QUEER

Originally a derogatory slur towards gay men. It has since been reclaimed by many members of the LGBT community as a self-affirming self-descriptive umbrella term.

SKOLIOSEXUAL

A person who is sexually or romantically attracted to non-binary people or those who do not identify as cisgender.

TRANS

A abbreviation for transgender. Sometimes used as a broader umbrella term to refer to people with a non-cisgender gender identity.

TRANSGENDER

A person who has a gender identity or gender expression that differs from their assigned sex.

TRANSGENDERED

An incorrect term for a transgender person.

TRANSITIONING

The process of a transgender person presenting themselves as their gender identity. This can include changing their appearance, name and pronouns. Medical transition changes the transgender person's body and can include hormonal treatment and surgical procedures. Social transition is the part of a transgender person's transition that is seen by the people around them. This can feature coming out, changing a gender expression, name and pronouns. Transition is not necessary for a person to identify as transgender.

TRANSSEXUAL

A term that is considered offensive by some transgender people. Sometimes used to refer to transgender people who have already undergone gender confirmation surgery. Previously an accepted term for a person with a gender identity that is inconsistent with, or not culturally associated with their assigned sex.

TRANSVESTITE

A person who dresses and acts in a style or manner traditionally associated with another sex. Now seen as outdated and often a slur, and CROSS-DRESSER is more commonly used, although some trans people have reclaimed it.

This quote from the Pink News helpfully outlines the best language that is to be used when discussing transgender matters. The author will of course use these terms wherever appropriate and will also endeavour to use generalist terms to avoid confusion. The author recalls very well a transgender patient he saw in clinic who was female at birth but was undergoing social transition prior to taking testosterone and was considering undergoing mastectomy. They kept referring to themselves as a "transfemale" during several appointments. What the patient should really have said was "transman" or "transmale". The author has occasionally noticed commentators in the Media being similarly muddled. The author will refer to transwoman for a male to female transgender person or transman for a female to male transgender person throughout the book.

Having clarified the terminology, the book will now consider the possible side effects of treatments used in gender transition medicine. It is only right that a doctor should make patients aware of the possible downsides of any treatment as part of the "consent to treatment" process. There are, of course, two major concerns in transgender medical practice:

1. The side effects of the treatments themselves.
2. The fact that a patient may have made a mistake in undergoing hormonal and surgical gender transition and will come to suffer a lifetime of bitter regret.

POSSIBLE SIDE EFFECTS OF GENDER TRANSITION MEDICATION AND SURGERY

PUBERTY BLOCKERS

At the age of puberty the pituitary gland (which is part of the brain) starts off the complex process of sexual maturation by producing "chemical messengers" that cause the female sex hormone oestrogen and the male sex hormone testosterone to be produced according to the sex of the child. Puberty blockers are medications that can block this pituitary gland function.

Very rarely, some girls start puberty before the age of eight and some boys before the age of nine - this is known as "precocious puberty". There are many problems with this occurring - an obvious example would be the difficulty faced by a very young girl in having an unexpected menstrual period in the classroom. Precocious puberty can also result in stunted growth. Puberty blockers can be used to halt precocious puberty and if prescribed for this purpose are of course, stopped at the normal age of puberty allowing it to take place.

Some doctors therefore came to believe that puberty blockers could be prescribed for children who are going through puberty at the normal age but were experiencing severe mental distress. Any mental distress at the time of puberty tends *quite naturally* to have gender associated elements to it and therefore readily comes to be labelled as "gender dysphoria" - because the *assumption* is that the distress is arising from gender issues - rather than just being associated with them. The doctors' reasoning was that once the distress had subsided the puberty blockers would be stopped, and things would carry on normally. This may at first seem a really straightforward idea but in reality, matters are far more complicated. These doctors also believed that the pause in any gender related distress would allow a child to choose which gender they wished to be. However, whilst "gender dysphoria" is often quite understandably blamed on puberty itself there are very often *other significant and complex psychological and social matters* occurring at the same time. It is all too easy to inaccurately blame *all* of the psychological distress onto gender matters and overlook "ordinary" mental distress. This is what can sometimes happen in paediatric gender identity clinics.

The development of the brain from the earliest stages in the foetus up to the middle twenties or beyond is influenced by numerous genetic, chemical, hormonal and social factors. The brain is a sexed organ, by which is meant that female and male brains are different - but there are more similarities than differences. The influences of testosterone and the male Y chromosome on the male brain are the main factors in the "maleness" of the developing brain. Oestrogen and the results of having XX chromosomes influence the development of the female brain. The reader may be surprised to learn that female and male bodies actually produce *both* sex hormones, but oestrogen is, of course, the main hormone in females and testosterone in males. These two hormones have a very significant effect on various areas of the body other than the brain and are responsible for the development of the reproductive organs and the overall femaleness and maleness of the body in general.

Puberty blockers would theoretically interfere with the sexual development of the brain as well as the body but there is no reliable evidence as to how far this is the case or if the brain will subsequently develop normally once they have been stopped. The effects at the current state of research are completely unknown and the treatment of "gender dysphoria" in this way remains entirely experimental.

Once puberty blockers have been started in a gender identity clinic, they can all too easily become part of an almost inevitably escalating treatment process. Please consider the following possible sequence:

1. A child is prescribed puberty blockers in a gender identity clinic for "gender dysphoria" but they may not result in a "cure" because the puberty blockers obviously have not dealt with any *other significant and complex psychological and social issues.*
2. So, if puberty blockers haven't made things better then the gender identity clinic staff feel they need to do something more and so they prescribe cross-sex hormones "as the next stage of treatment". These may also fail to "cure" the symptoms because they have not dealt with any *other significant and complex psychological and social issues.*
3. Now, if stages 1 and 2 haven't put things right the gender identity clinic recommends "the next stage of treatment". The patient undergoes gender transition surgery, but this may not help either as it hasn't dealt with any *other significant and complex psychological and social issues.* Of course, some much older patients are better off having stages 1 - 3 but others may find that they are no better off or end up in a confused and difficult state with the result that they then they progress to:
4. Detransition, which is a very difficult situation to be in. This is discussed in detail later in the book.

The progression from stage 1 to 3 not only takes place because each stage may not have yet "cured" the young patient but also because if a specialist doctor is offering it "it must be right" and so the parents and child go along with it in the hope that the next stage will produce the "cure". Also, there may have been suggestions that "a child is at risk of suicide if they don't undergo gender transition".

What is also totally unknown is the final status of the brain when the child has had *both* puberty blockers *and* cross-sex hormones - once again, it is not precisely known how the brain will be sexed.

If puberty blockers are given before the ovaries and testicles are properly developed and are then immediately followed by cross-sex hormones, *permanent infertility* will very likely be the result. This contrasts with the case of adult transgender people who are to undergo gender transition surgery as they can have mature ova (eggs) or sperm harvested and frozen in advance of surgery for future use, assuming the process works. In the case of children who had puberty blockers early in life then immediate cross-sex hormones *there may be no or insufficient ova or sperm to save* - this may be a cause of tragic gender transition regret later in life. Compare this to the case of children who are treated for cancer and lose their ability to have children due to the effects of chemotherapy or radiotherapy - this is very frequently a cause of a tremendous and all-consuming sadness later in life. Please bear in mind that a large proportion of adult transgender people do actually want to have children at some stage in their life.

Puberty blockers reduce the amount of tissue growth and development of the genitalia, which will result an immature appearance. If a child goes on to take cross-sex hormones after puberty blockers they will be left with infantile genitals. Therefore whether someone detransitions or not they might be left with a *permanent childlike appearance of their genitalia* and given the importance that is attached to the appearance of that part of the body in relationships, this can only be regarded as disastrous. Who as an adult would be content to have child-like genitalia? For those who wish to undergo gender transition surgery there will be less tissue available to reconstruct the genitalia. As a result, the surgical techniques will be far more complicated.

It seems that if children are given puberty blockers in early puberty and then take cross-sex hormones *they may not develop the ability to have an orgasm.*

Another highly significant theoretical concern about puberty blockers is related to the very fact that they block - *they may block the actual "psychological growing up" process that would enable a child to naturally pass through their assumed "gender dysphoria".*

Please contrast all this with children who are diagnosed as having "gender dysphoria" but a wait and see approach is taken and they are *not* given puberty blockers or cross-sex hormones. A very high proportion of these children will pass through what was labelled as "gender dysphoria" quite unremarkably although some just turn out to be lesbian, gay or bisexual.

Other side effects of puberty blockers include irregular periods (although menstruation is usually stopped), hot flushes, headaches, fatigue, general aches, pains and malaise. Anxiety and mood instability may occur, which can be quite severe. Puberty blockers can have adverse effects on bone development and strength. In susceptible children epileptic fits may occur. Puberty blockers may possibly have an adverse effect on the development of IQ. In animal experiments it has been noted that puberty blockers affect the brain structure but at present it is simply not known if the same changes will occur in the human - to repeat, it is just not known for sure.

Parents looking for more information will find a helpful article in the British Medical Journal by C. Dyer (please refer to the bibliography at the end of this book). For those who wish to research the technical aspects of puberty blockers in more detail the medical name for puberty blockers is Gonadotrophin Releasing Hormone Analogues (GnRHa).

TESTOSTERONE

Increased risk of strokes, high blood pressure, heart attacks, blood clots, joint problems, diabetes and dementia.

Permanent clitoral enlargement.

Permanent voice deepening.

Permanent facial and bodily hair growth - although may possibly be reduced with certain other treatments.

Permanent facial coarsening.

Male pattern baldness - permanence depends on duration of treatment and the types of medications subsequently taken.

Acne.

Increased aggression.

Mood disorders and other psychiatric conditions such as psychosis.

Increased sex drive (not always a problem but this can be very frustrating if for some reason orgasmic ability has been lost as a result of a gender transition surgery complication).

The lining of the womb (endometrium) breaks down and shrinks. Periods stop. Infertility results. The endometrium may become painful and hysterectomy (removal of the womb) may be necessary.

The vaginal lining breaks down, becomes dry and shrinks (atrophy). This can be very painful and may impair vaginal sexual gratification.

Testosterone is changed into oestrogen by the body's natural chemical processes and raised levels of oestrogen are known to be associated with increased risks of cancer in the ovary, the lining of the womb and the breast. Mastectomy performed on transmen does not always remove all of the breast tissue and therefore any remaining breast cells may be at risk of cancerous change.

OESTROGENS

Male breast cancer.

Prostate cancer risk should be reduced by the taking of oestrogens by transwomen but the risk is not eliminated entirely.

Mood changes.

SIDE EFFECTS THAT MAY COMPLICATE *ALL* FORMS OF SURGERY

All types of surgery are subject to possible anaesthetic complications, haemorrhage, blood clots, infection (including MRSA and flesh eating bacteria), scarring, scar breakdown and contracture (shrinkage and distortion), complications of blood transfusion, permanent pain in the area, loss of sensation and function. Numbness around the operated area can reduce the pleasure of intimacy. This is not generally the surgeon's fault as when skin is cut, many nerves that are too small to see are cut through too. Most seriously and tragically people have died as a result of transgender surgery although fortunately this is very rare. It is advisable to look at images of gender transition surgery on the Internet and even better at the surgeon's own photographic portfolio. Please be advised that there is no guarantee that the results of surgery will be the same as in the photographs. It is worth bearing in mind that many people can live very happily as the other gender without undergoing any gender transition surgery at all. It may not be necessary to have *both* "top" and "bottom" surgery to get the best out of life. Please do not rush to make the decision.

MASTECTOMY (BREAST TISSUE REMOVAL)

Asymmetry of the nipples, loss of nipple sensation, total loss of the nipple, painful collection of fluid where the nipple used to be as the original ducts are blocked. The large scars can be quite disfiguring particularly if there is scar overgrowth or distortion.

CLITORAL LENGTHENING

This may be done to make a clitoris that has been enlarged by testosterone treatment to look a little longer and to resemble a mini-penis.
Loss of sensation may occur if the nerves are damaged.

Clitoral damage or loss of tissue in the event of post operative infection.

METOIDOPLASTY

This is the placement of the urine passage through a clitoris that has been enlarged by testosterone treatment. The procedure allows urination while standing up.
Risk of damage to the clitoris.
Risk of narrowing of the urine passage.
It can never look, feel or fully function exactly like a natural penis.

PHALLOPLASTY

This is the construction of a penis shaped structure known as a neo-penis or neo-phallus. It is made from a skin graft taken from the thigh, forearm or abdomen - a large scar is left on the skin graft donor area. There is no guarantee that the delicate process of joining the nerves will work thus resulting in a numb neo-penis. In any case even if the process of joining nerves is successful the sensation from the neo-phallus will not necessarily seem to be coming from the neo-phallus itself in the same way it would from a natural penis. Narrowing of the urine tube may occur and further operations on this area are then required. There is no guarantee that the clitoris, which is at the base of the neo-penis will definitely still be able to produce an orgasm.
Surgically joining blood vessels is very difficult. If joining the arteries fails the neo-phallus will die or if the joining of veins is insufficient the tissues of the neo-phallus will become waterlogged.
It can never look, feel or fully function exactly like a natural penis.

PENILE IMPLANTS INTO A PHALLOPLASTY

These are implants that give a degree of rigidity to a phalloplasty - they can either be made of semirigid plastic or a piece of rib cartilage. The body may react to the plastic, which could then erode through the skin or the natural rib cartilage may be reabsorbed by the body. Either type of implant will result in a neo-penis that may give the embarrassing impression of an erection when wearing swimwear. This problem can be got around by the use of an inflatable implant.

SCROTUM CONSTRUCTION

There is generally too little skin in the labia majora to form a full-size scrotum but this in any case would look out of proportion to a metoidoplasty. However, there are techniques that can enlarge the labia majora so that a constructed scrotum would be in proportion to a phalloplasty.

BREAST IMPLANTS

Asymmetry is possible.
As there may be little natural fat tissue in the area to cover the silicone implants and as there is no natural "tail" of mammary tissue the implants can sometimes appear very artificial - as if "stuck on".

CONSTRUCTION OF A NEO-VAGINA

A neo-vagina is constructed by removing some of the internal structures of penis and then pushing in the skin of the penis to make an internal tube. Sometimes a length of bowel is used to add to the length of the neo-vagina. If there are surgical complications a colostomy may be necessary (although hopefully this would be temporary). If part of the lining of the neo-vagina is made of bowel, the neo-vaginal orifice may smell like bowel. It is theoretically possible that bowel cancer could occur in the neo-vagina's bowel tissue.

The neo-vagina tends to shrink due to natural bodily healing processes and therefore needs to be dilated (expanded) regularly, which can be very painful. A small amount of sensitive penile tissue is retained to preserve orgasmic function but there is no guarantee that this will be successful thus resulting in the loss of orgasm.

Narrowing of the urethra (water passage) can cause blockage of the urinary flow. There is no guarantee of the direction of urination. Increased risk of urine infections.
The scrotum is used to fashion labia majora, which may look more wrinkled than cisfemale labia. It has to be said that a good surgeon can produce a remarkably natural looking appearance.

There is a fortunately rare surgical complication that can result in a leakage of faeces into the neo-vagina. As the rectum is immediately behind the neo-vagina a surgical mishap can result in a hole being made between the rectum and the neo-vagina. It may sound as if it only needs repair with some sutures (stitches) but generally it requires a quite complicated form of surgical procedure.

A neo-vagina made only from pushed in penile skin cannot self-lubricate. Sex can sometimes be painful even with the use of lubricants. If bowel tissue is used to construct part of the neo-vagina in some cases it over lubricates and in others it under lubricates. The neo-vagina can be damaged by or be uncomfortable during rough sex.

All external skin of the body is at a slight risk of developing cancer - external skin is used to form the neo-vagina. Factors that increase the risk of skin cancer are infection with the genital wart virus, repeated trauma and the application of chemicals. These factors may of course, apply to neo-vaginal skin, the particular problem being that a developing cancer would be out of sight and not detected at an early stage.

BIOLOGICAL PRINCIPLES THAT RELATE TO FEMALE AND MALE SEX AS TRADITIONALLY FOLLOWED BY SCIENTISTS AND DOCTORS

The following are terms that are generally used by scientific and medical organisations:

SEX

Sex is often confused with gender. The two are technically different but of course, are very much related. From a strictly *genetic* point of view there are only two distinct *biological* sexes and these are dictated by the presence of the X and Y sex chromosomes in the cells of the body:

Females have two X chromosomes.

Males have one X and one Y chromosome.

The vast, vast majority of people are either XX female or XY male. Put simply, these sex chromosomes *biologically* determine which sex the person is (but we must bear in mind that a transgender person may have a deep inner experience of being the other sex).

XX or females produce eggs - known as an ovum (or ova in the plural).

XY or males produce sperm.

Ova and sperm are known as gametes. Gametes have 23 chromosomes - half the number of chromosomes of the other body cells. When a sperm combines with an ovum the resulting combination obviously has the full number of chromosomes (46).

Ova have a single X chromosome.

Sperm have an X *or* a Y chromosome.

Thus, the father's sperm determines the sex of a child.

Gametes define the sex of animals and humans - *this is one of the main biological definitions of sex.*

Sex can also be scientifically and biologically defined as the way a body has been "set up" by Nature (i.e. evolution) to reproduce. However, as above a person may feel differently to this.

For the vast, vast majority of people sex is clearly female or male, in other words it is one *or* the other - BUT THERE ARE SOME *EXCEPTIONALLY* RARE MEDICAL INTERSEX SYNDROMES TO CONSIDER:

In these conditions the biological sex of the person may not be obvious. This complex subject matter is beyond the scope of this small book, but a brief lay description of two conditions will be given.

There are people whose sexual characteristics differ from the mainstream population - they may have genitalia that are not obviously either female or male. They may possibly have features of both sexes. Overall, this applies to less than 1% of the World's population. These are medical conditions and should not be confused with being transgender. The basis of these conditions tends to be various disorders of sex hormone metabolism and/or sex chromosome abnormalities. The two examples will now be given:

1. One example would be congenital adrenal hyperplasia (CAH) in which an excess of testosterone is produced. An XX (female) individual with CAH will develop some male type characteristics such as an enlarged clitoris, a deep voice and facial hair.

2. The second example may be seen extremely rarely in people whose tissues are not sensitive to the effects of sex hormones, an example of such a condition would be testicular feminisation syndrome in which an XY (male) person's tissues do not respond to testosterone so that the tissues develop as female. This XY person does not develop a penis, but they have testicles that remain inside their body. They have no beard growth, and their voice does not drop. Their outside appearance is that of a woman but there is no womb.

For those who are interested, there are many other medical intersex conditions - an Internet search is recommended for readers who would like to learn more. The reference in the bibliography by D. DiGiglie is recommended.

A NOTE ON FOETAL BRAIN DEVELOPMENT

As mentioned before, it is the effects of testosterone and the Y chromosome on the foetus that are the main factors that determine whether a brain develops as male rather than female. It is technically incorrect to say that female and male brains are hugely different but female brains have more connections between the two sides of the brain and male brains have more connections between the front and rear of the brain. Certain brain structures involved with sex drive and aggression are sized differently in female and male brains. There are other structural and chemical differences between female and male brains - the male brain is bigger, but this is due to an increase of the supportive tissues. The differences in the way in which female and male brains are structured and the various areas are interconnected result in the innate differences between female and male personalities and attributes.

There are more similarities than differences between female and male brains. The degree of femaleness and maleness varies. *Figuratively* speaking, brains are not always totally female or totally male - there tends to be a mixture or overlap of female and male characteristics. This helps females and males to have a degree of mutual understanding and empathy for each other.

Please consider prehistoric times:

Empathic female multitaskers = Cavewoman looking after several children in a cave home.

Unempathic, single task focussed and aggressive males = Caveman hunter and protector.

Please excuse the oversimplification but this is how humans originated after all. Women and men evolved along somewhat different and divergent pathways that helped them to survive in their respective biological roles and of course, in terms of the survival of groups of their sex. In modern society such survival stresses are mostly irrelevant, but the author is sure the reader will appreciate how such evolutionary selection pressures operated in human history.

SEX HORMONES AND THE BRAIN:

You may find it interesting to note that both the female XX brain and the male XY brain are influenced by the female hormone oestrogen *and* the male hormone testosterone. The female brain is more responsive to oestrogen than the male brain - in some respects in the same way and in other respects in different ways. This is a very complex area.

A genetically XX person who has the medical condition of congenital adrenal hyperplasia and an excess of testosterone will have a more masculine type functioning brain than the average XX female.

A genetically XY person who has the medical condition of testicular feminisation syndrome will have a more female type functioning of the brain than the average XY male.

To repeat - *the above intersex conditions are extremely rare* and some may have caused difficulty in diagnosing sex at birth or thereafter because sex characteristics may have been mixed, confusing or poorly developed.

The presence of the above intersex syndromes have resulted in many tragic disasters when well-meaning but ultimately miscalculated medical attempts have been made in early life to hormonally and or surgically "assign" sex.

(Medically speaking, sex is not "assigned" at birth, it is identified and confirmed by biological and medical convention).

PEOPLE WHO FEEL THAT THEY ARE TRANSGENDER IN THE VAST MAJORITY OF CASES **DO NOT** HAVE ANY OF THE ABOVE MEDICAL INTERSEX SYNDROMES ... THEY *MAY* HAVE INSTEAD:

1. A brain that "tends towards" that of the other sex.
2. A tendency to be gay, lesbian or bisexual.
3. Suffered a number of adverse psychological experiences, particularly in their early life.
4. A neurodevelopmental condition such as autism.

Bearing in mind the miscalculated medical attempts to deal with intersex conditions mentioned above, this book aims to reduce the risk of medical interventions that might result in gender transition regret in the future. It is surely better for a person to undergo hormonal and surgical gender transition only if it will be helpful to them and that all attempts should be made to reduce the risk of regret.

BIOLOGY AND THE SEXED BRAIN AND BODY - THE "DOUBLE CURVE SEXUAL CHARACTERISTICS" GRAPH

So, why is it that some people feel that they have a male mind trapped in a female body or a female mind trapped in a male body?

The following describes a concept that is critical to *part of* the understanding of what are described as gender dysphoria and transgender feelings in some people.

As stated earlier there are more similarities than differences between female and male brains. The degree of femaleness and maleness varies. Figuratively speaking, brains are not always totally female or totally male - there tends to be a mixture or overlap of female and male characteristics. *We are binary but not totally binary.*

As the "double curve sexual characteristics" graph (below) shows there is up to a 30% *overall* overlap of female and male sexed personality characteristics and so either sex might have up to 15% of the characteristics of the other. Thus a 15% feminine male might *feel and believe* that he should have been born a female due to this variation in femaleness and maleness that occurs naturally in human beings. It of course, has to be said that this is only *part of* why they feel

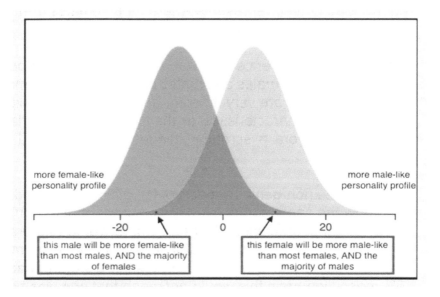

as they do.

(For the origin and acknowledgement of the graph please refer to the bibliography at the end of the book).

The "double curve sexual characteristics" graph shows that some males will be as feminine as some females and, of course, vice versa.

*However, this does not really mean that there is a true statistical continuous spectrum of the sexing of the brains of females and males as there is only a **partial** overlap of female and male characteristics curves on the graph. There are two curves: one for females and one for males. If there was a true continuous biological spectrum of sexualisation across female and male brains, there would only be a single long curve on the graph.*

We traditionally refer to the "opposite sex" but to a great extent that is a figure of speech. Females and males are not opposites but complementary beings. There maybe a range of sex characteristics but at each side the graph there is a "hump". Each hump represents where most females or most most males are statistically placed.

The distinct difference between the physical bodily characteristics of females and males is very obvious - female and male genitalia are very different and there is only a slight overlap of the characteristics of the sex organs: clitoris = penis, labia majora = scrotum, ovaries = testicles and so forth.

Of course, the non-genital aspects of female and male bodies also show the same sort of overlap as shown on the "double curve sexual characteristics" graph. Some women naturally have a far more muscular and "athletic" body than some men - *due to this natural variation.* Even if such a woman had a 15% masculine brain this would *not* mean that she was born in the wrong body - *this would just be the result of a natural variation and overlap of female and male characteristics.*

It has become apparent from brain scanning that some people who have cross-gender feelings may have a brain structure and function that *somewhat tends* towards that of the other sex. Note the word *tends*, no matter how a person may *feel* that they possess the brain of the other sex, biologically speaking - they don't, instead they may have up to 15% of the characteristics of the other sex. It can be said that the sexes aren't fully mutually exclusive - females can have a male side and males can have female side - but only up to a point. As mentioned previously this eanbles each sex to have some empathy and understanding of the other.

A very significant proportion of sex related personality and behaviour characteristics are genetically determined and do not need to be socially conditioned for them to be present but of course, social conditioning is a very influential factor. Society models and conditions female and male characteristics - sometimes helpfully but alas, sometimes unhelpfully. This brings us onto the next section.

WHAT MAKES US WHO WE ARE?

We are who we are as a result of:

1. Our chromosomes and the genetic material they contain - present in the ovum and sperm that combined at conception (fertilisation) and produced our body.

2. Factors that give rise to the changes in expression of the genetic code of our genetic material that are caused by environmental factors such as toxins, viruses and even psychological stress. (There are many other factors that affect genetic expression that are beyond the scope of a small book - the subject of epigenetics is huge).

3. The nature of the attachment we had with our carers, particularly in the earliest stages of life. Rejection, abandonment, frustration of needs are significant. Emotional, physical and sexual abuse are particularly influential. These factors have a major influence on how the personality develops, the amount of self-esteem that someone has and how they regard themselves in many other ways.

4. Continued learning and conditioning by social and cultural factors.

1 - 4 combined dictate:

      a. Where we are on the "double curve sexual characteristics" graph.
      b. How we deal with the emotional and practical stresses of life.

To decrease the emotional pain from the stresses and strains of life the mind uses various "mental defences" as will be discussed in the next section. To be frank, this may be somewhat technical and tedious to read but it will hopefully give an understanding of human emotions - but this is essential to be able to understand how thoughts and feeling develop.

MENTAL DEFENCES - SOMETIMES THEY WORK TO OUR ADVANTAGE AND SOMETIMES THEY DON'T

We all have many psychological strains in life, the most obvious are the stresses of day-to-day practicalities and the difficulties of dealing with the awkward personalities of other people. Most people put their own practical and emotional needs before those of other people.

Another often unrecognised mental strain is the "psychological ghosts of the past" - these include:

1. Mental traumas of earlier life that lurk in the *unconscious*. They may not be thought of or remembered in daily life, but their emotional pain may invade our consciousness in the form of anxiety and other feelings. As a result, we may experience a vague sense of unease or anxiety but not be able to put a finger on what it is or where it comes from.
2. Every interaction that we have with people in the present will have echoes from the past - sometimes good and sometimes bad. The appreciated characteristics of a dear friend may *unconsciously* remind you of some of the loving aspects of your mother. The discomfort you feel with your boss might *unconsciously* remind you of a father who punished you out of spite and anger about his own life rather than because you just needed guidance or loving discipline.

Our "mental defences" help to reduce the amount of psychological pain we feel in day-to-day life *and* from the effects of the *unconscious* "psychological ghosts of the past". Even those of us who do not have formal psychological training can instinctively spot the use of mental defences by others as shown by the following examples.

Whenever the various mental defences are referred to in this book, they will be written in capitals.

DENIAL

"He's fooling himself, he blamed his wife's personality for the marriage break up but in reality the divorce was all due to his drinking and violence. He is in complete DENIAL".

PROJECTION

This is a feeling of what is actually occurring *inside* the mind being experienced *as if* it comes from the *outside* world. "The man in the social club *felt* inadequate because he *assumed* the others were criticising him - he *blamed them* for *his* feelings". In actual fact he *already* had feelings of inadequacy and was *already* self-critical but he PROJECTED these feelings *away from himself onto others*. He then believed that the others were being critical of him.

There may also be a whole variety of things you inwardly criticise yourself for but then PROJECT them onto others and assume that they are judging or criticising you. In a similar way, you may secretly blame yourself for something but then PROJECT the blame onto someone else and so it *feels as if* things are their fault.

PROJECTIVE IDENTIFICATION

"She hated her neighbour who was in reality a very pleasant woman. The way she kept annoying and insulting the neighbour *made* the neighbour dislike her in return". PROJECTIVE IDENTIFICATION is a process where a person has a certain emotion but the way they behave to someone else makes the *other person* have the same emotional experience or behave in a similar way. Perhaps the simplest example of how behaviour by one human can influence the feelings of another is that of a child crying. The other well known example is that of a lovers' tiff - one partner may feel rejected and angry and the way they behave to their partner in return is an *unconscious* way of making their

51

partner feel similar emotional pain. They are "putting" some of their own emotional pain *into the other person* as a way of punishing them and making them feel what they feel so they know what it is like - or as revenge.

IDENTIFICATION

"That thirteen year old boy was so obsessed by the gang leader that he wanted to be like him and copied everything about him. He wanted to *be* him, he IDENTIFIED with him". IDENTIFICATION may occur when someone takes on a certain identity to cover up or compensate for uncomfortable feelings or a sense of lacking something. If this new assumed "identity" is challenged, it feels very threatening and uncomfortable.

AVOIDANCE

We are all very familiar with this defence! We all indulge in AVOIDANCE of things we just cannot face - we keep putting things off - sometimes for a little while or even long term. Sometimes we consciously realise we are using this defence but at other times we do it *unconsciously* when we put things out of the mind or just fill the mind with a more pleasurable thought or task.

UNDOING

"At first he kept washing his penis after having sex with the man he met in the gay club. He was initially unsure about his sexuality but later became comfortable with it when he realised he was in love with the man". It is literally as if a certain physical action can "wash away" or "UNDO" something that you have done or a feeling that you are uncomfortable about.

DISPLACEMENT

"She was really angry with her mother for the way she had spoken to her. When she went to work she had an angry outburst with her older female boss". She had redirected and DISPLACED her anger from her mother to somebody who *unconsciously* represented her mother. This process changes the target of feelings to someone who just happens to be available and who *represents* the real target of those feelings. Sometimes the feelings are redirected to someone who is a "safer" target - in other words someone who cannot or will not retaliate as in "The man who beats his wife having been punished and humiliated by his boss".

You can also DISPLACE bad feelings about yourself onto someone else. For example, you may have secret greedy or sexual desires but you can DISPLACE them onto someone else and so it seems as if it is the other person who has the feelings.

If you have self-critical thoughts, it is more emotionally comfortable to DISPLACE the criticism towards others so that you believe that they have the faults. For example, "It's obvious that she sees her own faults in other people and gives them a hard time about it".

Scapegoating is also a form of DISPLACEMENT of feelings or blame and can be the basis of long-term grievances and accusations between people.

RATIONALISATION

"He never achieved much in his business but pretends to people in the pub *and to himself* that his failure was due to market forces rather than his poor planning. In reality he was just useless in business but tried to explain away and RATIONALISE his failure".

REACTION FORMATION

"She really fancied her co-worker and deliberately sat provocatively with her knees showing but when he spotted her legs, she covered her knees". REACTION FORMATION is doing the opposite of what you would actually like to do. The action reduces the sense of discomfort, inner conflict, embarrassment, shame or guilt.

SUBLIMATION (Physical)

"He tried to get rid of his (mental) stress by (physically) punching the wall".

SUBLIMATION (Emotional and sexual)

"He never had much of a sex life and puts all his (emotional and sexual) energies into charity work".

USING HUMOUR

"He coped with his disappointment by making a joke about the situation and putting all his energies into helping others". SHOWING ALTRUISM is also a mental defence as it helps soothe the feelings by doing a good deed - so that you can feel good about yourself. Sometimes SHOWING ALTRUISM is sometimes done to compensate for previous bad deeds or other feelings of guilt.

THOUGHT SUPPRESSION AND COMPARTMENTALISATION

"The judge had to keep her mind on the difficult actual bodily harm case and kept pushing out of her mind the fact that her husband had punched her in the chest - she SUPPRESSED HER THOUGHTS". "The judge had also to separate her distracting thoughts about her husband by COMPARTMENTALISING them in her mind".

Now, who hasn't used such "mental defences"? We all have of course!

By casting an eye down the list it can easily be seen that some mental defences seem more mature and sophisticated than others. As you would expect, the more mature and sophisticated the person, the more they will utilise mature defences. The difficulty we *all* face is that the more stressed and threatened we are, the more we abandon the use of mature defences and instead resort to the use of immature defences - the very defences we would have used at an earlier stage in our life.

There is an old phrase, "The best method of defence is attack". This is seen on a day-to-day basis in the workplace and at home and we are all familiar with it:

The jilted lover hit their partner.

An insult to someone's dress sense is responded to with a retaliatory insult.

The workings of the *unconscious* mind can cause a defensive physical, verbal or emotional response *before the conscious mind can control it*. We have all seen examples when impulsive violent actions are taken, or hurtful words are blurted out. These are all examples of how we are at the mercy of our *unconscious* mind - *things "just seem to happen".*

MENTAL DEFENCES THAT ARE PARTICULARLY RELEVANT TO THE MENTAL LIFE OF CHILDREN AND ADOLESCENTS

It is readily obvious to parents that their child's appreciation of reality is very limited and that children frequently indulge in fantasy play and wild imagination. Children are totally reliant on their parents for everything - safety, food and affection to name but a few. Being completely dependent on their parents makes children feel vulnerable and in order to cope with their precarious feelings use the following very immature mental defences. The names of these mental defences are once again in capitals:

IDEALISATION

Examples of IDEALISATION: "My mother is the most loving in the world", "My Dad is the toughest and richest in our street". Young children and particularly teenagers may IDEALISE a parent in one moment then in the next breath may say they "hate" them - this is the opposite defence of DENIGRATION. DENIGRATION can allow someone to emotionally leave a person behind - for example a teenager who is trying to psychologically separate and differentiate themselves from their parents. DENIGRATION will make it easier to get over a lover who rejected you. Unjustifiably criticising someone by means of DENIGRATION can be used to make you feel better than them - and can be a defence for feeling bad about yourself.

SPLITTING

Dividing people into purely good or purely bad with no shades of grey is the defence of SPLITTING. An awful socially divisive and toxic example of SPLITTING is prejudice in which *all* people of one group are believed to be bad. Clearly, *every* group of people in society has its proportion of exceptionally good and exceptionally bad people - but most people are pretty average and reasonable.

There is another way in which SPLITTING functions - if there are aspects of life or of the self that are not liked, they can be SPLIT OFF from consciousness and be "put out of the mind". Most people are familiar with "putting things out of the mind" and this involves a combination of SPLITTING, DENIAL and COMPARTMENTALISATION of thoughts and feelings. Thoughts and feelings of disgust about the self can be SPLIT OFF and PROJECTED onto parts of the body - "my ugly breasts", "my weird shaped penis", "my smelly vagina that bleeds" and so forth. In the examples given the breasts may be quite normal, the penis also normal and the vagina only has the normal slight odour of menstruation but if the person has a lot of self-hate and disgust about their personality then the parts of the body PROJECTED onto will seem similarly "bad".

ACTING OUT

"The toddler was angry because he couldn't stack his bricks and his mother was ignoring him because she was busy preparing a business spreadsheet. He threw his Teddy bear out of the door". His actions helped him to vent his frustration. ACTING OUT is a way of releasing or redirecting the emotional energy of mental angst. Vandalism is an example of this. Please remember - *behaviour can also be a form of communication* and is particularly used by those who cannot maturely process powerful emotions and then express them words - toddlers and teenagers would be a good example but of course, adults can also do the same - don't we all at times?

INTROJECTION

This is a process in which very young children seem to automatically mentally "take in whole" and copy a parent's characteristics in order to be like their parents although of course, their overall similarity to parents is a mixture of copying and heredity. This is a process in which what is in the *outside* world is experienced *as if* it comes from the *inside* mental world. This is therefore an *unconscious* mental defence mechanism that occurs in the *opposite* direction to PROJECTION.

MAGICAL THINKING & FANTASY THINKING

"The six year old boy still completely believed that Father Christmas would bring him absolutely anything he wanted". "The five year old girl totally believed that if she was wrapped in her mother's favourite pink cardigan it would protect her from her abusing uncle". This is MAGICAL THINKING, which tends to be used less after reality has repeatedly debunked the fantasy i.e. Father Christmas is known to not exist. MAGICAL THINKING is also used less and less once a person has developed more mature mental defence mechanisms. We often use the term "wishful thinking", which is similar although this can result in a less strongly held belief. MAGICAL THINKING is the basis of FANTASY THINKING but the actual degree of belief in the FANTASY THOUGHT can vary according to maturity and psychological need.

DELUSIONAL PROJECTION

"The four year old boy had no doubt that the shadow in the corner was a monster who would take him from his parents and he would never see them again". DELUSIONAL PROJECTION is perceiving everyday objects as something other than what they really are.

REGRESSION

The human mind is in a continuous process of maturation and development from the earliest moments of life up to the time of life when ageing and degeneration cause the brain's function to deteriorate. A striking feature of the mind is that when it is under considerable duress it functions as if it was working at an earlier stage of development. Many of us feel we need a hug when distressed and can cry at times. People in war zones when under attack can feel like rolling up in a ball into the foetal position. Returning to an earlier stage of mental processing and behaviour is known as REGRESSION. Most of us can recall people who were very distressed "acting just like a child". Absolutely *every* one of us can REGRESS if our resilience has been overcome by severe stress. There is no shame in admitting this, after all, we are all human and have our frailties no matter how much we may try to DENY it to others and ourselves.

To recap, when we are under psychological stress, we all use mental defences. Mental defences defuse, redirect and modify our psychological pain *but as a result our mental defences can distort our reality*. Mental defences operate without us knowing it - they are *unconscious* processes. The use of mental defences can modify someone's behaviour, but not always for the better. The more *immature* the type of defence that is being used, the more *dysfunctional* the result and the more that reality is distorted.

As has been referred to and is obvious to older parents, the maturation of the mind continues well into adulthood. In general terms, the more emotional and physical trauma a person experienced in their early years, the more they come to rely on immature mental defences such as DENIAL of reality, MAGICAL THINKING or indulging in FANTASY THOUGHT. The more a particular mental defence is habitually used, the more it becomes ingrained. Traumatised individuals are particularly prone to push away unpleasant feelings from themselves by DISPLACEMENT, PROJECTION and PROJECTIVE IDENTIFICATION.

Sophisticated and mature mental defences can only develop in childhood as a result of an environment that:

1. Feels safe.
2. Has an atmosphere of constant love and acceptance.
3. Has good mature role models.
4. Has parents who can "absorb" and "cope with" a child's anxiety and reassure the child that there is no need to be anxious. You could say that good parents are able to "contain" their child's anxiety. (The psychoanayst Wilfred Bion wrote extensively about containment of a child's emotions - please refer to the bibliography for more information).

The important point to emphasise once again is that the greater the psychological stress a person is under in the present moment, the more they resort to using immature defences - even if they do actually possess mature mental defences. *We all do this at times.*

Please keep in mind that *the more that **immature** mental defences are used, the more a person's reality is distorted.* This is why at times you will have difficulty understanding someone or have difficulty "getting through to them" - what they are saying or doing just does not seem to make sense, but this is simply due to their dysfunctional use of mental defences that is distorting their reality. This is why some people can seem to be completely exasperating to deal with.

When considering our minds, it is once again important to remember that human thought is *not* primarily controlled by the conscious mind - even though it might feel or seem that way. In reality, thoughts and feelings originate in the *unconscious* mind and are a result of the interaction between the complex *unconscious* automatic actions of the mental defences and the stresses the person is experiencing. These stresses maybe either current external social pressures from other people or inner anxieties resulting from buried memories of previous mental trauma. It can therefore be concluded that:

"No one is a captain of their own ship".

This is why people "cannot just pull themselves together" or "get a grip of their emotions". Even apparently mentally mature and sophisticated people can at times seem to behave quite bizarrely and inexplicably when they are under certain extreme types of stress. In other words, although mental defences are there to help they can also be a hindrance by clouding reality and allowing the mind to deal with internal mental distress in unhelpful or counterproductive ways.

If you come across someone who seems to be "deceiving themselves", this may well be due to the action of their mental defences and as this happens *unconsciously* the self-deception might be more obvious to the onlooker than the person themselves. In other words, it can sometimes be seen by an independent observer that a person is DENYING a concrete reality or indulging in FANTASY THOUGHT and FANTASY problem solving.

When someone is experiencing strong emotions or a painful reality that their mental defences cannot adequately deal with, the reaction they give can be exceptionally powerful. The person on the receiving end of such a reaction is in no doubt about the power of such emotions - parents of teenagers will know all about this. The display of emotions by a bereaved person is another heart-wrenching example. The reader will have already noted that the mental defences involve a process of self-deception or modification of reality that aims to reduce psychological pain.

To emphasise a profound difficulty for parents - a young child's version of reality will often be remarkably inaccurate, and this most definitely still applies to teenagers and even some young adults.

The hard truth is that no matter how hard they try, a parent or health care professional will not be able to

gauge with absolute certainty how well a young child or teenager is able to make life changing decisions.

This is important to bear in mind as some gender transition treatments can dramatically affect the later stages of life - areas about which an immature child or teenager is extremely unlikely to fully understand. Generally, all an immature mind can focus on is the wants and needs *of the moment* - and generally the focus is on the *emotional* wants.

A COMPARISON OF FEMALE & MALE SEXUALITY AND WHAT EVERYBODY WANTS - BUT SOMETIMES IT MAY NOT BE "CONVENTIONAL"

One of the most overwhelming human needs is that of emotional, sensual and sexual contact with another person. Emotional, sensual and sexual feelings are all interrelated but they all vary according to the personality, sex, gender expression and sexual orientation of a person. However, to put it bluntly, sometimes people just want to have sexual satisfaction and it just does not matter too much how they get their sexual relief. At times it is just such an overwhelmingly strong need and desire that they will go to any lengths to get it or alternatively may take any opportunity that presents itself - this of course, applies to both cisheterosexual and LGBTQIA+ people.

Men tend to be quite sexually simplistic with a main focus on just having an orgasm and at a primitive psychological level having feelings of being protective and ownership. The latter is an evolutionary throwback to Caveman days and now considered old-fashioned, inappropriate and politically incorrect.

Female sexuality is far, far more complex and is not just centred mainly on the genitals but may involve many or even all areas of the body. The female sexual experience is very psychologically sensual as well as physically sensual. The psychological part of female sexual enjoyment and attraction is comprised of factors that are essential to an enduring relationship and are a complex mixture of feeling valued, being cherished, being cared for, being nurtured, being protected, being found sexually desirable and being loved. The male partner's social status, physical attractiveness and other factors related to his potential to be a biologically good father are also factors that can make a man more sexually desirable to a woman.

Of course, men can also enjoy the sensuality of general bodily and psychological contact but *either* sex can also just fancy an orgasm - self-pleasuring by masturbation or "quickie" sex.

Someone's particular sexual taste may not necessarily be cisheterosexual and the fact that it is not sexually mainstream may heighten the desire and the intensity of the pleasure for that individual - such is the lure of pleasures "forbidden" by society. Many couples, whether they are cisheterosexual or transgender can heighten their pleasure by indulging in sex that is mildly paraphilic in nature. Virtually no one is without this potential as is discussed in the section about Freudian principles under the heading of Anything Goes - Polymorphous Sexuality. *(*Paraphilia is discussed later in the book).

GENDER, GENDER IDENTITY AND GENDER EXPRESSION

Gender and sex are of course, related to biological femaleness or maleness. Your gender identity and your gender expression are the ways you *feel* and ACT OUT your femaleness or maleness - as to what you *believe* and *feel* is your gender. How you *express* gender is a very much a socially learned mental phenomenon - it might *feel* individual but is very much constructed from components of other people's characteristics due to IDENTIFICATION and INTROJECTION in addition to genetic factors.

Gender stereotypes in the earliest periods of human history were originally very much due to biological factors but became modified by innumerable years of social influence layered on top. Some aspects of gender identity and expression can be consciously and *unconsciously* altered - as happens during teenage years and during the progress of gender transition.

Yes, gender *identity* and *expression* can be consciously and *unconsciously* changed, but scientists and biologists continue to take the view that sex cannot be changed. It is therefore respectfully suggested that scientifically and biological speaking the term "gender transition" is more accurate and appropriate than the often-used terminology of "sex change". Of course, anyone can form their own personal viewpoint on terminology and use it accordingly - but at the end of the day, for it to be best understood, there should be a broad consensus about its use.

There are those who say that they naturally *feel* that they are another gender to what their physical body would suggest - and for them this a totally authentic experience of themselves. There are others, particularly in the much younger age groups who come to feel this way because it appears to be able to help them deal with a number of discomforts they experience within and about themselves. As will be repeatedly stated, some people are truly helped by gender transition but for others, especially in the younger age groups the notion that gender transition "will" help is an inaccurate belief that is a result of the action of mental defences.

It is incredible how quickly our *feelings* can become our "facts" - they then become our firm *beliefs* and then part of our *identity*. We have all experienced this at some stage and is why when your *feelings* and *beliefs* are questioned it is felt to be a personal attack on your *identity* - it may *feel* like a direct insult against who you believe you are. This explains why even in the face of science, logic and what is actually in front of their eyes, when challenged, some people give a very heartfelt response about particular matters under discussion. They may be regarding their beliefs as if they are profound insights without realising that they are sometimes based only on *feelings*. On the other hand, scientists welcome a challenge to their views - they like to keep an open mind and are guided by evidence. Having said that, it has to be repeated that many people who have undergone full hormonal and surgical gender transition *feel* that they are under no illusion that they are actually living as the other sex. They say that although they still have the chromosomal sex they were born with - they feel quite able and content to ACT OUT their particular mode of gender expression as the other sex. If this improves their experience of life and is their genuine feeling, who could object? Some transmen may quite understandably wish to be referred to as a man but would be frank enough to say that they are not truly a man. One of the world's best-known transmen, Buck Angel has said as much. Most understanding cisgender people would and indeed *should* be polite and reasonable enough to *refer to* them as a man in a social situation. Some people who have undergone hormonal and surgical gender transition express no doubts that they have actually changed sex. It would of course, be extremely impolite to challenge them in a social environment and this should be borne in mind by cisgender people.

FEELINGS OF BEING NON-BINARY, AGENDER AND GENDER FLUID

There are some people who *feel* that they are neither one gender or the other and describe themselves as "non-binary". There are others who say that have no gender at all and are "agender". As was mentioned above, it is correct to say that not everybody is 100% feminine or 100% masculine but is what being described as being non-binary or agender does seem to relate to a deep personal experience rather than something that pure physical biology can necessarily explain on its own. The psychology of this will be explored later in the book - or at least attempted as best as a cisgender author can do so but of course, the accounts of patients and psychological literature were taken into consideration during writing.

There are also those who have the experience that their gender can actually be changeable, which is referred to as "gender fluidity". Of course, biologically, *actual* sex is not technically fluid or variable. It is of course, once again deep subjective experiences about the gender and the self that are being "fluid" due to complex *changeable* deep *unconscious* psychological processes taking place. To repeat, a sense of "being" non-binary, gender fluid or agender is due to an inner subjective experience and is not technically entirely rooted in biology. Whilst these feelings are not technically associated with biology, it can be fully appreciated that we all *feel* differently about ourselves at different times depending what is going on in our existence and therefore our *unconscious*. However, if this feels to the person as if it is a totally intrinsic and authentic experience - it is important to acknowledge and respect what other people are feeling and how they wish to live their life.

It is very concerning that very young women who *feel* that they are non-binary, agender or gender fluid may choose to have their breasts removed at a particularly young age. Surely, many of them could not possibly be certain that they will never want to have children and breastfeed at a future point in life. They will tragically lose a fundamental part of motherhood, the mutual mother-child joy of love and nurture during breastfeeding.

MORE IDEAS AND TERMINOLOGY IN TRANSGENDER THEORY THAT MANY CISGENDER PEOPLE FIND DIFFICULT TO APPRECIATE. WHERE DO TRANSGENDER FEELINGS SOMETIMES COME FROM AND SHOULD THEY ALWAYS BE FOLLOWED?

Cisgender people could perhaps be forgiven for not understanding some transgender terminology - it is becoming increasingly complex. It is helpful for cisgender people to have some form of understanding in order to avoid causing offence. There are unfortunately some very confusing statements regarding transgender matters and they sometimes appear to clash with each other. To add further to difficulties, terminologies change - some that were formerly felt to be insulting have been "reclaimed" for use in certain circumstances. There are others, which previously seemed innocuous or even considered polite have now become regarded as insulting. If it turns out that offence has been inadvertently given to a transgender person an apology should obviously be given followed by a request to know the preferred terminology.

Please consider the following somewhat confusing viewpoints that many cisgender people may find very difficult to understand:

1. Some transgender spokespersons directly refer to one gender *or* its opposite. They say that gender is innate and immutable. They are clearly referring to one gender *or* the other in an *entirely binary* way but confusingly...
2. Some say that they are non-binary, or even agender and
   ...
3. Others say that they are gender fluid.
4. There are suggestions that there is an almost infinite spectrum of genders.
5. Another view is that gender is completely a social construction.

6. When asked the question, "What is a woman?" some transgender spokespersons answer in terms of factors that only relate to the function of reproduction or the presence of certain female reproductive organs. This clashes with a frequently made assertion that the body doesn't matter and it is instead the *"feelings* of being a woman" that are important. As stated previously, female and male minds evolved over separate evolutionary pathways for very different biopsychosocial roles.

So, what is going on?

Please consider the following:

1. The most scientific and medical point of view would be to say that sex is biological and immutable but that ...
2. Gender identity and the expression of gender characteristics can be influenced by society, a person's personality type, their sexual orientation and the exceptionally complex workings of their *unconscious* mind.

Mental state is potentially very changeable for everyone. Sometimes any of us might be content with ourselves one moment but at other times feel dissatisfied and may therefore DENY or COMPARTMENTALISE certain emotions and features about ourselves that we don't like. Wishing we were a different person to who we are is a common thought for many, if not all people. This applies to both the mind and the body. Some examples: "If only I wasn't so shy", "I wish my nose wasn't as big", "I would feel better about myself if I wasn't so overweight", "If I had a better sense of humour I would get on better in life", "I would be more confident if I had bigger breasts", "I wish my testicles didn't look like that" - the list is endless. Given that gender is such a large part of our identity, if we are uncomfortable about ourselves, our gender is one of the most important identity factors that we might *unconsciously* DENY or consciously wish was different -

particularly if we have a feeling of struggling in our traditional role as a female or as a male. We might instead then be *unconsciously* or consciously motivated to *express* our gender differently.

We are all "different people" at different times depending on our current psychological situation. People can therefore feel differently about their gender identity at different times and they may be attracted to different genders at different times - this can all give a *feeling* and experience of gender fluidity. As is mentioned throughout this book, feelings of discomfort as a person and as a sexual being can sometimes make us wish to become a different person and this can be translated into feeling the self to be transgender.

Please consider the following confusing viewpoints that might lead to someone making unwise decisions about hormonal and surgical gender transition treatments:

1. If someone *feels* they are non-binary, is it advisable for them to undergo hormonal and surgical gender transitioning treatments? What would they transition to?
2. How can it necessarily be the best thing to provide cross-sex hormones or conducting gender transition surgery on those who *feel* they are gender fluid? What would they transition to?
3. If gender is a social construct as some gender theorists state, why does it need to be permanently changed surgically? What would they transition to?

Just because someone is a masculine woman, or a feminine man does not suggest that a change of gender expression is definitely the best way forward. *After all, in the current world shouldn't diversity and the range of human types be celebrated?*

Particularly in the case of very young people who are experiencing life stresses, self-doubt and are considering hormonal and surgical gender transition is it perhaps not a more psychological healthy approach to:

a. Become accepting of the self - the personality, sexual orientation, physique and gender but also to ...
b. Improve psychological resilience and skills in handling life's unavoidable difficult emotions and stresses by means of psychotherapy and self-development processes such as resilience building, mindfulness, self-help books, yoga, exercise, creative activities, more community living and so forth. Religious faith is valuable in gaining an inner sense of contentment *rather than* by means of an over reliance on Social Media for life guidance. It is of note that some parts of society in the Western world have become diminished in terms of religious faith and as a result other supporting systems have filled the vacuum. Transgender ideation has to an extent become a sort of faith system that is filling this gap for *some* young people. Young people are particularly susceptible to INTROJECTING belief systems just as they latch onto political and other ideologies and identities. Political and belief systems give a sense of certainty and provide explanations for why life is as it is. They also give a sense of hope and control. They also provide a sense of rebellion - something that *unconsciously* appeals to a teenager who is establishing their identity and differentiating from the older generation.

By perseverance with a and b, younger people who have transgender feelings may well find that they can get on with life through self-acceptance and personal development without the need for puberty blockers, cross-sex hormones and surgery.

It is appreciated that someone might be dissatisfied with certain aspects of their body and would wish them to be permanently changed - but the problem is that the mind changes and evolves throughout life. What may have seemed appropriate at one time of life might be totally the wrong thing when the mind has "moved on" and personal circumstances or emotions have changed. The author has come across people who were glad that they had not subjected themselves to cross-sex hormones and surgery but equally he has also come across those who became happier having undergone hormonal and surgical gender transition processes. Unfortunately, he has come across examples of terrible medical gender transition regret. *It is all about making the correct decision.*

GENDER DYSPHORIA - IS THAT *REALLY* THE PROBLEM IN YOUNG PEOPLE *OR* IS SOMETHING ELSE GOING ON PSYCHOLOGICALLY - COULD IT BE *GENERAL* DYSPHORIA *OR* "SENSUAL-SEXUAL" DYSPHORIA?

It would be helpful to explore the medical term "dysphoria". *General* dysphoria is an experience of psychological discomfort, in other words it is an abnormality of mood, thought and perception and is often accompanied by anxiety. In non-psychiatric terms it means that something just "doesn't *generally* feel right emotionally".

Every single stage of human life can be associated with feelings of emotional distress and discomfort. It is often possible to point a finger towards the cause of mental pain but sometimes it is just not that obvious. There may be factors within someone's mind that they just don't understand or are unable to acknowledge - this is because mental defences are covering things up in the *unconscious* and of course, these mental defences are working *unconsciously* - without us realising it.

There has been an explosion of the number of young people attending clinics who are experiencing what is labelled as gender dysphoria. It is well known that the years around puberty are filled with self-doubt, confusion and conflicts within the self. In the teenage years there is an inevitable discomfort with and opposition to the older generation - this is actually a part of growing up and differentiating from parents. It is a way of establishing a personal identity and moving away from parents. This is normal even though sometimes painful for all concerned.

It is important to emphasise to parents that if their transgender child is being assessed in a clinic, the staff will not be critical of their parenting or "think the worst" of the parents themselves.

Members of the modern youth are subjected to a bombardment by Social Media of how wonderful other people's lives *supposedly* are. As a result, many young people may feel that they lack the exciting life of those who wildly exaggerate their lifestyles in the Social Media. They feel that they are "supposed" to live up to these overstated lifestyles but are unable to do so because it's just not possible to match up to what is actually someone else's lies and pretences. This can nevertheless become a major source of dissatisfaction. Not having as many likes, friends or followers as the "starlets" of Social Media may result in feelings of inadequacy.

Another area of concern is body perfectionism and looking at faked and modified images in the Social Media will inevitably also cause many young people to have feelings of physical inadequacy.

Please consider the combination of:

1. A teenager who is not feeling content with their life and is unhappy with themselves - in other words they are feeling *generally* dysphoric. They may not be entirely sure why they feel this way but they almost certainly have vague underlying feelings of poor self-esteem and of not matching up to others of their age group.
2. A teenager who is uncomfortable about the physical changes of puberty: "Do my breasts look OK?" "Is my penis big enough, is its shape OK?" "I wish I wasn't so spotty", "I'm really embarrassed about my periods".
3. A teenager who is under confident about their sexual attractiveness.
4. A teenager who is feeling insecure about romantically approaching the other sex and fears rejection.

5. The "double curve sexual characteristics" graph showing that nobody is 100% female or 100% male - the teenager may not feel totally female or totally male because they have up to 15% of the characteristics of the other sex.
6. An explosion of very convincing publicity in the Social Media regarding transgender issues put out by confident, convincing and "cool" YouTubers, Instagrammers and other "influencers".

1 - 6 make all too easy for a teenager to conclude that they are transgender *although in reality they are really just taking refuge in the idea* - it seems to be an explanation for what they are feeling and it may be a way of expressing a mental pain that they don't have a better way of putting into words. The human mind is always on the lookout for explanations or solutions to problems and it will readily latch onto appealing ideas, particularly if many other people are doing the same. Fashion can be comforting, exciting and gives a sense of being in vogue. Young people may therefore incorrectly believe that what is actually "life dysphoria" or "*general dysphoria*" is the "gender dysphoria" that is so often talked about in the Social Media. But this maybe nothing more than a self-diagnosis and an assumption based on the content of Social Media. The origin of their mental distress will often really lie in a variety of other mundane and ordinary unsatisfactory parts of life but because of the many convincing transgender messages in the Social Media, it is all too easy to wrongly conclude that it is all due to having gender dysphoria and being transgender.

Taking on a self-image that is transgender results in instant *attention, approval, acceptance, appreciation and acknowledgement* by online transgender groups - the very things that are often missing from many a teenager's life. This finding of solace, connection and being (virtually) noticed is very *addictive*. Most of us like to be noticed and to "belong".

Gender identity is often *felt* to very flexible in the time before and during puberty. This can be regarded as a completely normal part of that period in life and also part of the process of working out who you are. It will pass - but not if it is given rewarding attention. Furthermore, a soupçon of same-sex attraction can be experienced by many people in this age group, which is often just a part of passing through puberty. Those who experience same-sex attraction are often innately non-gender conforming. In spite of the current libero-diverse times there is often an undercurrent of homophobia in society. Unfortunately, this homophobia can be incorporated into the mind of the teenager by INTROJECTION - every one of us *unconsciously* "absorbs" the values and ideas of our society into our mind, for better or for worse. This all just adds to the already perturbing feelings of pubertal insecurity - but none of these factors truly indicates that the young person is living in a body of the wrong sex.

In the even younger age group, if a very young boy says, "I *feel* I'm a girl" or a young girl says, "I *feel* like a boy" it is most likely just a phase or in fact no more than a *phrase* - not a disorder. There is absolutely no way a very young boy knows how a girl truly *feels* or vice versa - other than just superficially given their limited understanding and knowledge of the other sex. Children often behave in ways that they have picked up from other children or television but if it this more than just a phase, persistent cross-gender behaviour requires professional assessment to pick up any *conventional* and non-gender related mental wellbeing matters.

Children like any attention - and a lot is even better. In this modern world in which both parents may need to work, the adults will understandably want some time for themselves, and their own spare time may be consumed by Social Media and Information Technology screens but as a result their children may be ignored and therefore craving attention. It is well known how young children like to commandeer their sibling's toys and anything else they can get their hands on.

A girl who repeatedly wants to play with her brother's train set may simply be coveting a sibling's toys as children do, or she may have noticed that playing with trains gets plenty of Daddy's attention. Imagine a young boy making a feeble attempt at putting on his father's tie or work boots - he might obtain approving but minor attention. Consider the same young lad who purely out of sibling devilment puts on his sister's dress - he will obtain quite intense attention. He may well put on the dress again for obvious reasons - not because he's transgender, he just likes the degree of attention. He does not need a gender identity clinic appointment.

Very young children will say a whole variety of nonsensical things such as, "I have special powers and can fly like a superhero" but this merely demonstrates their ability to fantasise and their occasional detachment from reality - in other words MAGICAL THINKING. This is why we regard children as children - vulnerable, immature and ignorant of the realities, dangers and responsibilities of life. It is therefore an important parental role to guide and protect children from themselves. When a young child refers to *feelings* of being of the other sex or frankly states that they are transgender, its perplexed and concerned parents will wonder what they should do. A very young child's cross-gender ramblings can generally be disregarded as the outpourings of an immature mind that cannot possibly fully comprehend sex and gender at their age.

Due to the amount of pro-gender transition material that exists in the Social Media some parents may feel that it is the "right and progressive" thing to allow their child to follow the transgender pathway. Other parents will be horrified and conflicted. However, to repeat, their child's use of Social Media or just following what their young friends are doing will almost certainly have actually been the cause of their transgender ideas. Parents will be in a quandary as to what to do and how to seek help. They will almost certainly find that many institutions such as health services are under the pressure of political correctness to be pro-gender transition. Of course, the transgender organisations putting this pressure on the health services are doing so with good intentions but as in most aspects of making a diagnosis it is essential to consider all possible causes. Putting the words, "I think my child is transgender" in an Internet search engine will almost invariably bring up very pro-gender transition websites. In order to find a balance of viewpoints and then weigh matters up accordingly helpful alternative views can be obtained by reference to www.transgendertrend.com, www.genspect.org and www.sexchangeregret.com. YouTube can also provide some useful balance if a search is made under "transition regret" and "detransition". Reference to the website of The Society for Evidenced Based Gender Medicine is also very strongly recommended. For those who feel there is a need for an expert psychological exploration of transgender feelings reference to the website www.genderexploratory.com (Gender Exploratory Therapy Association - GETA) can provide contact with psychotherapists who specialise in this area. For those who have same sex attraction and are considering gender transition a very useful website is www.genderhq.com (Gender Health Query). Another helpful resource is www.4thwavenow.com. In terms of what can be read to or read with a four to nine year old child there is a particularly helpful children's book called "Johnny the Walrus". This publication makes clear the mindset and mental immaturity of a young child. Whilst this book has received a number of accusations of being transphobic and bigoted its overall rating on Amazon has been astonishingly good. Anything that can protect the welfare of children can only be to the good.

Once they have passed through puberty the majority of young people find that *feelings* of what may have been believed to be gender dysphoria naturally subside. Some of those who eventually *feel* that their gender identity has been particularly difficult to come to terms with may turn out to be lesbian, gay or bisexual, which is of course not a problem. It has become evident through brain research that brains of lesbian and gay people may in some instances tend to be slightly shifted towards the other sex as indicated on the "double curve sexual characteristics" graph. Why on earth shouldn't those who tend towards the other sex on the graph be permitted follow their sexual preferences and act accordingly by being gay, lesbian or bisexual rather than rush into cross-sex hormonal or surgical treatments? After all, society has at long last become more accommodating and understanding of non-cisheterosexual relationships. It is also encouraging that society is becoming more accepting towards transgender people but to repeat, the concern of the author is that immature young people can inappropriately embark upon medical transgender treatments when their underlying problems are of a *general* psychological nature, which have not been properly explored prior to receiving irreversible hormonal and surgical cross-gender treatments.

Young people who are not gay, lesbian or bisexual but whose assumed gender dysphoria doesn't subside once they have passed through puberty will be expected to have underlying psychological discomforts of a *general* rather than a specifically gender related nature. Any lack of mental wellbeing should be the subject of very careful clinical assessment.

The sad reality is that many people may ultimately never receive the psychological care they needed in the first place to help them accept their personality, sexual orientation and body *as they are* because they had gone straight into hormonal and surgical gender transition treatments at the outset.

As above, it is becoming increasingly apparent that sexual orientation has both biological and psychological origins. Attraction is obviously a good indication of sexual orientation although societal taboos can prevent or influence expression of particular sexual tastes and directions. The important thing is that people can enjoy their sexuality as best they can without societal disapproval. A person's overall sense of identity as a "sexual being" is a mixture of their orientation, sexual tastes and how they have come to view their gender identity - we could invent a term for this such as, "sensual-sexual direction". If their "sensual-sexual direction" is felt to be at odds with society's mainstream cisheterosexual direction it can be understood how they will feel uncomfortable about this - due to internalised homophobia as referred to above. Humans are instinctively driven to "fit in" to society and if for some reason they do not correspond to the mainstream this can be very uncomfortable. Someone's sexual desires and how they are perceived as a sexual being are major and sometimes overwhelming preoccupations in their day-to-day thoughts and feelings. A "sensual-sexual identity" that does not fit in with that of the majority of the population will result in uncomfortable *general* dysphoric feelings - but these can easily wrongly be put down to gender dysphoria because gender and sexual matters are *associated with* those uncomfortable *general* feelings.

Somewhere on the misty border between conscious and *unconscious* feelings due to the conditioning received from cisheterosexual society there may be a sense that, "If I desire a man, I must be a woman" or "If I desire a woman, I must be a man". We could again describe this as "sensual-sexual dysphoria" and it does appear that many pre and post-gender transition patients describe this but regarded it as gender dysphoria. As repeatedly stated in this book, many patients who have gone through hormonal and surgical gender transition say that what they originally believed to be gender dysphoria has not gone away. It does seem that what they are continuing to experience is "sensual-sexual dysphoria" and other deep psychological conflicts rather than actually living in a body of the wrong sex. It is people in this category that can be particularly prone to gender transition regret - purely because it was not that they were in the wrong body but instead felt that their "sensual-sexual" feelings did not fit in with the mainstream cisheterosexual conventions or with their expectations of themselves.

To repeat, launching headlong into puberty blockers, cross-sex hormones and gender transition surgery is likely to be inappropriate for most young people in the above categories as many of them just have normal variations of femaleness or maleness with or without feelings of same-sex attraction. They may have also have been experiencing general dysphoria *rather than* gender dysphoria. More considerations of "dysphoria" will now be discussed.

SOME COMPARISONS: 1. SUPPOSED RAPID ONSET GENDER DYSPHORIA (BUT NOT) 2. SUPPOSED GENDER DYSPHORIA (BUT NOT) 3. TRUE GENDER DYSPHORIA

1. SUPPOSED RAPID ONSET GENDER DYSPHORIA (BUT NOT)

Some young people appear to have the somewhat newly formulated diagnosis of Rapid Onset Gender Dysphoria (ROGD). Given that puberty may *rapidly* descend upon an unsuspecting youth, a time in life when there are almost inevitable identity issues and sexual insecurities, it is all too easy for a diagnosis of ROGD to be made. The supposed "rapid onset" can *seem* to occur suddenly (i.e. rapidly) after a period of teenage emotional distress and an overindulgence in Social Media. Supposed ROGD appears to be more common in young girls than boys in the same way as it is with anorexia nervosa - it does seem that girls are somewhat more susceptible than boys to certain types of peer online fads. Most other trends and fads of youth can have a similarly "rapid onset" and no teenager's parent is surprised by things such as bizarre hair colours, slashed jeans, music choices, joining cult groups and gangs - the list is endless, but all are of "rapid onset" in the very same way as supposed ROGD. The older the reader, the more trends and cults that came and went will be recalled - some with considerable personal embarrassment. Just as joining a cult or dressing in novel ways can be part of "teenage rebellion" - so can stating to their parents that they are transgender. In fact, being transgender can be a "micro-cult" within some schools and wider teenage social groups.

It is well known that coming out as LGBTQIA+ throughout history has been extremely difficult and requires considerable courage. Some people from former generations never, ever came out during their whole life and only their closest friends or lover(s) knew. Fortunately, due to the work of LGBTQIA groups coming out is now much easier but even now, it can be an agonising and slow decision making process. It is of note that children with supposed gender dysphoria come out remarkably rapidly, which indicates that they are not truly coming out but instead are more than likely just joining a youth cult.

2. SUPPOSED GENDER DYSPHORIA (BUT NOT)

Please consider some entirely expected teenage psychological factors:

1. Teenagers need to feel they are differentiating from their parents - and shocking their exasperated parents is just part of that stage in life.
2. Teenagers are still children and therefore still like to have parental attention - and pocket money, have their clothes washed, food on the table etc..
3. Teenagers certainly need to be protected from themselves - they are at a stage of life in which impulsiveness is at its height.
4. Teenagers may be particularly under confident - especially about their bodies.
5. Teenagers may have up to 15% of the characteristics of the other sex as shown by the "double curve sexual characteristics" graph - in both their mind and their body.
6. Teenagers tend to be shy in relation to the other sex - in terms of their attractiveness and approaching sexually.
7. Teenagers may have early awakenings of same sex attraction - in fact transient same sex attraction is remarkably common in this age group and this will often naturally be accompanied by a temporarily confused gender identity. It is important to remember that these two factors may just be normal *phases*.

A fourteen year old girl saying that she wants her breasts removed as she hates them fits into categories 1, 2, 3 and 4 remarkably well as does a boy saying he wants to wear makeup and a dress to school. (Particularly when it is known that the latter behaviour can bring fame and fortune for stage show and cinema "stars" - an example of which is the show and film, Everybody's Talking about Jamie).

Factors 4 - 7 may give rise to conscious and *unconscious* emotions in a teenager of "Not feeling quite right" in a way that at first they cannot really put into words but they may also feel that they don't fit well into the binary femaleness or maleness of their classmates. This phenomenon has been a teenage psychological reality for generations but it doesn't mean they are in the wrong body.

Girls wanting to wear trousers to school on the grounds of equality and safety is, of course, perfectly normal and reasonable - if that's why they are doing it.

The apparent mystery is that some children who claim to be transgender may say that, "I have always known I was in the wrong body" to the puzzlement of parents who cannot recall even the slightest cross-gender behaviour at any time. But there is no real mystery at all, it often seems that this is a Social Media based phenomenon. It is likely to be due to the mantra like regurgitation of the, "I've always known I wasn't a girl/boy" statements on YouTube. The *unconscious* processes are also likely to actually be, "I've always been a bit of an outsider and I can now be part of a cool (albeit online) group" plus the need to shock parents or simply become the centre of attention. If all these factors are combined with self-deceiving ACTING OUT it easily comes to be believed by the child that gender dysphoria has "always" been present. Please recall the earlier comment about feelings becoming beliefs and then "facts".

However, it is only with:

a. The recent advent of transgender messages in the Social Media.
b. Medical developments in hormonal and surgical gender transition techniques.
c. The increased societal acceptance of people adopting a transgender lifestyle.

... That the trend of being a transgender teenager has become so evident and indeed possible for such young people.

Given factors 4 - 7 and a - c, a teenager may quite genuinely once again put their emotion of, "Not feeling quite right" into regurgitated words such as, "I have always known I was born in the body of the wrong sex". It is quite understandable how this *seems* to be an explanation about their feelings for a young person. It is of course, extremely perplexing and worrying for parents to hear this. They cannot explain it and have no idea what to do about what their child is saying. To remind the reader - reference to the websites www.transgendertrend and www.genspect.org are strongly recommended where many useful reference sources will be found. The website of the Society for Evidence Based Gender Medicine also has invaluable information. For those who feel there is a need for expert psychological exploration of transgender feelings reference to the website www.genderexploratory.com (Gender Exploratory Therapy Association - GETA) can provide contact with psychotherapists who specialise in this area. For those who have same sex attraction and are considering gender transition a very useful website is www.genderhq.com (Gender Health Query). An interesting and helpful website is www.4thwavenow.com.

Children who are on the autistic spectrum are particularly prone to seizing upon niche concepts and thus parents of such children would be well advised to be particularly aware of this phenomenon. Autistic children may be in the "out group" at school and might find that their "outness" is compensated for by the sense of belonging that YouTube transgender virtual groups provide. Children with attention deficit and hyperactivity disorder (ADHD) and other neurodiverse conditions may also end up in the "out group" and seek acceptance in online transgender groups.

It is entirely normal to have daydreams of how life will turn out but in the Internet age such hopes for the future maybe based on Internet fantasy and can therefore be entirely unrealistic and as a result there is a good chance that such ambitions will be frustrated in some way. Ambitions for personal development are often traditionally gender specific and feelings of failure for not being an adequate female or an adequate male can ruin dreams of success. For a young person who *unconsciously* feels that they have some characteristics of the other sex as shown by the "double curve sexual characteristics" graph it is very easy to take refuge in a notion of being in a body of the wrong sex *as the reason for struggling in their own sex* by means of RATIONALISATION. When life disappoints it is particularly important to remember that it is only a dream that is broken, not the self. Wishful MAGICAL THINKING about gender transition is unlikely to be the answer to a broken teenage dream. The reality of life will always turn up at some stage no matter how much someone may wish to escape it.

The above paragraphs illustrate that there are many factors that cause or underlie what may be *assumed* to be gender dysphoria. This shows the absolute importance of a practitioner asking themselves, "What's *really* going on here?" rather than just labelling a condition as gender dysphoria because it's happening during puberty and there are *some* gender factors. It is essential to look at *all* of the contributing psychosocial factors so as to not miss the point of what is *really* going on and *really* needs to be dealt with.

3. TRUE GENDER DYSPHORIA

True diagnosable gender dysphoria is exceptionally rare and is present in a vanishingly small proportion of the population. It *will* have been very evident for many years - it would have been impossible to miss. However, people who have what may be correctly diagnosed as gender dysphoria will often also have other associated complex but conventional developmental trauma and psychiatric symptoms. It may be difficult for a psychotherapist to unravel cause and effect as such people will often be on extreme positions on the "double curve sexual characteristics" graph both physically and mentally. People with true gender dysphoria are the *least* likely to suffer from gender transition regret.

Once again, it is important to be sceptical of the teenager who just happens to say, "I have always known I was in the wrong body" when they never before shown any consistent cross-gender features.

There is absolutely *no* need for a parent to automatically "diagnose" their child as having gender dysphoria *now* but the difficulty for a parent is understood and appreciated as there are so many vocal but well-meaning transgender spokespersons out there. Parents, please ask yourself if these Social Media experts will be able to help you heal the relationship with your child when it turns out that your child detransitions but has been irreversibly damaged.

A curious footnote to this section:

As women know, it is normal for girls to have thoughts and fantasies of having babies even before puberty but increasingly afterwards. It is very striking that a number of males who say, "I have always been in the wrong body and am really a woman" do not generally report prior fantasies of pregnancy and motherhood. Their focus is usually mostly on actual bodily and sexual matters, although extremely rarely some men do have fantasies of bearing children. Envy of the wonder of childbirth is understandable and some males who have poor self-esteem and suspect that they will not achieve much in life as a man may incorporate the fantasy of the ability to conceive, by becoming a woman into their mental processes. From another perspective, the author has interviewed pre-operative transmen who used to have thoughts about having children but much less so after becoming transgender. It appeared that they had COMPARTMENTALISED and DENIED their wishes to bear children, but it is not known whether testosterone supplements and lowered oestrogen levels may also have been a contributory factor.

REAL VERSUS SUPPOSED MENTAL ILLNESS - UNDERLYING LACK OF MENTAL WELLBEING IN YOUNG PEOPLE THAT MAY LEAD THEM TO CHOOSE THE "TRANSGENDER SOLUTION"

So, what is going on in the world that has caused such an explosion in the number of young people presenting to gender identity clinics with the belief that they are in a body of the wrong sex? Cross-gender feelings have been with humankind for millennia, but it is only recently by the means of modern medicine that attempts can be made to alter physical sexual characteristics. However, just because something can be medically attempted does not always mean it is necessarily for the best. Clearly, prior to the invention of current cross-gender medical procedures transgender people of former times "just had to get on with life" and we will never know how badly they actually suffered. Of course, prior to the existence of the Internet and Social Media the explosion of transgender feelings could just not possibly have occurred in the way it has in present times. How much anguish will be relieved and how much will actually be caused in the long term by medical cross-gender procedures will only be truly known in the future.

Many young people have aspects of themselves that they are very unhappy about and would rather be a different person or have a different life to the one they have. In former times, prior to the current increase of transgender feelings in society, if someone was unhappy with themselves, they could re-invent themselves but within their own sex. This could be quite successful, and an example would be someone working and training hard to develop a skill or profession and having done so there would be a degree of conscious and *unconscious* remaking of the self - hence the traditional old saying, "Job maketh man" or rather in this day and age, "Job maketh person".

There is a diminishing ability for young people to show resilience and acceptance of their situation in life without somehow automatically believing that things "should be" better for them - after all, *other* young people *seem* to have it better on Social Media.

There is currently frequent mention in all forms of the Press and other news outlets of increasing levels of "mental illness" in young people but in many instances what is being labelled as "mental illness" is actually something that is within the *normal range of human emotional experience*. Just because such emotions are particularly unpleasant does not necessarily indicate the presence of an actual true "mental disorder" or "mental illness". How does comfortable modern Western life compare to the bombing of civilian areas in London during World War Two or the situation in Syria, Afghanistan, parts of Africa or Ukraine? There is no comparison. However, it has to be said that there has nevertheless been an astonishing rise in the number of young people being referred in the United Kingdom to the Child and Adolescent Mental Health Services (CAMHS). There are of course, many possible factors causing this but two of the main factors are:

1. The isolating effects of overuse of IT screens and Social Media that prevent children from learning how to interact with real people and how to cope with the stresses of real life.
2. Changing patterns and styles of parenting (discussed in detail in other sections).

What is sometimes labelled as "depression" is in many instances simply the mental state that results from not having the type of life that has been wished for or fantasised about - in other words this is *unhappiness* rather than true depression, but so many young people are nevertheless put onto SSRI antidepressants for what is really *unhappiness* and a lack of life coping skills.

There are more and more public pronouncements that state that it is acceptable to have a "mental illness" and that there is no stigma attached. This is all to the good as it helps people with true mental illness to feel able to approach the mental health services rather than experience shame or embarrassment and fail to receive treatment. They can now obtain the care and treatment they need and deserve. But as stated, many people are only experiencing the normal range of human emotions for which they have not developed coping mechanisms - perhaps in part because they have not had the opportunity to learn how to cope with real life and real people as they have spent too much of their young lives online or in overprotective families. (Of course, not having coping mechanisms for life's normal range of stresses can eventually result in mental illness).

The downside to the lessening of the stigma of mental illness is that it "allows" some young people to "over-emote" and self-label as having a mental disorder when they actually don't. It is almost as if some are *unconsciously* or even consciously getting onto a "mental illness bandwagon". They simply say that they have a "mental illness" rather than attempting to demonstrate resilience, resolve or resignation to their situation. Some *feel* they have become "victims" and throw in the towel instead of getting on with life (AVOIDANCE). Others may take on a "sick role" and say, "It's my mental illness" as a justification for doing nothing, not going to school or even getting out of bed. They are using "mental illness" as a "reason" and one that is surprisingly difficult to argue against - and they know it. If you say to a young person that they don't seem particularly anxious or depressed, they can quite reasonably say, "How can you know how I feel?" In some instances, they have a good point but others maybe taking advantage of the situation. How can anyone really be sure? It is nevertheless important that mental health staff do not overlook the possibility of a young person having something similar to the resignation syndrome (please search this on the Internet and also look up learned helplessness) or severe depression rather than assuming that their patient is just "skiving".

It is only fair to say that even if someone does *not* technically have a true mental illness, they can still be mentally suffering - but it would be advantageous if the mental health services can teach them helpful mental skills with which they can improve their approach to life.

It is also important for patients to realise that even if they have been given a "psychiatric label" (i.e. a diagnosis) this doesn't by any means indicate that this is a "life sentence". In many instances the "psychiatric label" just applies to a particular phase in life that is due to circumstances and a lack of resilience and coping skills. Focussing on recovery, often with psychotherapy rather than medication is the best way of improving life.

Transgender processes have become a channel of thought and behaviour that might be seen as a solution to both the minor forms and also the more severe forms of psychological distress in young people. Transgender feelings may also seem to explain to someone why they are feeling as they do - due to the amount of transgender information that is present in the Social Media.

A high proportion of young people who present with what is *believed* to be gender dysphoria and with ideas of being transgender will have some form of pre-existing psychological complaint that is aggravating their difficulties with puberty or with life in general. Of course, *it can also be the other way round* - puberty can add an extra mental pressure onto an *already* troubled mind. Whichever way round things are happening, many young people *do feel* real distress but, in most cases, the most appropriate treatment is psychological not with puberty blockers, cross-sex hormones and most certainly not surgery. They will benefit from psychological treatments and resilience building whether they are just badly suffering from "normal" mental distress or a true mental illness.

The current ever-increasing incidence and prevalence of transgender thought is for many young people a fashionable way of expressing emotional issues that they cannot find any other way of putting into words. Teenagers have always been prone to fads, crazes and novel identifications and for many, this is what their "transgender identity" may actually be - a fad and a craze but unfortunately one that can lead to some totally inappropriate forms of treatment. It may have started with mental distress, but this can lead a young person to get onto a perilous transgender hormonal and surgical treatment pathway.

The belief of being in the wrong body can *seem* to be the underlying problem and then gender transition *seems* to be the way forward. The underlying *unconscious* mental processes can be something like this: "I am not happy or content with myself and if I leave my old self behind and reinvent myself I will be happy". This is in essence MAGICAL THINKING taking place in a young person's *unconscious* mind. It now seems there are as many gender identities as there are forms of mental distress. As previously stated, quite often, matters simply start with a *self-diagnosis* of "gender dysphoria" or "being transgender" as a result of watching YouTube or similar.

Having declared their self-diagnosis of (suposed) gender dysphoria and saying that they are transgender, a child has the satisfaction of not only receiving attention and feeling special, they can in some cases control those around them such as parents, teachers and so forth. *This is a mostly unconscious process.* It will be the transgender child that gains the most attention from parents, relatives and teachers. The transgender child will also notice the anxiety and distress that they cause in adults and the child may *unconsciously* use this to punish or control the adults in their life - they can then become the centre of a family's emotional world.

The important and sometimes difficult distinction to be made by medical and psychological practitioners is between:

1. Young people who are having transgender feelings as part of their preexisting psychosocial distress.
2. Those for whom being transgender is a social fashion accessory and a "cult" they enjoy being part of.
3. The exceptionally rare young patient who has true gender dysphoria.
4. The presence of body dysmorphic disorder. (There is a "complex relationship" between true gender dysphoria and body dysmorphic disorder. The phrase "complex relationship" relates to the disagreement regarding the definitions of these two experiences and how they are interrelated. Body dysmorphic disorder is discussed in the next chapter).

Who can forget cults such as hippies, goths, punks and emos? But these were only left with embarrassing photographs not the permanent effects of puberty blockers, cross-sex hormones and gender transition surgery. Trying out different identities is a part of growing up. For a young person it is surely a safer option to temporarily transition into a cult figure than to subject their body irreversible modifications during what is really a stage of maturation.

The recent explosion in the numbers of people who have real or assumed mental illness is due to many factors. The changing nature of the style of modern parenting is a factor as this in some instances leads to children who are:

1. Less resilient.
2. Less able to tolerate delayed gratification.
3. Less able to accept their fate.
4. Less self-reliant.

5. Less self-motivated.
6. Less equipped with social skills.
7. Less able to appreciate and cope with reality.

If you add to factors 1 - 7 the messages of Social Media, which show the apparently wonderful lives of people who "have it better" it is hardly surprising that there are high levels of *unhappiness* with life in young people. *Unhappiness* is not best treated with medication and certainly not with "self treatment" with street drugs or alcohol as often now happens. Nor can it be treated by leaving the unhappy self behind by leaving behind the gendered body in which a young person feels they are unhappy.

It is all too easy for a young person to *believe* that if they are unhappy in a female or male role, it is not being in their female or male body that is the problem. But it's actually unhappiness in life that is the problem, not which gender of body that is inhabited.

Looking at what is wrong with the actual realities of life points to what actually needs to be directly tackled.

Given the publicity devoted to transgender matters in the Social Media it is all too easy to jump to the "obvious" conclusion that life's problem are related to gender rather than mundane life matters or in some cases deep psychological difficulties.

It is clear that there are many other exceptionally complex factors that result in people adopting a transgender mode of life - some of these will now be discussed in the next few sections.

A MIX OF COMPLEX FACTORS THAT MAY UNDERLIE TRANSGENDER FEELINGS. AN INTRODUCTION TO BODY DYSMORPHIC DISORDER AND VARIOUS OTHER DISSATISFACTIONS WITH THE BODY

IT ALL STARTS IN THE *UNCONSCIOUS* MIND - AFTER ALL, EVERYTHING DOES, BUT HOW CAN IT BE BETTER UNDERSTOOD?

People who suffer from mental pain aren't always able to understand where their emotions come from because complex mental factors and previous mental trauma are deeply buried in the *unconscious* by mental defences such as REPRESSION. On the other hand, it *is* sometimes possible to point a finger at obvious *conscious* causes such as unmanageable current social and home life stresses. Either way, someone may suffer crushing depression or feelings of anxiety from these factors.

To remind the reader what was said earlier in the book, someone's mental state is due to a combination of genetics, prior emotional experiences, current stresses and the way in which mental defences developed and are currently being utilised.

Transgender desires generally result from *unconscious* mental processes and therefore those who experience them will not understand or realise where they come from - they just seem to "be there". Transgender individuals are sometimes *unconsciously* and/or consciously blaming what is actually the mental pain of a dissatisfaction with the self and how they fit into life onto matters of sex and gender. This is of course, very understandable.

You might ask yourself the valid question, "If if something is in my *unconscious* how on earth can I know what is going on and do something about it?" This would be a very good question and the answer is that you won't automatically know. But the way to have an inkling of what is happening in the depths of your mind is to read through the sections on mental defences and other thought processes in this book. You might then be able to ask the question, "Is this what is happening in the mind?" A "lightbulb" moment might occur, and then thoughts and feelings can be looked at differently. This can be difficult to do as the mental defences themselves can get in the way - it is far more effective if this is done with the help of a psychotherapist who can also help to give a reflective viewpoint. If a psychotherapist is not available a close friend or family member who has read this book maybe able to help.

Body dysmorphic disorder is an over concern about appearance with a belief that the body is abnormal in some way. A body area may be *believed* to be misshapen or that other people might consider it ugly or abnormal even though an examining doctor would regard it as perfectly normal. Body dysmorphic disorder most commonly affects the face (especially the nose) but also the genitalia, breasts, buttocks and abdomen.

Body dysmorphic disorder can also affect the body more generally in terms of body weight, for example the feeling of being overweight (when not actually so) - therefore anorexia nervosa is a form of body dysmorphic disorder (although there are generally other factors involved). On the other end of the scale there may be an extraordinarily strong belief of being too puny leading to a need for muscular development through weight training - usually in males. This is referred to as "bigorexia" by the popular press, in which sometimes massive muscular development with the aid of steroids is carried out.

Body dysmorphic disorder can also result in particular parts of the body being regarded as disgusting, revolting and even diseased - this particularly applies to the genitalia.

99

Sometimes the belief cannot be altered by even the strongest logical argument or reassurance and therefore takes the form of what is known in psychiatric terms as an overvalued idea or even delusion. Reading this paragraph might make the reader conclude that body dysmorphic disorder will be somehow linked to gender dysphoria as in both there is dissatisfaction with the body. *Connecting the two in this way is a very controversial approach.* Transgender commentators tend to take the view that body dysmorphic disorder is a psychological disorder as the name would suggest but that gender dysphoria is not. Psychotherapists and psychiatrists tend to consider that both stem from complex *unconscious* forces. This is therefore one of those areas where it maybe difficult to find agreement with transgender spokespersons about these two definitions and the relationship between them. However, it would be reasonable to say that some transgender people might experience both phenomena.

Long before the current increase in the number of people wishing to adopt a transgender life-mode, doctors had been aware of people with body dysmorphic disorder wishing to undergo for example, facial plastic surgery but found that they were never satisfied and often wanted "just one more procedure". Once the face was "done" the body dysmorphic focus then moved to another area of the body. The same compulsive and continuing desire to change the body most definitely can also apply to other aspects of appearance.

Body dysmorphic disorder most commonly tends to start during puberty or early adulthood although it can even show itself in middle age. There is often an underlying dissatisfaction with the *self in general* - poor self-esteem and reduced self-confidence that generally date back to earlier childhood experiences, but which may not recalled by the child (or their parents) due to REPRESSION. The affected person may also have features of obsessional-compulsive disorder.

Some forms of body dysmorphic disorder can result in someone having extreme tattoos, piercings or other dramatic body modifications. These examples may indicate a dissatisfaction with the body, which is disguised by such forms of body art (there is often also a dissatisfaction with the deeper sense of self that goes along with this). These are attempts to make the body as the person wants it even if to onlookers things seem out of the ordinary. Tattoos and other body modifications in many ways are a conscious and *unconscious* statement *and* a way of reinventing or reclaiming the self. They can sometimes also be a form of self-harm or self-punishment. Obviously, not every tattooed person has body dysmorphic disorder but many people with large numbers of tattoos and other body modifications may have a history of previous mental trauma and severe dissatisfaction with the self.

To repeat, it is important to be mindful of the controversy surrounding how the two conditions of body dysmorphic disorder and gender dysphoria are defined and interrelated - and that transgender spokespersons can take a very strong view of this. Body dysmorphic disorder is a condition that is only occasionally mentioned in relation to people who wish to adopt a transgender life-mode but may be a very relevant factor in some. In fact, a number of transgender people will also have some of the other body dysmorphic conditions mentioned above - anorexia, a desire for huge muscle development, escalating numbers of surgical procedures, tattoos and other body modifications. Disgust about breasts, male or female genitalia may feature as a conscious or *unconscious* reason for wanting transgender surgery but psychotherapeutically exploring the reasons for such disgust about the self could be regarded as a good and helpful first step.

A significant number of transgender people do not have actual diagnosable body dysmorphic disorder but have instead a much lower level of disgust with their body.

The important clinical transgender practice point to bear in mind is that if someone has a significant degree of body dysmorphia, they are particularly prone to finding fault with their body *and are therefore more likely to find fault or be dissatisfied with the results of surgical gender transition procedures.*

The increasing frequency of body dissatisfaction amongst young people may also be contributing to the recent astonishing increase in the number of young people saying that they hate their bodies and/or announcing that they are transgender. There are two factors that are contributing to body dissatisfaction or that may worsen a pre-existing deep dissatisfaction with the inner self:

1. Body perfectionism in advertising, feature films, fashion magazines, the use of faked or modified online images and so forth.
2. The fact that so many young people *are actually* overweight, some being morbidly obese.

Each sex is consciously and *unconsciously* hyper-alert to:

1. The inner psychological need to be attractive to the other sex (or a member of the same sex if lesbian or gay).
2. What is *currently* regarded as attractive to the other sex (or a member of the same sex if lesbian or gay).

In the past someone who lacked body confidence may just have remained single as a way of avoiding body embarrassment or alternatively they may have made the effort to get themselves fit, smarten themselves up and make a point of acquiring some social skills.

Being transgender offers a different form of approach about dissatisfaction with the body. How can you or a partner regard your breasts as "ugly" if you have them removed? How can you be uncomfortable with yourself when your old self has been ghosted? But does this necessarily seem like the best option for a developing young person in the longer term?

Therefore it can now be understood that dissatisfaction with the body and the self in general may underlie the belief of being transgender. Thus, it is not so much a case of being in the body of the wrong sex but rather a profound disgruntlement or sometimes even disgust with the body and the self *as they are*. A feeling of failure in their original gender can seem to be dealt with by DENYING its existence and ghosting that too. However, in the current climate of transgender life modes the RATIONALISATION of being in the wrong gender can occur all too easily. Clearly body improvements such as toning up but remaining within normal body mass index limits *and* the use of psychological techniques to promote self-acceptance of body and mind can be more appropriate and certainly less damaging than puberty blockers, cross-sex hormones or surgery for young people.

A FURTHER CONSIDERATION OF PSYCHOLOGICAL PROCESSES THAT *EVERYONE* USES WHEN THE MIND IS UNDER DURESS

Now that we have considered some of the basic workings of mental defences and some of the background to gendered thinking and feeling, we can explore more deeply what maybe going on in the mind of a young person who is having transgender feelings.

FANTASY THINKING

We will revisit the mental process of FANTASY THINKING. Just like the rest of humanity transgender young people can be subject to elements of fantasy. Which one of us hasn't had a fantasy of being successful or wealthy? Of course, such wishful thinking tends to bump into reality, and we realise it was nothing more than that - just wishful thinking. If for example you work in a factory on the minimum wage why not fantasise about winning the Lottery? As stated earlier, fantasy is of course, related to the mental defence of MAGICAL THINKING. It is obvious to all that the younger someone is, the more they indulge in and enjoy some fantasy. This is why fantasy films and novels are most popular with the younger age group whether the topic is magical characters, superheroes or outer space. Such films and novels are an enjoyable escape and reverie from the pain and tedium of everyday life. Of course, all age groups can enjoy such forms of entertainment, but it is the younger age group that tends to "believe" it or IDENTIFY themselves into it whereas the older age group just regards it as light entertainment and harmless escapism. The concern here is that younger people are less able to be objective about FANTASY THOUGHT and they maybe more prone to seizing upon the idea of being in the wrong body as a way of escaping or dealing with conventional psychosocial pain of difficulties at school or with puberty. As we all know, children are less able to analyse and be objective about their thoughts and feelings in general than are adults.

When thinking and fantasising about sex and gender there are no limits to the imagination and what now seems possible, particularly in a modern world in which there are so many cross-gender treatments and IT based ways of meeting people with non-cisheterosexual desires. Sexual options have become enormously expanded as can be seen in the astonishing variety of cisheterosexual, lesbian, gay and transgender porn and Internet sex hook-up sites - but if this allows adults to get the best from sensual-sexual experience, so much the better. The idea of becoming someone else and leaving the old self behind by means of reinvention of the identity *and* indulging in particular exciting sexual tastes can be very alluring to a pubertal teenager who is just starting to explore sexual experience. In summary, FANTASY THINKING can lead to unrealistic fantasy solutions to ordinary and conventional problems in teenagers.

DELUSIONAL THINKING

If someone is told that they are "deluded", they would probably find it insulting. *But every single one of us will have had at some time beliefs that don't match reality in some way.* DELUSIONAL THINKING can be a way of protecting our feelings and believing that the world is as we would like it to be - we believe what we need to believe for the sake of our psychological comfort. Some people's false belief of being loved by someone can fall into this category and can become a total obsession. Many of us have had the long-term belief that someone who completely rejected us in love could in the end become our romantic partner once again. When such a faith in regaining a lost love has become an obsessive belief it has resulted in many a pathological case of stalking.

We *all* tend to have, "The lies we tell ourselves". We indulge in this to make life feel easier to bear. These lies to ourselves may become completely unshakable and the rigidity of such beliefs relates to:

1. Our degree of underlying conscious and *unconscious* psychological pain.
2. The way we employ our mental defences.

In classic psychiatric terms a delusion is a totally unshakable belief that cannot in any way be changed by contact with reality - it therefore goes beyond just a fantasy. DELUSIONAL THINKING results from the combined use of the mental defences of MAGICAL or FANTASY THINKING and DENIAL of reality. Delusional belief is more "concrete" and unchallengeable than FANTASY THINKING. In its most extreme form delusion can be a feature of psychosis such as schizophrenia (a now somewhat outmoded term). As was said previously, every one of us has their own personal limited fantasies and limited delusions as a way of handling the psychological pain of life.

Some people who are members of cults can develop unshakeable beliefs. Please recall that younger people are particularly prone to joining cult groups as they are developing their personality. The members of certain cults around the world have become so convinced by their beliefs that some of their members have taken part in group suicide rituals. If you wish to read of an example of the power of cults over the mind please refer to the Jonestown ritual suicide in 1978 in which mental processes had resulted in the CONCRETE BELIEF of the need to die for the cult. Over 900 people killed themselves for their belief.

A most important point to emphasise is that anyone experiencing self-harming or suicidal thoughts and feelings should urgently obtain support and assistance.

An isolated delusion may possibly be a factor in some transgender young people as such DELUSORY THINKING can be an escape from the pain of puberty and their current social situation as well as providing a perceived solution to the psychologically precarious time of entering the adult world.

There are seemingly cult-like elements to the psychological experience of being in certain online groups and in some respects there are similarities with religious practice:

1. Rites of passage: Displays of allegiance such as having undergone certain ritual (e.g. medical) procedures that are ranked according to their extremity. Suffering for the belief is positively regarded.
2. Acceptance by a group is part of the attraction.
3. Loyalty to the in-group and distain of those who don't follow the group's principles i.e. the out-group.
4. A sense of being able to control destiny through following the code of practice of the group.
5. As the cultism becomes a major part of someone's identity, if the cult or its principles are questioned this is seen as a direct and insulting challenge to the new identity. A challenge to the individual's identity and cult is therefore uncomfortable, threatening and therefore reacted to strongly.

In spite of such a departure from reality in other respects the mind can often function well socially and practically because the unreal beliefs and feelings are SPLIT OFF and COMPARTMENTALISED from the rest of the mind's healthy functioning.

DISSOCIATION

We all daydream. The depth of the daydream can range from being on a train thinking of a beach holiday through to complete loss of contact with consciousness as if in a different world or persona - in psychiatry this is known as DISSOCIATION. DISSOCIATION into another personality state can be a form of an escape from a painful conscious state of the moment. DISSOCIATION can also be used to escape traumatic memories of the past that are torturing the conscious mind. DISSOCIATION is a mental defence that can come about in childhood as a way of mentally escaping from severe abuse and other forms of extreme psychological pain. DISSOCIATION is at the extreme opposite end of the spectrum to daydreaming. The author has interviewed young transgender patients who have an academic understanding of psychological processes and they believe that DISSOCIATION can be part of their cross-gender experience. It is important to note that this in no way devalues their transgender experience or their life.

MEMORY DISTORTION

Memories of events are remarkably mouldable, malleable or "plastic" - chose your preferred terminology. Memories can be altered by the influence of repeated internal mental conversations and *unconscious* processes such as the mental defences of MAGICAL THINKING and DENIAL or REPRESSION of the truth. What are "quite honestly" thought to be memories can have been invented or distorted using these entirely *unconscious* mental defences. We *all* do this. We *all* like to think about memories that validate our ideas about ourselves and DENY those that don't. Frequently running a better version of past events through the mind can remodel memories to become a "new truth", which for all intents and purposes becomes "genuinely" believed.

The statement that, "I have always been in the wrong body" may either be the result of *unconsciously* altered memory or conscious statements made to gender transition practitioners to obtain cross-sex hormones and gender transition surgery. Practitioners would be advised to be ultra-aware of this in order to ensure that they are not over-diagnosing true gender dysphoria.

A TWO WAY PROCESS THAT CAN OCCUR IN THE COMPLEX AND UNFATHOMABLE *UNCONSCIOUS* HUMAN MIND

Please recall that our personality and how it appears to others is due to the combination of:

1. The workings of complex *unconscious* mental defences.
2. The effects of deep *unconscious* memories of experiences.
3. Our current mental stresses and anxieties.

Please remember that:

A. Our *personality* affects the way we deal with our anxieties and psychological pain but ...
B. Our anxieties and psychological pain affect the way our *personality* shows itself.

In other words, there is a two-way process going on in our minds: A affects B and B affects A.

There is nothing simple or easy to explain about the workings of the *unconscious* mind, but all activities of the mind seem to be interrelated. Nobody but nobody has a complete understanding or explanation of human nature. On a day-to-day basis we see examples of the curious qualities of the human mind and how unfathomable human nature is. The extremes of human behaviour are most dramatically and painfully shown in love, seeking power and war. Our behaviour is often our way of trying to deal with or expel psychological pain and torment from our minds. If you see someone behaving bizarrely or inexplicably - they are probably trying to deal with some form of terrible mental torment. Nobody is without such potential illogical behaviour whether they are cisgender or transgender. Most people are familiar with the phrase, "We do all sorts of things when in pain or in love".

We have now considered the majority of mental defences that we *all* use. (For more information on the mental defences please see the reference by Vaillant in the bibliography). It is now possible to conclude that:

1. Every thought, feeling and everything that is said or done is influenced by our *unconscious* mental defences.
2. Every thought, feeling and everything that is said or done may actually be a mental defence in itself to shield ourselves from the mental pain of life.

"A BRAIN IN THE BODY OF THE WRONG SEX" - CAN SUCH A FEELING BE DUE TO A MISTAKE OF NATURE OR CAN IT BE DUE TO COMPLEX *UNCONSCIOUS* MENTAL PROCESSES?

It can be understood why some transgender spokespersons may be opposed to the suggestion that an underlying lack of mental wellbeing may be a relevant factor in cross-gender feelings. It is also possible to appreciate that it will instead quite naturally feel as if transgender desires result from a "mistake of Nature", which has put someone in the body of the wrong sex.

Unfortunately, statements that suggest that there is no connection between being transgender and a lack of mental wellbeing can be unhelpful. This is because such statements might discourage a young transgender person who is actually suffering severe mental pain from seeking treatment. Anybody can suffer severe mental pain whether they are cisgender or transgender.

Scientists state that it is difficult to argue against the genetic reality of the body - a female body has XX chromosomes throughout and a male body has XY chromosomes throughout. Scientists would suggest that it does not fit in with proven biological principles to say that Nature has "accidentally put" a brain with XY chromosomes into a body with XX chromosomes *or* "accidentally put" a brain with XX chromosomes into a body with XY chromosomes. Of course, occasional genetic mutations do actually occur that result in cancer, certain deformities, metabolic problems and other disease processes, however, it is difficult to biologically understand how a DNA "mishap" could result in a brain of a foetus developing in a body of the wrong sex - the genetics of the brain and body are far too complex for a genetic glitch to cause such a mishap in only the brain. *All* the tissues of the body are sexed in the same way by genetic and hormonal mechanisms and to say that Nature somehow gets it wrong with *only the brain* being of a different sex is difficult to understand in a scientific sense. It is therefore left to the reader to consider how the action of various psychological process in a stressed mind can lead to the *experience* of a brain being in the body of the wrong sex. It must not be overlooked that some people have natural characteristics that mean without doubt that they are best helped by hormonal and surgical gender transition. However, it is essential to avoid errors of choice by overlooking purely psychological factors - particularly in the younger age groups.

For some young people in a particularly difficult mental state, a transgender solution to life's difficulties may be the only thing that *seems* to be the answer to their life's current problems as it provides a sense of certainty and reassurance in an uncertain and difficult world. After all, it is so often presented this way by very convincing and confident sounding transgender spokespersons in the Social Media. Being transgender is seen as both the issue *and* the solution.

Transgender spokespersons are quite correct when they refer to "inequalities in the provision of mental healthcare" and there is much truth in statements about transgender people having poor results from the mental health services. As will be discussed later in the book, there is a definite need for improved psychological support services for transgender people (and of course, also for those who decide to detransition). Even though the stigma of mental illness has quite correctly been reduced, in many respects it is preferable to describe oneself as having the "misfortune of being born in the wrong body" rather than having a mental illness - it then becomes an issue of "biological fate" rather than an issue of perceived "mental weakness". (A lack of mental welbeing is not an actual weakness of course, the complex causes of someone's mental state were discussed earlier). Those who are on certain extreme points of the "double curve sexual characteristics" graph are likely to experience more psychosocial stress than the average person. The sad thing is that there are incredibly long waiting lists for young people who are awaiting assistance from the mental health services and gender identity services in the United Kingdom's National Health Service. On grounds of safeguarding the roles of these two services should be to *explore* a young person's transgender feelings and *not* just affirm their beliefs and feelings.

A noticeable number of transgender young people have autistic traits and as a result have impaired symbolic thought - this can be an important factor underlying their transgender choices. Generally speaking, other people are represented in the mind in an abstract and "symbolic" form that is a "mental image" of them - this is how we can have a "picture" and a "feel" for other people in our mind. This ability is important in that it enables someone to imagine how other people exist and feel in the world and how everybody relates. A lack of ability in symbolic thought results in it being difficult to empathise with other people and to understand them - this is because in order to empathise with another person it is essential to hold in the mind a mental image of them and to have a sense of what they are thinking and feeling. In order to have an idea of another person's emotions it is also necessary to be able to read their body language - something that someone with autistic traits may also have difficulty in doing. If a person with autistic traits feels a sense of general dysphoria it is difficult for them to put it into words and express it in a way that other people can understand - precisely because it can be hard for them to psychologically link in with other people. Also, people with autistic traits can very readily seize upon niche concepts by way of an explanation and can hang onto them very tenaciously.

It would be best for young people if transgender feelings are carefully evaluated as they will most often have a basis in a lack of mental wellbeing, something which requires understanding and the appropriate form of assistance.

Therefore, such assistance should not automatically be puberty blockers, cross-sex hormones or surgery. The latter two maybe helpful for some carefully selected mature people, but the fullest psychological exploration is recommended first.

FREUDIAN AND OTHER PSYCHOSEXUAL CONCEPTS

THE IMPORTANCE OF UNDERSTANDING SEXUAL PSYCHOLOGY

In order that we can understand ourselves - and each other it is important to be acquainted with the workings of the mind. Those involved in healthcare can best do their job if they understand their patients' states of mind. If healthcare professionals understand the underlying causes of someone's anxiety or depression, they can help their patient understand themselves much better rather than only acting in a superficially supportive role. Likewise, if practitioners in transgender medicine are familiar with the psychology of those under their care and any pain, they experience they can be more helpful to them.

ANYTHING GOES - POLYMORPHOUS SEXUALITY

Most people have heard of Freud (born 1856), the originator of our modern understanding of psychological processes. Love him or hate him, he has given the modern world some very useful psychological principles and has completely changed the way in which the human psyche (mind) is viewed.

Although the concept of the *unconscious* had been hinted at by earlier philosophers it was Freud who really laid the foundations for making the wider public aware of its existence and importance. Freud has often been criticised for overstating the significance of sexual desire in the origin of mental illness although he did also emphasise the importance of childhood experiences in the development of the personality. There is no doubt that Freud was correct in saying that deep redirected sexual desires and energies are highly relevant to *unconscious* psychological experiences, but it is *also* the other way around - certain *unconscious* mental processes can have a significant effect on the way in which sexual desire is experienced.

Freud referred to "polymorphous sexuality". (Polymorphous simply means "many shapes or forms"). By this he meant that many forms of sexual desire and orientation are naturally "programmed" in our *unconscious* minds. In other words, we *all* have laid down within our psyche various forms of polymorphous sexual desire, identity and orientation. This, however, is generally kept deep within the *unconscious* and the majority of people consciously have a cisfemale identity or a cismale identity and a cisheterosexual orientation. The term polymorphous sexuality fits in with there being a spectrum of sexual desire and orientation and this is very suitably illustrated by the use of the rainbow symbol by LGBTQIA+ organisations. Mature adults can of course enjoy aspects polymorphous sexual pleasure whether they are cisgender or LGBTQIA+.

Credit where due, Freud was ahead of his time in accepting homosexuality at a time when the Viennese society he lived in was particularly hostile to same sex love.

CHILDHOOD SEXUALITY

One of Freud's other ground-breaking realisations was the existence of childhood sexual feelings. This was a very controversial notion at the time and is one that remains instinctively uncomfortable to think about. Freud noted that young children can demonstrate a "prototype" form of sexuality and that this is polymorphous in nature. Young children have a lack of understanding of gender and the polymorphous nature of their sexuality is a factor in them showing apparent gender-muddled behaviour in their sexual play. Young children have an instinctive curiosity and wonder about their own genitalia and those of the other sex. This is "sexuality" in its most immature and basic form, but that's all it is. Before puberty children of similar ages can get up to all sorts of sex play. This is normal but it's not truly sexual - just partially. Young children may take part in cross-sex play - penis tucking in boys and girls using a pen, lavatory paper tube or whatever as a "penis". This is what children naturally do. Parents need to use the most delicate discretion and tact when dealing with this, assuming it needs to be dealt with at all. It would of course, need to be dealt with if there is an inappropriate age gap between the children and the potential for physical or psychological harm - in other words, abuse or if it is incestuous.

Please also be aware that fantasies in early childhood of either being the other sex or wanting to be the other sex are an expected part of childhood mental exploration of the child's own mind and the wider world. The child should not be chided for this but more importantly parents should not show any great interest in this form of natural explorative or playful cross-gender expression or in any other way reward it as to do so will guarantee recurrence after recurrence. *A very young child will not require a gender identity clinic appointment - it's just play.*

TWO DIRECTIONAL PROCESSES

Transgender people quite understandably tend to believe at a conscious level that the main cause of their psychological distress is related to sex or gender matters and of course, they naturally feel that transphobia is also a significant factor in this distress. However, it is a striking feature when talking to transgender young people that they often suffer from quite severe *conventional* underlying mental distress *in areas that are completely separate from matters of gender and sex or are parallel to those matters*. This is the very same psychological stress that may of course, be experienced by absolutely any person at any stage in life. These areas of lack of mental wellbeing include: persistent worries, anxieties, panic, phobia, morbid thoughts, paranoia, feelings of isolation, emotional variability, avoidance, obsessive-compulsive disorder, depression and so forth.

As Freud stated, it can be observed in clinical situations that two *unconscious* processes can be in play and that they work in opposite directions:

1. *Conventional mental distress* such as anxiety and depression can be redirected or "converted" into sex and gender matters. (The notion of psychological stresses being "converted" from one type into another is discussed later in the book under the heading "Conversion Disorders").
2. The psychological distress of sexual and gender matters (as around the time of puberty) can result in *conventional mental distress* such as anxiety and depression.

SEX IS EVERYWHERE

Freud observed, quite rightly that there is a thread of sexuality running through every female to male interaction and every male to female interaction. But as he also pointed out, a thread of sexuality runs through so many aspects of life that do not seem to be sexual at first sight. The world *is* very gendered, and many aspects of society relate to matters that are typically female or typically male. These stereotypes exist precisely because we have sexed brains. This sexual element is of course, either fleeting or at first seemingly irrelevant to a social situation, but it is still there. Who hasn't worked with a colleague of the other sex and at some time even briefly considered the desirability or otherwise of having sex with them? A thought about sex may only have cropped up at work as a way of dismissing it, "Ugh, I don't fancy them very much". But it's always there. So much of our day-to-day lives has a sexual connection, it is often very obvious: gendered clothes, gendered roles, changing rooms, power play and flirting. Many of our day-to-day activities are related to making a society that is conducive to preparing for the next generation - so it is therefore sex related even if only indirectly. One of the major factors in our identity is, to state the very obvious - sex/gender, "I am a woman and a mother", "I am a man who is in a romantic relationship with a man" and so forth. The author is merely trying to illustrate that, there is rarely no sex/gender in our mental processes. Freud was right.

 EROTIC FOCUS, FANTASY, OVERWHELMING DESIRE - JUST AS YOU LIKE IT

Both ciswomen and cismen can have polymorphous sexual desire. In cismen the sexual attention is often focussed on a sexualised object or image rather than the whole being of a ciswoman. A cisman's attention may be directed to part of her: breasts, vulva or a *representation* of femininity such as underwear, a shoe, perfume and so forth. Such an item of focus is known in psychoanalysis as a "part-object". Ciswomen can, but are less likely to have only "part-object" sexual desire - their desire tends to involve wider sensual and psychological areas.

For a cisman, his basic erotic focus is obviously very penis and orgasm centred. (In more romantically involved sex it becomes penis *and* whole partner focussed). Cismale sexual behaviour can merely be focussed on achieving psycho-sexual relief using a part-object - a fantasy image or even a self-image. As is clearly demonstrated in transgender porn a transwoman or male cross-sex dresser may have desires during sex that they are a woman while having sex with a ciswoman or transwoman partner in lesbian fashion or they may fantasise during sex with a transwoman or ciswoman that they are being penetrated vaginally or anally. They may of course have sex with a cisman or transman. Transgender porn illustrates many variations of such themes using various types of clothing, sex toys with actors in various stages of gender transition. Cross-sex desires and fantasies are also illustrated by the types of clothing and appliances that are readily available in not only sex shops but also quite ordinary Internet selling sites - penis tucking gaffs and tapes, silicone breasts, vulvas and vaginas etc..

The author's patients have provided him with descriptions of the following desires and fantasies. A woman who has female to male transgender feelings may fantasise during sex and masturbation that she is receiving fellatio (yes, fellatio, not cunnilingus) from a female or male partner. In her mind she might be receiving oral sex to a "penis in her imagination", a testosterone enlarged clitoris or a phalloplasty she is yet to have. Such fantasies can be lived out using silicone sex appliances that are readily available on Internet selling sites. (The author will never, ever make any reference to patients in a way in which they could be recognised).

The drive to have sex as we know is exceptionally strong and is based on deep and very powerful conscious and *unconscious* forces, which as was said can be polymorphous in fantasy and in action. Due to social conditioning and social codes, if the sex being indulged in is not "mainstream sexual activity" (i.e. it is not cisheterosexual) there may be some form of regret, remorse or even shame afterwards. This shame does not prevent a future desire for more non-cisheterosexual sex and there may even be compulsive elements to having sex of various polymorphic types. Of course, cisheterosexual sex can also driven by compulsion and compulsive features are also seen in other areas of human behaviour. This is due to the mind's desire for a quick fix period of excitement and anticipated reward.

MERGING

During sex there may be a desire to "merge" with a sexual partner. This is often referred to in classical cisheterosexual romantic literature, "It is as though we were one". In early emotional terms this is similar to the infant's desire to merge with its mother for comfort, safety and milk. Deep within our minds our childhood sensualities and desires remain with us. Do men not really enjoy feeling and sucking breasts? (REGRESSION). The merging mechanism quite naturally leads us to have in fantasy the feeling as if we have become a "merged" being with our sexual partner as if there is no barrier between us. The mind has retained this sensual feeling from childhood. The mind is also quite readily able to imagine itself as the other sex - to put it figuratively the brain "wiring" and "programming" are there for this to happen in partners of any sexual orientation and this process of imagination is aided by the fact that very few brains are 100% female or 100% male, there are many similarities between female and male brains, which gives us our ability to empathise. Put together these inbuilt wishes of merging, being able to imagine being of the other sex combined with our natural sexual polymorphism mean that deep down we have within us the potential to have a whole variety of sexual desires and activities - *in other words to have sex as either sex, with either sex*. However, these *unconscious* drives are generally constrained by societal convention and an overwhelming innate cisheterosexual desire. As a result, the majority of people tend towards having a cisheterosexual orientation. However, if a transgender person or cross-sex dresser is able to enjoy mutually acceptable polymorphic sex with pleasurable fantasy, then why shouldn't they have this particular pleasure of life? It is incredible how many cisheterosexual partners do not manage to have a blissful and mutually consenting sexual relationship.

Unfortunately, there can be a pathological version of merging in which one person wishes to engulf, possess and totally control another person *or* be possessed by them. Outwardly seemingly non-sexual examples of this can be a pathologically over possessive mother or a pathologically dependent or controlling partner - but there will often also be associated *unconscious* sexualised feelings. The *unconscious* fear of an over possessive mother can persist throughout life and result in an inability to become emotionally close to other people due to a fear of becoming dependent upon them or being engulfed and entrapped by them. These factors clearly impede the development of a loving and trusting relationship - a cismale may have *unconscious* fears of being engulfed by a cisfemale partner who psychologically represents the mother figure.

This section leads us onto a psychosexual phenomenon that is key to understanding some aspects of male to female transgender desire.

AUTOGYNAEPHILIA

This is a relatively new term but one which names the long known psychosexual phenomenon of men enjoying and becoming sexually aroused by dressing as women. Very many men have such a desire. The term when translated means, "loving the self in female form". It is a term that was effectively introduced by Ray Blanchard (a clinical psychologist). To state the incredibly obvious, most cismen enjoy touching their own genitals and those of ciswomen. They also enjoy touching or feeling many other feminine things - breasts, the female body in general and especially if clothed in sensual feminine garments. Ciswomen of course, enjoy cismen caressing them and a ciswoman's own sensual pleasure is heightened by wearing softly textured and sexually inviting clothing. For cismen, even just visualising these highly feminine sexual images in the mind can be very sexually arousing. Touching these feminine items on a ciswoman when accompanied by fantasy images can result in even greater levels of arousal. (Obviously, both sexes can enhance their sexual pleasure by means of mental fantasy images). Ciswomen themselves may feel aroused by the process of dressing seductively for a romantic liaison but not when putting on day-to-day female garments.

Autogynaephilic men can be aroused by quite a wide variety of activities and other factors that *relate* to women - putting on makeup, wearing female wigs, the idea of menstruation, images of women passing urine, high heeled shoes and many other obviously feminine items or activities. The arousal that occurs during cross-sex dressing may be a prelude to obtaining sexual satisfaction by masturbation. A man who enjoys cross-sex dressing and feels like masturbating may or may not put on women's clothes to heighten his pleasure. As an aside, it is far, far rarer for women to wear male clothes and masturbate than for men to wear female clothes and masturbate.

Surely but surely, no one should be ashamed of having sexual fantasies. There is no law against having sexual fantasies that may not be cisheterosexual and then enjoying some self-pleasuring.

Autogynaephillic behaviour can start around the age of puberty. Some boys and adolescents who are generally masculine in their behaviour, already attracted to females and aroused by female bodily characteristics can also become aroused by a variety of things *associated* with femininity such as clothing, makeup, long hair and painted nails. Just like their older cross-sex dressing adult counterparts, they become aroused when putting on women's clothing, makeup, nail varnish and so forth. To say it again, there is no shame in being sexually aroused in this way.

Another group of male teenagers which cross-sex dresses is those who are less masculine than those described above. These less masculine or perhaps even effeminate cross-sex dressing boys may initially have found wearing women's clothes comforting because of *unconscious* memories of motherly contact but subsequently found them to be sexually alluring at the time of pubertal sexual awakening. These less masculine cross-sex dressing boys may have had a very possessive and smothering mother. Many such effeminate young males may experience same sex attraction, which could be referred to as androphilia. Some may become exclusively gay, others bisexual or of course cisheterosexual.

Mothers who have weakly masculine partners or no regular male partner may consciously crave male to female sensuality and as a result their sons can *unconsciously* become a psychological substitute with there being subtle elements of sexuality in the mother-son relationship. In a sense, the weakly masculine father has already "sacrificed" his maleness and he will have modelled to his son the concept of relinquishing masculinity. Sons only tend to strongly identify with a father who is admired in the family, particularly by the mother figure. These factors combined can result in a destabilising and conflictual influence on the son's sense of maleness and his ability to sexually relate to ciswomen later in life.

Alternatively, some effeminate boys who have overtly macho fathers that they cannot not match up to might be able to find solace in the sensual and comforting feminine world of motherly and sisterly love. During puberty some of these boys may enjoy cross-sex dressing and have autogynaephilic desires as this gives a sense of comfort and excitement. Both weakly and strongly masculine men may have started cross-sex dressing when a boy to obtain a comforting feeling of being in contact with something maternal and loving and/or for autogynaephilic pleasure. As we all know, many childhood habits persist into adulthood. Men should not feel criticised for this or feel it is some form of "weakness" - it should be borne in mind that every person's actions in life stem from *unconscious* ways of trying to feel comfortable, safe and have some enjoyment in life.

If a mother feels intimidated by an overly macho cismale partner and resents or fears his maleness, she might *unconsciously* reward her son if he showed feminine characteristics and *unconsciously* discourage him from demonstrating strongly male characteristics. Some teenage boys may seem innately effeminate and this does not seem obviously related to parental modelling factors - it is just due to natural genetic femaleness.

Whatever the background factors in feminine men, whether the nature of their personality is genetically based, a result of family factors or both, some such males may have a lifetime quest to become female. Many feel that they cannot possibly be at peace with themselves until they have undergone full hormonal and surgical gender transition and can then take on the psychosexual and physical characteristics of a woman. The way they conduct their sexual lives and express their feminised gender is to an extent affected by the culture that they live within. It would be hoped that cisgender people could appreciate, understand and accommodate this desire. Many non-Western cultures have their own ways in which such males can express themselves - ladyboys in Thailand are a well-known example (although for many of these, their transition would have been for the purposes of sex work to escape from poverty). In former times in Western society such a man would discretely cross-sex dress and perhaps be secretly gay but due to changes in modern world and the power of Social Media they might nowadays consider hormonal and surgical gender transition and live openly as a transwoman, perhaps being able to pass particularly well.

Again, it must be said that if this improves the quality of life, society should not be critical or discriminatory in any way whatsoever.

Thus, cross-sex dressing can be carried out by both strongly and weakly masculine males and so no generalisations can be made about the degree of masculinity present in cross-sex dressing males - *please do not judge the way they express and enjoy their sexuality*. It is of note that some cross-sex dressing males, whether strongly masculine or effeminate can become aroused by the notion of being subjugated in the way that women have been by men throughout history (and of course, regrettably still are in many situations).

The more strongly masculine cross-sex dressing boys quite often tend to retain their heterosexual desires and do not necessarily wish to undergo hormonal and surgical gender transition although some do eventually start to have a desire for gender transition as discussed below. Weakly masculine cross-sex dressing boys who were over-attached to and over-identified with their mothers may find comfort in wishing to "become" female and dispense with physical reminders of the male role they felt uncomfortable in.

Some men may feel *unconsciously* disgusted with their own male sexuality if they had experienced an inappropriately sexualised relationship with their mother or had been directly sexually abused as a child by someone else - be that by a male or by a female. Others may feel disappointed with themselves because they feel that they have struggled in their male role in the world. They might seek solace by leaving their uncomfortable maleness behind by entering the female world in fantasy (FANTASY THINKING). Their self-disgust may be DISPLACED onto their overall maleness or particularly onto their genitalia and in order to symbolically remove the focus of their self-disgust they adopt a cross-gender lifestyle. If they then wish to fully rid themselves of this focus they may wish for gender transition surgery. As these mental processes are *unconscious*, such a man may not be able to put into words why he finds his genitalia disgusting but it maybe technically a form of body dysmorphia in some instances. Such men may be able to live their best life by means of hormonal and surgical gender transition and why shouldn't they? However, this needs to be a very carefully made decision.

Middle aged men who have struggled in their sexual life or lost a significant woman in their life due to rejection by a female partner or her death may start to indulge in comforting cross-sex dressing and/or autogynaephilia. This allows a form of psychological fusion with the lost female loved one, sexual release or both. Hormonal and surgical gender transition in this latter group can be at a high risk of regret.

This all reinforces the mental association of cross-sex dressing and cross-sex fantasy with pleasure and needless to say, this leads to an ever-increasing desire to cross-sex dress and have sexual release. This can become a failsafe route to orgasmic pleasure and may be relied upon if the cross-sex dressing is off-putting to a female partner. Of course, it should not be overlooked that some ciswomen really enjoy sex with a cross-sex dressing male or a transwoman.

It must be said that for some male cross-sex dressers their motivation to cross-sex dress is to psychologically leave behind a personal identity that they are not comfortable with rather than purely for sexual enjoyment. They find a certain form of confidence and an ability to express themselves in their cross-sex dressed state that they cannot feel in their masculine state, which they are glad to leave behind, even if only temporarily. At an *unconscious* and even at a conscious level, it does not feel like a drag image - "It *is* me". If such men gain a good degree of life satisfaction in this way then why on earth shouldn't they?

Some men who do not feel particularly powerful as a man in a male environment can completely alter the social dynamic by becoming a transwoman or a cross-sex dresser who is overtly sexually dressed. This is because cismen are sometimes intimidated by powerfully sexual ciswomen. (Cismen may not like to admit this). Being in the company of a very sexually dressed transwoman or cross-sex dressing male can unsettle cismen in a way that is quite dissimilar to being in the company of a sexually powerful ciswoman. This is something that they may find difficult to put into words but it relates to the fact that men have laid down in their *unconscious* mind a particular mode of feeling and interacting with women or men - it is different for each.

Thus, transwomen can invoke extremely confusing and unsettling emotions in cismen but this is not necessarily because the cismen are being transphobic, it is just that they are innately uncomfortable and emotionally conflicted - it is the way their brains are programmed together with a lifetime of social conditioning. Transwomen may also have unsettling effects on ciswomen who likewise are not being transphobic when they have feelings that are difficult to fathom out. Some transgender people could exploit this phenomenon in a power play as they know all too well that anything that could conceivably be interpreted as transphobia can result in sanctions on the cisgender person. Let's face it, most people take advantage of a situation if they can!

The complexities of autogynaephilic psychosexual experience are revisited here:

1. Some cross-sex dressing males may experience a sense of conflict between alternating desires of autogynaephilia, androphilia and heterosexual sex. Straight cross-sex dressing males tend to not want to go through hormonal and surgical gender transition particularly in the earlier stages of their sexual life although a some do wish for full surgical gender transition in the longer term.
2. Some autogynaephilic males are not mostly sexually driven, just partially. They may instead desire to experience themselves in female form because they wish to leave their "male life" behind - perhaps because they feel that they are not particularly masculine or feel as if they have struggled in life as a man. This may therefore be a powerful but not primarily sexual motivation for hormonal and surgical gender transition - in order to allow them to live their life more comfortably as a transwoman.
3. Men who have felt intimidated by their mother or women in general can compensate for this by cross-sex dressing

in an overtly feminine and hyper-sexualised way - thus feeling that they are outdoing women. In some instances, they can feel that they are a more powerful and womanly woman than their mother.

Whichever is the case, if a someone can achieve an improvement in their life by means of cross-sex dressing or hormonal and surgical gender transition then the author hopes that they can make the very best of their life. *The psychological reasons for doing this just do not matter - it is getting the best out of life that matters. This also applies to cisgender people - whatever the psychological factors underlying their life choices, what matters most is living their best life.*

However, the author sincerely hopes that the correct gender transition decision is made and particularly in the case of younger people that sufficient time is given to the complex decision making process. If someone thinks, "It's quite straightforward, I definitely need hormonal and surgical gender transition, there's absolutely no doubt about it" this very concrete and inflexible thought is a red flag and an indication that much more thought is needed. To have absolutely no doubts can be a pointer to the fact that the mind is being clouded by the powerful action of *unconscious* mental defences.

If you happen to be a reader who is considering hormonal and surgical gender transition, please just be very careful and make the decision that gives the best possible life. Please explore this question with someone who takes a neutral viewpoint on transgender matters.

L, G or B FEELINGS - WHERE DO THEY COME FROM?

This is a very thorny question and one that tends to be avoided ...

The jury is out as to the relevance and proportion of the following listed factors in being gay, lesbian or bisexual. There has been very much discussion about this but as yet, science has been unable to provide the answer:

1. Whether being gay, lesbian or bisexual is innate and due to genetic factors. Whether it is significantly influenced by the parental factors described in this and other sections.
2. Whether it is sometimes related to being an effeminate man or masculine woman (as indicated on the "double curve sexual characteristics graph" - although there are obviously both genetic *and* child rearing factors in where someone is on the curve). But it must be remembered that many gay men are very masculine and some lesbians very feminine.
3. Or a variable mixture of 1 and 2.

As sexual beings we need sensual-sexual relief and comfort no matter what our gender expression and sexual orientation may be - this is only natural and nothing to be ashamed of. There should be no discrimination, disapproval or intolerance shown by anyone about this.

MORE ON MOTHER TO CHILD INTERACTION AND EARLY LIFE EXPERIENCES THAT MAY RESULT IN POOR SELF-ESTEEM AND TRANSGENDER EXPERIENCES. THE EFFECTS OF ABUSE BY THE FATHER FIGURE OR THE MOTHER HERSELF

Someone's mindset or rather "the way that someone's mind works" originates in early childhood experiences - but please remember that genetic factors should not be overlooked in the development of a person's character.

Further factors in the relationship between mother and child that can predispose to transgender leanings are discussed here. These are generally factors that make a child feel insecure in its self-worth and in its identity. There is absolutely no intention to criticise any mother in this section. Any mother who feels that she is perhaps recognising her style of mothering when reading this should not feel criticised. We are all struggling through life as best we can and the way we do things is a result of our own childhood experiences and of course, our own mother's childhood experiences and so on down through the generations. If a mother does recognise something, her only reaction could be to consider how things might perhaps be done in a different way that may be better. When any of us become aware of the unhelpful things that we *all* do in life, we can stop in our tracks and change the way we do things and hopefully be better off in the long term. The author certainly looks back painfully and regretfully on the way he has conducted his life. He tries, but often fails to improve himself even at the age of retirement.

It is important to emphasise to parents that if their transgender child is being assessed in a clinic, the staff will not be critical of their parenting or "think the worst" of the parents themselves.

The following examples are situations that can so easily develop but there are many more that can do so as life is for most people an incredibly hard practical and psychological struggle. We can all recognise how easy it is to get ourselves into difficult and unhelpful situations - we have *all* done it at times. The examples that follow are perhaps extreme but are designed to illustrate the principles of what can so easily happen. To repeat, in no way is the author saying that a finger can be pointed at families or suggesting this is what is generally happening in families with children who take on a transgender identity.

Please consider for a moment a mother who wanted a child of the other sex to what was born to her. It is perfectly natural that she will consciously or more likely *unconsciously* give praise and other forms of positive response to features of the child's gendered behaviour that match the sex of the child she wanted. Some mothers will go to the extremes of dressing an unwanted boy in female clothes or school uniform and try to pass him off as a girl. There are well known cases of this that only came to light once the boy's voice dropped, he started growing whiskers or inbuilt male psychosexual factors took over and he rebelled. There is the possibility that such a mother might have shown *unconscious* disgust of her son's genitalia, which could then make him feel a sense of disgust and dissatisfaction with his genitalia. It is necessary to take a compassionate view of a mother whose daughter died but the next child born to her was a boy. It would be quite understandable for her to *unconsciously* regard the boy as a form of replacement for the girl and to positively focus on and reward any feminine traits that the boy showed.

A mother might have masculine traits herself, which she *unconsciously* feels uncomfortable about as she doesn't feel "feminine enough". This could lead to her *unconsciously* rejecting male characteristics in herself and perhaps also in her young son. To repeat, the processes just described would be entirely *unconscious* but at the same time very understandable. A mother like this might possibly raise a boy who cross-sex dresses or has fantasises of being both sexes. Furthermore, being brought up in a feminised way may ultimately lead to the boy wanting to be attractive in a feminine way - possibly to men.

A mother who was sexually abused as a child by a man might *unconsciously* fear the same might happen to a daughter and would wish to protect her. The mother would then *unconsciously* not reward her daughter's feminine characteristics but praise any male traits thus sowing the seeds of male characteristics being preferable.

It is all too easy for psychologically difficult situations to develop in the case of single mother families. Again, no criticism is intended here as many women feel that they can give their child(ren) a better start with a troublesome man completely out of their life. For most people there is a totally overwhelming desire to have a partner in life for companionship, support and sensual-sexual contact. This can become an all-consuming craving in and it is not uncommon for single mothers who may have previously said to themselves, "I've finished with men, they are all bastards" to very easily find themselves in a new relationship. Who can blame them? It's what we all need very deeply. The trouble with relationships is that quite unwittingly we (all) keep finding ourselves in the same old situation - there seems to be a "relationship roundabout". This is because without realising what we are doing, we keep *unconsciously* finding the same type of partner and things just go the same old way. Freud referred to "repetition compulsion" in which we *unconsciously* recreate the "same old situations" in life - and there is the hope that *next time* we can get things right. In fact "the same old situation" can give us a comfortable sense of security and even control due to the sense of familiarity - even if the situation isn't particularly nice. Freud's message was *what cannot be remembered and/or emotionally processed is destined to be repeated.* It is of note that adult child abusers tend to abuse children at the same age they were abused themselves. Of course, we all tend to do things the same way because we use the same old mental defences and other mind habits and therefore things work out badly time after time. In other words, being the same person, we don't change our approach. Looking back, most of us will recognise this. The older you are, the more painfully obvious it is.

It is an all too well known reality that men keep coming into and then leaving single mother families in the fashion of the "relationship roundabout" due to the "repetition compulsion" process. The author does not wish to use stereotypes, but he has all too frequently observed the following sequence of events. It often happens that a man, who has a personality profile that includes predatory characteristics will spot a vulnerable single mother and charm his way into her life, possibly mostly for sex. The mother's quite natural personal craving for companionship, support and sensual-sexual contact may result in her, at times, directing her attention and time towards the man rather than her child(ren). She's only human. In the mind of her young offspring this may be perceived as abandonment, rejection and frustration of their needs. These factors, together with any child abuse that may occur at the hands of the male partner are the classical ingredients that make a child feel unworthy of love. Feelings of unworthiness lead to poor self-esteem and for the child to feel that it is "unsatisfactory" to other people in some way. The mother may of course, sense that she has emotionally and practically neglected her child(ren) and may then overcompensate. An alternately "hot and cold" emotional environment is another factor that is detrimental to the development of a child's confidence in their sense of self-worth. The mother's male partner may be coerced into "being nice" to the child(ren) - "If you're not nice to them, no sex". To repeat, this form of "on-off" process of affection then abandonment has a remarkably negative effect on the development of a child's sense of security in its own sense of self. Indeed, it does appear that the more "temporary stepfathers" that a child has in its life, the worse it is for a child - few people would doubt this is the case and is a factor in the development of a personality structure that is characterised by poor self-esteem and self-hate. Feeling dissatisfied with the self in this way results in a tendency to grasp onto anything that provides acceptance and approval - because, after all the child had learnt to do this during the succession of new "temporary stepfathers". This dissatisfaction with the self may result in a desire *to be a different self* - the Social Media based transgender groups can appear to provide an alternative self and a way of remaking the self.

Transwomen may have a strong IDENTIFICATION with women and this can come about in various ways:

1. If a young boy had repeated fears of being abandoned by his mother, he will *unconsciously* increase his IDENTIFICATION with her. A young son needs to feel loved by his mother *and* to love her. He may not be able to consciously distinguish between loving and IDENTIFYING with her - he feels that IDENTIFYING with her "is" to love her. Furthermore, he may not be able to distinguish between IDENTIFYING with and "becoming" her - hence a desire to wear her clothes and to "be her" by dressing in her clothes.
2. If the father figure is frequently threatening to mother and son, the son might over IDENTIFY with his mother as a way of increasing his feeling of closeness to her in order to feel safe.

These two examples demonstrate how some males can develop female IDENTIFICATIONS.

Alternatively, sons may IDENTIFY with an aggressive father as a way of feeling stronger and therefore safer. This is known as IDENTIFICATION WITH THE AGGRESSOR, a concept proposed by Freud's daughter, Anna who helped to pioneer psychoanalysis of children.

Please also consider the situation in which a father of the family frequently criticises and denigrates the feminine characteristics of his wife - a daughter may then DIS-IDENTIFY with her mother and from female characteristics.

IDENTIFICATION with a parent is a vital component in a child's self-esteem and personality development and it can be said that boys have a more difficult time with establishing a proper male identification than girls have with establishing a female identity. This because boys have to first go through a stage of DIS-IDENTIFICATION from their mother who was their first object of IDENTIFICATION. For some boys the psychological journey of DIS-IDENTIFICATION from their mother can be emotionally unsettling and wearing their mother's clothes can help them to maintain a sense of contact with the person they are differentiating from even though in other respects they are developing increasingly male characteristics.

Another area in which IDENTIFICATION WITH THE AGGRESSOR is relevant is the development of sadomasochistic behaviour. Both cisgender and transgender people who have complex self-esteem difficulties may have elements in their sexuality that can be sadomasochistic. There may be a predominance of either sadism or masochism but often both can occur in the same person. The full topic of sadomasochism is beyond the scope of this small book but suffice to say that it often takes origin in childhood abuse in which the child has been humiliated, brutalised, over controlled, made to feel worthless and unloveable. Approval and a loving relationship would have been craved but not experienced and a sense of control of the situation would have been totally absent. Repetition compulsion as mentioned earlier in the section also applies in adult sadomasochistic behaviour. Situations that occurred in childhood are *unconsciously* recreated in the hope that "this time things will work out better" by use of IDENTIFICATION WITH THE AGGRESSOR in sadism and recreating a vulnerable situation in masochism. It is obvious that a sense of control of a sexual and/or brutal act is present in sadism, but it is not so obvious that a sense of control is also present in masochism - but it is. A child being mercilessly physically, emotionally or sexually abused would have lacked any sense of control over their destiny but recreating the vulnerable situation in adulthood gives the *unconscious* hope at least (even if a false hope) that some control is possible - "this time things will work out better". As a sense of control is all important, it is hardly surprising that both sadism and masochism can occur in the same person as they can both give an *unconscious* sense of mastery over the situation as just described. This perhaps explains why the wish for sadomasochistic sex does not at first always start with sexual desire but instead originates in a desire for closeness and control *but then* sexual desire arises. This is because by *unconsciously* bringing in sexual desire to an interaction between two people produces the sense of a relationship existing. Single, lonely and isolated people sometimes initiate sex as a way of feeling some form of emotional connection with others - it is sometimes the only way they can feel close to someone and feel of significance as a person. This is why for some desolate and rejected people, casual sex with various partners can become compulsive such is their craving for close human contact.

A history of sexual abuse can result in a renunciation or rejection of sexuality and a feeling of disgust with the body's sexual features. It can therefore be understood how someone might feel that they are agender or need to have their sexual characteristics surgically changed. Requests for transgender treatments can give someone the sense of control over their sexuality that they had felt they lacked in the past when being sexually abused. These processes, as do so many other transgender processes work on an entirely *unconscious* basis and are therefore not recognised by the individual.

When considering the detachment and separation of a teenager from its parents in order to enter the adult world it is important to note there is a particular problem if parents cling onto their child. In its early years a toddler has the conflicting desires of clinging to its mother for safety and succour but at the same time wanting to separate from her in order to explore - much later on a teenager will also show some ambivalence but really does need to separate in order to grow up. Some children start life as being particularly "clingy" and some mothers are over "clingy" to their children. Mothers sometimes nostalgically cling to the earlier stages of their child's life and when it comes to puberty can find it particularly difficult to let go. Mothers who cling to their children at the time of puberty, may *unconsciously* want to keep them as children so that they feel they "can't" leave - to achieve this the mother might try to make the teenager feel guilty if they try and leave. These processes create a high degree of insecurity in the child about separation and entering adulthood, which can of course, result in the AVOIDANCE of separating from the mother. The AVOIDANCE of the precarious feelings of taking on an adult gender role may be achieved by *unconsciously* taking on a transgender identity and therefore not entering the destined adult gender form. Becoming transgender *unconsciously* gives the child a form of sense of control over how puberty happens and how their life develops.

Freud referred to the notion of a psychosexual interaction between a mother and her son and because of this there can be a sense of sexual jealousy between the son and his father as the father is obviously more able to sexually "possess" the mother. (This again is an *unconscious* process). Such jealousy is magnified should the son witness or otherwise become aware his parents having sex and the son may wish to take his father's place, if only in *unconscious* fantasy. This may just seem to be another fanciful Freudian notion but without doubt it does happen and is most definitely not as rare as might be imagined. (The term, "Mother fucker" didn't come from nowhere). This might make you ask yourself, "What of the relationship between fathers and daughters?" As awful as it is, and all too well known, fathers can sexually abuse their daughters or stepdaughters. The difference between mother to son sexuality and father to daughter sexuality is along the same lines as mentioned in the section "A Simple Comparison of Female & Male Sexuality and What Everybody Wants". For a man (the father) it is mostly about sexual release and for a woman (the mother) it is more about a far more complex and encompassing sensuality. Quite astonishingly, mothers abusing their own child can be a form of self-harm - this is because they are *unconsciously* harming part of themselves in the form of the child which is an extension/product of their own body.

This psychological blurring of generational barriers can be carried into later life with the result that when these sexually abused children become adults, they have the potential to commit sexual acts against children.

SONS AND DAUGHTERS OF INFORMATION TECHNOLOGY SCREENS AND SOCIAL MEDIA. SOCIAL MEDIA OVERUSE RESULTING IN SOCIAL ISOLATION AND SOCIAL INEPTITUDE. THE EFFECT OF TRANSGENDER INFLUENCES IN THE SOCIAL MEDIA

Society currently has a generation of young people who in some cases appear as if they are affected as much by the influences of Information Technology screens and Social Media as they are by their parents. There is now an entire generation that has had access to the Internet for all if its existence - it is known as Generation Z. According to some surveys 1 in 6 of Generation Z identify as LGBTQIA+. This begs an obvious question regarding the influence of the Internet on transgender choices and the answer is perhaps equally obvious.

There is a modern trend for both parents to go out to work and the need for this is to financially get by due to the rapidly and ever-increasing cost of living. When parents return home from work they may be exhausted and have to deal with home practicalities and chores but understandably also need some restorative "me-time". This may result in children being put in front of a television or various types of IT screen. In all due fairness to modern working parents, workplaces can be far more emotionally draining than in former times. For previous generations there was far less geographical mobility and so working relationships were more stable and could be better developed, particularly in comparison to the present gig economy, the current trend for people to frequently change jobs and to spend much of the day commuting. Former working environments were less bureaucratic and not at the mercy of Human Resources departments, which so often do not give the impression of having a good understanding of the psychological complexities of the workplace. In former times personnel would work their way up from the bottom ranks so that once they became a foreman, they really knew their working environment and the personalities of their colleagues. This is in strong contrast to the modern trend in so-called "management" where the "managers" are often put into positions in which they have little no background knowledge, experience or training. These "managers" may come up with ideas without consulting the hands-on staff who actually know best how the workplace runs and how to do the job. Frequently the "managers" have only theoretical training in the complexities and psychology of management - if they have had any at all. If financial cuts need to be made, it is often the hands-on staff who are sacked - the "management" is hardly going to vote to sack itself. Quite often, after such sackings, even more "management processes" are put in place to "solve any problems" - these problems themselves being caused by the very lack of hands-on staff or mis-"management" in the first place. This entirely unsatisfactory "management" situation is all too often seen in over-corporatised private companies, Government organisations and *particularly* in the United Kingdom's National Health Service (NHS).

The above was mentioned to illustrate how the author has full sympathy and an understanding of at least some of the difficulties that modern working parents labour under. It is important not to lose sight of the fact that in former times when the West was more industrialised and less reliant on being a "service economy" the workplace would be incredibly physically arduous and often extremely hazardous. There is no doubt however, that even though the modern working world is less physically demanding and dangerous, it is still exceptionally emotionally draining for the reasons just discussed - the author fully appreciates how and why modern parents are exhausted and feel the need to put their children in front of IT screens.

IT screens reduce the desire for solitary imaginative play as the imagination is done for the child and this seems to have the unfortunate effect of preventing the fullest development of symbolic thought and problem solving ability. Fantasy play and imagination are critical for the development of abstract and innovative thought. If such abilities are not developed it leads to a mindset where fewer viewpoints of a problem or a solution to it can be effectively formulated and as a result thinking can become very "concrete" and inflexible.

Developing a grounded sense of the actual reality of the world can obviously only come about from direct contact with that *real* world. Some young people are spending so much time immersed in a fake or virtual reality that they have a distorted impression and grasp of actual reality. Some children spend considerable amounts of time looking at IT screens and this can become their "life's reality" for several hours per day, every single day for years. As a result, at some level they come to believe or at least fantasise that certain things are possible, which in the real world they are most definitely not. This sets them up for inevitable disappointment due to their distorted view of the world and what is actually feasible. They may have a view of the world that is based on MAGICAL THINKING - "You can be what you want to be just as you can in a computer game or computer-generated image". "You can even change your body into anything you wish".

Screens can also seem to reduce the feeling of the need for actual contact with people, albeit artificially. This is again unhelpful as there is an absolute and critical need for direct contact with peers for the proper development of social skills and the personality. This lack of *real* contact with *real* people also reduces the sense of belonging, that most critical human emotional need and which is also essential for the proper functioning of wider society. Throughout history, the older generation has looked down on and criticised the younger generation but in the present time, it really does seem that many youths of the current younger generation are particularly devoid of individuality and psychological resilience. It is not necessarily the direct fault of the children or their parents - a huge societal change has crept up unseen on all of us.

Figuratively speaking, we communicate with each other through our personalities. To state the very obvious, our personalities define who we are. We have an inbuilt conscious and *unconscious* tendency to strive to develop our individual character - but this is being inhibited in the current youth by excessive immersion in IT devices. It really does seem that personality development is being impaired by the tendency of the modern youth to be "alone within their Social Media" in their bedroom. Even when within in a crowd of other young people they are transfixed by their own smartphones and ignore the person next to them. However, one form of marking themselves out as individuals but at the same time gaining some sense of approval within their Social Media world is by taking on a transgender identity - even if this is only a cult-like behaviour.

This excessive time spent on Social Media or IT screens in general results in reduced time with real people and it is only by intensive interaction with other people that an ability to read body language and to learn to handle the stresses of interacting with other people can be developed. It can be seen how an over immersion in IT can lead to the following:

1. An inability to read other people and interact with them.
2. A lack of social and communication skills.
3. A distinct feeling of social discomfort and therefore a preference of being alone with IT.
4. Carrying out the same old repertoire of activities on an IT device.

These factors give the impression of a form of behaviour that *seems* autistic, even if not actually autistic. Please compare 1 - 4 above with the characteristics of autism by looking at an Internet search engine where you probably see the following features of autism:

"A" Symptoms - Reduced ability in two-way social interaction.

"B" Symptoms - Reduced verbal and non-verbal communication. Reduced ability in imagination.

"C" Symptoms - Limited range of interests and activities.

It is quite conceivable that many children who have been given the label of autism actually have difficulties that in reality are due to IT overuse and a lack of social and family person to person interaction.

To summarise - excessive Social Media usage results in five dysfunctional steps:

1. Prevents the actual *real* physical and emotional belonging to a group of *real* people but at the same time:
2. Provides a sense of human contact, but which actually somehow feels false and empty because humans are hardwired to be social beings and interact with other real humans. The survival of Cavewoman and Caveman very much depended on group behaviour.
3. The fact that the sense of belonging feels false and empty makes the person return again and again to Social Media in a futile attempt to try to fill that emptiness - the law of diminishing returns thus comes into play.
4. The person is then hooked on and in some cases badly addicted to Social Media in the continued vain hope that it will fill the emotional void.
5. This reliance on Social Media for "social contact" as opposed to having face to face contact results in a failure to develop *real* social skills and resilience to the inevitable knock backs from interaction with real people.

This lack of a feeling of true belonging results in a feeling of loneliness, which can then result in a sense of "grievance" or "resentment" or "anger" against "something" although that "something" is not always something that can be put into words. This feeling can morph into a form of hatred against any group into which the young individual feels they do not fit. A feeling of not fitting in can also cause a feeling of failure and this can result in self-hatred. Such emotions of being a misfit may of course, be experienced by IT obsessed transgender young people who live in an overwhelmingly cisgender world.

This raises the question, "What can happen to the feeling of self-hatred experienced by the apparently transgender young person who doesn't fit in?"

The answer - It is turned outwards, in other words it is externalised by the mental defence of PROJECTION. You will recall from the section on mental defences that by means of PROJECTION, what is actually originally an internal feeling can be redirected to the outside. By this mechanism, a self-hating transgender young person accuses the cisgender people around them of hating and the cisgender people are described as "haters" or "transphobes".

A general dysphoric sense of unhappiness can result from discomfort in real face-to-face social contact that is a due to a lack of development of social skills. Good social skills and real human contact can help to prevent a child becoming emotionally isolated. Those who are already social misfits are of course, more likely to spend time on Social Media than face to face with real people where they would be able to learn to function socially. **This is why there is a certain tragic irony to the name Facebook - it is just the very opposite of face-to-face.** Those who are socially uncomfortable and isolated maybe drawn to Social Media because that is where they can find groups to which they feel they can "belong". Such Social Media groups are where they feel accepted and acknowledged or can even obtain a feeling of status. If a socially uncomfortable and generally dysphoric young person self-diagnoses themselves as having gender dysphoria their "social" life starts to revolve around transgender groups on Social Media.

The so called Social Media have actually been a cause of much social misery in many aspects of life - and much more to come.

Acceptance within a social group is a major human psychological need and this requires the individual to be "similar" to the others of the group and to conform to certain behaviour, appearances and rules. The mental defence of IDENTIFICATION can be very relevant. To recap, IDENTIFICATION between people is a process in which they consciously and *unconsciously* notice characteristics in each other and make them part of their own character. Noticing features in other people that are similar to ourselves is pleasing and therefore consciously and *unconsciously* making ourselves even more like others in order to feel closer to them is just another part of the process of IDENTIFICATION. IDENTIFICATION between friends and group members will be familiar to most of us. However, there is also a very strong desire to be "just that little bit different" to others so that a person can still feel that they are actually an individual. This is possible within the rainbow spectrum of the transgender world, it just needs a little self-invention, which can also take place consciously and *unconsciously*. This is something that can be behind the extremely colourful, flamboyant and unconventional dress styles adopted by young transgender people on Social Media - of course, for some this will be a form of rebellion. *The fact that for many young people being transgender is a form of rebellion is often overlooked.*

Unfortunately, many modern teenagers do not seem to have any realistic career plan, if they have a plan at all. Becoming a "celebrity", a football star, a music idol or an IT millionaire as seen on Social Media or television is what they refer to rather than more realistically becoming a mechanic, architect, nurse, builder, lorry driver or lawyer. Finding fame and fortune via a quick fix rather than hard graft and years of training is what they often seem wish for whilst not realising that being a professional sportsperson or a music star generally requires a very rare specific talent and a great degree of application. An area in which being transgender, or a male cross-sex dresser can provide a career advantage has been shown in certain high profile LGBTQIA+ musicals, films, television shows and publications. The drama and film "Everybody's Talking About Jamie" has been mentioned elsewhere. This may have a conscious or *unconscious* influence on transgender choices - becoming a famous transgender person or cross-sex dresser may be seen as a way to fame and fortune.

Indulgence in Social Media may at times feel good as it is a distraction from real life anxieties but can actually serve to worsen psychological problems whereas psychotherapy can feel either good or extremely challenging but it can help to explore and resolve psychological difficulties instead of deepening them. At some time, we all need to face our conscious and *unconscious* pain if we are to improve our mental wellbeing. By not exploring a young person's transgender feelings by means of psychotherapy loses the opportunity for them to find an acceptance and understanding of certain feelings relating to themselves, their gender expression and their sexual orientation. The next step may be to embark upon a complex, difficult and potentially perilous transgender medical pathway. Even becoming a transgender YouTube superstar or a film star and gaining a large income may not be adequate compensation for a life damaged by puberty blockers, cross-sex hormones and surgical gender transition procedures. If it turns out that a transgender lifestyle is the right thing for a (mature) person, this is clearly a very good thing but it is worth investing the time in the decision making process - to be sure.

Another negative effect of Social Media is "body perfectionism" and "lifestyle perfectionism". Preened, plucked, pencilled, posed, faked and modified images are posted together with messages that give the impression of those doing the posting are leading a wonderful, interesting and exciting lifestyle. The Social Media provide far, far more people for a modern young person to compare themselves to than before the invention of the Internet as prior to this a young person's social world would have been more confined to actual face to face contact with their local peer group. Teenagers naturally tend to feel insecure but will now be able compare themselves unfavourably with so many more people than would previous generations. This all leads to the lonely and socially isolated young person feeling even more isolated and disconnected from the world. Many of those posting such exaggerated images on Social Media will often only be doing so precisely because of their own feelings of social and sexual inadequacy that they are attempting to compensate for. How many young people (or indeed people of any age) don't have some feelings of inadequacy about their appearance or their sex life?

The teenage years and early twenties are critical for the development of the personality and for many, this is an uncomfortable journey. It is a stage of life in which the mental ability to carefully thinking things through before acting is not fully developed, hence the tendency for impulsive and unwise behaviour that may be based on nothing more than a Social Media post or copying peer behaviour. YouTube and Social Media are filled with confident statements that cross-sex hormones and gender transition surgery "will" improve someone's life. It is suggested by some YouTube transgender spokespersons that even the slightest feeling of being transgender "must" be followed up by social and even medical gender transition. Such statements are made as if they are concrete facts rather than matters that should be extremely carefully thought through and analysed before acting. It is often claimed that following a transgender life-mode is the "only way" to improve mental wellbeing and reduce risk of suicide once someone feels they are transgender. There are also warnings that anyone who detransitions would be regarded as a traitor to the transgender population.

The *perceived* support from Social Media is, as the word suggests, nothing more than a *perception* as after all it is only *real* person to person contact that truly helps someone who is psychologically suffering. There are many LGBTQIA+ groups and subgroups and even these aren't always supportive of each other. Indeed, there is sometimes a considerable degree of disagreement and even infighting between some of the various L, G, B, T, Q, I and A elements of the LGBTQIA+ population. This is perhaps because there can be quite a difference between the L, G, B, T, Q, I and A subgroups - their needs and viewpoints can be quite dissimilar. An important example of this occasional possible conflict is mentioned elsewhere - lesbians, whether Feminist or not are concerned about the risk of sexual assault on ciswomen in women's spaces from a very small minority of men who identify as women but have not undergone male to female transgender surgery and wish to sexually predate on ciswomen. This has caused an unfortunately unpleasant rift between some lesbian groups and some transgender groups - *discussion to find a safe and comfortable compromise is surely the only way forward.* It is of course very important that unity is shown between the various subgroups of the LGBTQIA+ population so that it can carry on its good work globally - after all there are over 60 countries in the world where people can be arrested for being LGBTQIA+.

An excellent and balanced alternative viewpoint to the pro-gender transition websites for parents to refer to can be found on the websites www.transgendertrend, www.sex-matters and www.genspect.org, which have many useful articles and reference sources. It is likewise worth searching under "transition regret" and "detransition" in YouTube. For those who feel there is a need for expert psychological exploration of transgender feelings reference to the website www.genderexploratory.com (Gender Exploratory Therapy Association - GETA) can provide contact with psychotherapists who specialise in this area. For those who have same sex attraction and are considering gender transition a very useful website is www.genderhq.com (Gender Health Query). It is also very worthwhile consulting www.4thwavenow.com.

A LACK OF "GOOD" GENDER ROLE MODELS, GENDER INSECURITY AND A LACK OF KNOWLEDGE OF SEXUAL ETIQUETTE

One factor that can help the development of a secure sense of self in a gender is the influence of "good" gender role models but in current society this is a controversial area and begs the two obvious questions:

1. What is a "good" female role model?
2. What is a "good" male role model?

Young cisgirls and ciswomen are quite correctly reminded of matters regarding their equality with cismen and this may motivate them to enter and even take over traditionally male domains. An increased "pushiness" is often necessary in traditionally "blokey" or "macho" environments. But of course, you don't have to be the same to be equal. In a progressive society women and men can not only be equal but their differences in aptitudes can be entirely complementary to each other - "the sum is greater than the parts". Whilst the world in general hasn't reached a desirable degree of equality of opportunity between women and men, it is a most worthy aim and further progress is essential.

Young cismen are quite rightly given the message regarding the undesirability of showing "toxic masculinity". In soft Western society where there are now fewer rugged male role models as there are fewer and fewer men working in tough, dangerous jobs such as mining, sea fishing, extreme heavy industry and the military. Cismen currently often work in comfortable offices where they may still try to project their maleness, but this can butt against powerful ciswomen and result in unpleasant consequences for all concerned.

Ciswomen may consciously and *unconsciously* flaunt their sexuality to catch the eye of cismen - the survival of the species has always depended on this. Cismen of course, also make sexual displays but as we all know, these are invariably less subtle and clumsier than those made by ciswomen, The innate nature of these displays is a consequence of evolution. These days, young cismen can be unsure how to react to ciswomen, if at all. They want to respond "as men" but feel conflicted as they will not want to be disciplined for any politically incorrect behaviour - they may therefore fluff their approach to the disappointment of all. Successfully fulfilling female and male sexual roles has always been difficult and the interaction between the sexes has always been a complex interplay of powerful desires versus social convention.

Both sexes will be affected by the conflicts between:

1. The influence of *newer* role models and *older* social conventions.
2. Influences of *older* role models and *newer* social conventions.
3. Instinctive behaviour.

It is difficult to be a female and it is difficult to be a male. This begs the question, if there is an overall difference between a female's difficulty in her role in life and a male's difficulty in his role in life? Many factors in modern life have resulted in a rapid and significant change in gender roles and social attitudes, which means that older role models may seem outmoded and irrelevant - this results in it being difficult for developing adolescents to know how to act and behave as their parents are generally modelling older modes of behaviour.

An apparent psychological "solution" to the inner mental and social stresses of how to be a female and how to be a male can be to *unconsciously* "refuse" to accept your role by saying you are not of the gender that you are struggling to be. In other words to "cop out" - a form of AVOIDANCE. This would seem to be a psychologically viable option to an anxious and insecure person. We all know the feeling of relief when a dreaded work task or social event is cancelled. Many people will have felt some sense of relief when they have phoned in "sick" even though they were not particularly unwell. The sudden removal of any of life's major psychosocial burdens can be very welcome. Letting go of a female or male gender role that is being struggled with would be another example of something giving a sense of relief. The wide rainbow-like spectrum of sexual roles and identities within the transgender world has just that type of appeal as it is a world that seems to remove the pressure of traditional gender roles - you can be just as you like. This may be a factor in why there is an increasing number of gender expressions and identities being described and in fact the same applies to new terminologies for sexual orientations. However, the difficulty with this is that there is often an instinctive deep psychological discomfort between the transgender world and the cisgender world as discussed elsewhere - the greater the number of newly named genders and sexual orientations the more difficult it is for cisgender people to comfortably relate to transgender people. Most cisgender people will want to know how to politely interact with transgender people, *but cisgender people may need to be helped to know how best to interact*. Everybody can help everybody else with a statement of preference but unfortunately sometimes cisgender people will accidentally or unintentionally say the wrong thing.

Socially insecure and Social Media dependent young people are less likely to have had actual sexual contact with people of their peer group. In some cases, they may only have had "sexual" contact with their former abusers - another complicating factor discussed elsewhere. Possible reasons for their lack of or avoidance of sex are:

1. Being socially and sexually under confident and naïve.

2. Being afraid of sexual rejection or failure - taking on a transgender or agender identity may be an *unconscious* form of AVOIDANCE.
3. They may be under confident about their developing bodies, "I hate the shape of my boobs", "My labia hang too low", "Someone might laugh at the shape of my penis". "Stay in the bedroom" young people are hardly likely to be fit and toned. Their time wasted on Social Media may be accompanied by comfort eating excessive quantities of junk food - this is often an unfortunate part of modern lifestyles.

Please consider the above with these additional factors:

4. Large amounts of transgender material and unconventional gender role models in the Social Media.
5. Having some features of the other sex as shown by the "double curve sexual characteristics" graph.

1 - 5 can all mean that it is a short step to "be" transgender and to opt for the "transgender solution."

To repeat, this in itself may be an *unconscious* but understandable AVOIDANCE of the risks of failure or being uncomfortable in cisheterosexual sex.

Having good contemporary sex and gender role models would perhaps go some way help reduce the above discomforts and insecurities - but where are they? Parental guidance and advice about sexual roles and their complexities might help to reduce such anxieties by ensuring that young people know about sexual courtesies and relationship pitfalls. It is surprising how often, when asked, transgender young people say that they have had little or no parental guidance in these areas. Some parents actually (optimistically) say that their children obtain all the advice they need from the Internet (whereas a generation or so ago there was much less sex on screen).

It is important to note that girls and young women can develop fears about sex if they have viewed Internet pornography in which appalling violence towards, and degradation of women are frequently shown. Internet pornography also has the negative effect of linking sex and violence in the minds of boys. Furthermore, there are relatively frequent news reports of male on female sexual assault in wider society and this can also serve to reinforce the mental connection of sex being associated with violence in various ways. These Media factors can of course, serve to cause both conscious and *unconscious* fears surrounding sex in cisgirls and young ciswomen and can result in further discomfort in their sexual role - they might therefore *unconsciously* wish to avoid sexual fear by taking on a male role.

In conclusion:

1. The importance of parents giving guidance and education about sex during the time of puberty (or better still, just before) cannot be overemphasised so that fears about sexual relations can be dispelled. Knowledge of the importance of mutual sexual etiquette is essential. Adequate sex education and role modelling will help to minimise insecurities about sex and interacting with the other sex. A good grounding in these factors will help to decrease the likelihood of AVOIDANCE of an adult sexual role by *unconsciously* rejecting it by taking on a transgender identity. Parents are recommended to counsel and advise their teenage children about sexual relationships. An excellent helpful reference on this topic has been written by Flo Perry and is strongly recommended (please see the bibliography).
2. Without adequate female and male role modelling it is difficult for a cisgirl to become a ciswoman and a cisboy to become a cisman - they will have significant insecurities about how to act during the very self-conscious time of puberty. If they do not know how to

155

behave in the eyes of their peers and wider society, they may *unconsciously* "cop out" by AVOIDANCE of their true social role by declaring themselves to be transgender.

MORE ABOUT FAMILY DYNAMICS THAT MAY RESULT IN POOR SELF-ESTEEM, A LACK OF RESILIENCE AND REDUCED SOCIAL COMPETENCE IN CHILDREN

It seems that children who decide that they are transgender frequently come from families where there are certain family dynamics in play. It must be emphasised that such a family environment is not the only cause of a transgender mindset in a child, merely that there is an association and that it is an important factor. There is absolutely no intention to criticise any form of parenting. Any parents who feel that they recognise their type of parenting in this book should not feel criticised and then feel guilty or even offended. Their main reaction could be to consider how things might be done differently having recognised how some features of home life could perhaps be contributing to their child's mindset. Parenting is the most difficult job in the world and there has historically been no instruction manual although having said that, perhaps one of the very best new references is by another member of the Perry family, Philippa - this is also strongly recommended (please see the bibliography).

Some examples of home and parenting factors that maybe seen in many modern families (again, no criticism is intended - parents will be doing their best):

1. It is a parent's commendable and understandable instinct to protect their children and it is very difficult to find a happy medium between overprotecting and under protecting. Some modern children maybe be metaphorically wrapped in physical and psychological bubblewrap or cotton wool - they might be overprotected and not given the opportunity to take responsibility for themselves. Everything is done for them and every material thing is provided. It is important for children to learn how to do things for themselves by trial and error - so that they can learn from consequences of their actions

- obviously, safety does need to be ensured. If children have everything done for them, they maybe left with an overdeveloped sense of entitlement or feel that they cannot be trusted to do things for themselves, which reduces their self-confidence in tackling tasks in the future. They may be academically spoon fed and whilst this may result in good exam results it does not allow a child to "learn how to learn" by themselves. Bullying of children is of course, unacceptable, but some children may be overprotected from others and therefore cannot learn to maturely stand up for themselves against difficult people.

2. No criticism is intended of those parents who both need to work to financially survive. In order "to make it up" to their children for being absent they may be over generous with material goods but then the ability of children to accept delayed gratification might not be developed. (It is quite reasonable to state that instant gratification does not make anyone happier in the long term). As compensation for their absence, parents may not wish to discipline their children for misdeeds but instead may allow them to over-emote rather than encourage them to show self-restraint - they may instead learn to rant, rave or adopt a victim status. It is all too easy for stressed, tired and exasperated parents to let their children "call the shots". This is very understandable in stressful modern life - but the adults must be in charge. Children cannot automatically know how to behave - they have to be taught by the older generation.

3. Children may be brought up by their grandparents due to 2.

4. There is a pressure towards high achievement for everyone in the family.

5. Parents may like to be "progressive", "modern" and "liberal" in their outlook towards transgender matters.

6. Due to high rates of relationship breakdown, many children may be brought up by step, foster or adoptive parents.

7. Some parents may allow their children too much screen time due to being absentee working parents. This again is understandable but will reduce the influence of parental role modelling and equally as importantly diminish the child's feelings that their parents have time for them - resulting in feelings of rejection, abandonment and frustration of needs. Feeling that their parents *do* in fact have time for them is a major factor in a child feeling valued, appreciated and that the child is worthy of love - these factors are essential for a child's self-esteem.

A common phrase to be heard these days is, "Childhood seems to last much longer than it used to". Quite understandably, parents feel the need to "give" as much to their children as possible on the basis of "wanting to give my child more than I had as a child" and to "better protect my child from the difficulties and dangers of life than I was". This is of course, very commendable although may actually be something that stems from parental guilt.

Parents may also wish to spare their children the hardships of school and may criticise teachers for disciplining their child. In this instance there may be an element of "there's nothing wrong with my child" on the basis that their child being in trouble can be painfully felt by parents as if it is some form of criticism of their parenting. It may not actually be a criticism although it may just *feel* as if it is. Teachers do need to enforce discipline in order to teach effectively.

Often, whether they actually have ability or not, children may be regarded by their parents as having a good career potential - they "must" become top barristers, brain surgeons, wealthy bankers, astronauts and so forth. Any hint of not living up to this is another pressure on the child that may make them retreat into their inner world and be unhappy with themselves. Again, teachers may be directly criticised by parents if their children aren't top of the class and this may of course, be the case if the parents had academically failed themselves and they are trying to live out their own frustrated ambitions through their children.

Some modern schools do try and cushion children from any sense of failure in the classroom or on the sports field. Some schools have notoriously stopped any competitive sport or use euphemisms for poor performance. The problem here is that children do not learn to accept failure or not winning - something which is required to develop resilience in forms of employment where dog-eat-dog competition and severe stress are part of the job.

On the subject of stress and anxiety, there are some children kept at home because of their "terrible school anxiety" but there is only one way to develop the ability to cope and this is by actually facing the anxiety, hardening up to it and by using mind techniques - old fashioned support and coaching. Avoiding the "terrible anxiety" by staying off school merely makes it progressively harder and harder to handle the stress when the child finally attempts to attend class. An immature child's mind cannot be expected to stage by stage rationalise what has caused their anxious plight or how to deal with it. It is all too easy for anxious, stressed and excluded children to become school outcasts or misfits and therefore at severe risk of latching onto online groups, which offer a supposed "explanation and a solution" to their feelings. Such online groups may be promoting the transgender "explanation and solution". (The author does of course fully accept that in very specific situations home schooling can be the best way for certain children).

There are *particular problems* resulting from:

1. Children being lavished with whatever material goods they demand.
2. Being protected from any sense of failure.
3. Not being disciplined and firmly guided.

4. Being allowed to over-emote without being told to exercise self-control.
5. Not having the ability to tolerate delayed gratification,

A wise great grandmother of the old school would perhaps describe them as "spoiled children". This is clearly not in a child's best interests and is a recipe for a child to become "difficult", "demanding" and "entitled". These three factors result in the child being disapproved of, excluded and then ultimately feeling dissatisfied with themselves. The mention of a former generation brings to mind that during those times there were greater degrees of:

1. Self-discipline and resilience. (Whilst it is clearly beneficial that those with true mental illness can now present themselves for treatment without stigma, in current times increasing numbers of people are able to consciously and *unconsciously* languish in the "sick role" of having "poor mental health". This maybe painful to hear and regarded as insulting - but it is not in their best interests of their self-respect and personal development in the longer term).
2. Societal discipline. (Modern society is beset by a decline in personal standards of decorum and courtesy, not to mention increasing amounts of antisocial behaviour, loss of self-control and crime).
3. Educational standards. (In comparison with formerly much stricter times teachers in many modern schools have increasing difficulties in educating children due to their inability to control bad behaviour that can prevent learning. This is partly but not wholly related to 1 and 2. In spite of children generally being kept in school longer than a generation ago, many children now leave school without even properly mastering the basics of grammar, arithmetic and other core subjects.

There is no intention whatsoever to lay all of the blame for 1 - 3 at the feet of parents for what is now happening. There has been a societal shift as a whole that has many factors in its origin but it is nevertheless resulting in a general "dumbing down" or "levelling down" of educational and social standards.

The parental style described above is all very understandable because parents don't want to "lose their child's love" - as they see it. In reality parents wouldn't actually lose a child's love by giving them loving discipline and expecting their child to honour certain obligations, boundaries and chores. A *particular problem* is that children who demonstrate factors 1 - 5 develop an astonishing sense of entitlement - they feel should have exactly what they want, to have what they want now, *nobody should question their viewpoint* and if they do, they feel that it is quite reasonable to rant and rave - after all this is exactly the behaviour that is so often unwittingly encouraged. Such "difficult" children can readily become "difficult" at school and then end up class outcasts. They may then take solace in Social Media.

The well known phrase in relation to children, "Their emotions are all mixed up" is a good one and gives a feel for what is being experienced. Even as adults many of us know that terrible feeling of being "all mixed up" when life seems to be an anxious mess and that it is extremely difficult to think clearly enough to come up with rational solutions. When "all mixed up" it is just too easy to grasp at any available apparent solution to emotional distress. For some young people opting for a transgender lifestyle may seem to provide a solution to emotional problems and also be a way of expressing their emotional difficulties.

Please remember in relation to children the phrase, "Behaviour is often the only way for a child to communicate".

A child may say to its parents that it "is" transgender. Parents who quite understandably feel that they should be progressive and move with the times may be swayed by the idea of using gender neutral parenting techniques and allow or even encourage transgender behaviour - but it must be borne in mind that children are very impressionable and suggestible. A child's parents may have incorrectly assumed that a few minor *apparent* cross-gender statements or actions made by their child indicate that their child "is" transgender. If this is followed up by allowing or worse, encouraging their child to adopt cross-gender or gender neutral dress and activities a child may then go along with it purely because it is impressionable and children do like to please their parents and to have parental attention. In these ways parents are thereby unwittingly encouraging transgender behaviour - but there will unlikely to have been a true problem with gender in the first place.

There is no scientific evidence to suggest that gender neutral parenting is of any benefit but it is highly likely to make a child a social misfit and an outcast at school - this may then actually take away from a child an important part of its gender related social and pubertal development. Worse still, some children may end up heading towards what will be totally inappropriate medical gender transition processes. If parents somehow realise that they have made a mistake, it will understandably be very difficult to own up to it.

Children have a certain psychological need for it to be *their parents* who care for them. (Note the plural). That is how evolution has hardwired the brain so that the very vulnerable human child is very strongly emotionally pulled to its parents for the very sake of its survival. This is also especially nourishing psychologically. (Please consider the perilous Cavewoman/Caveman era). Of course, grandparents, other family carers, step, foster and adoptive parents may be excellent and loving carers. It has to be said that in some instances substitute carers can be far more beneficial to the child than its biological parents if the biological parents are only able to provide dysfunctional care. Having good biological, attentive and loving parents in a child's life is the best way of preventing the child having feelings of abandonment that can lead to poor self-esteem and feelings of worthlessness. Parenting does not have to be "perfect all of the time", far from it. So long as it is loving and attentive around 50% of the time, a child can develop a good sense of self-worth and have confidence in themselves. The parenting just has to be "good enough" - a phrase coined by the pioneering paediatric psychoanalyst Donald Winnicott (please see the bibliography).

It is doubtful that men could fully understand the conflict that takes place within a working mother's mind between her desire to be an excellent mother and her wish to advance in a career. Quite rightly, many countries are striving to give women the chance to fulfil their career potential and have pay equality but this will clearly do little to ease a woman's inner conflict relating to her drive to fully care for her children.

Childhood life factors that repeatedly make a child feel less than valued and unloved give the child a long term sense of being unloveable in the personality that it has - this is especially the case if a child is subjected to mixed and or contradictory messages of love. It is emotionally harmful to a child if a background of consistent emotional warmth is lacking. This is particularly likely to occur when one or both parents have their own mental health problems, which might result in an inability of the parents to provide constancy and make the child sufficiently feel that it is loved, protected and wanted. Messages given to the child that mix love and hate or violence can be particularly unsettling and greatly impair its own ability to feel, give and receive love in later years. A child that is given constant love is more able to deal with the normal stresses of life in comparison with the traumatised child who latches onto any available apparent source of solace and protection of its feelings. The unloved and undervalued child may be purely reactive in its behaviour and impulsively seek out any psychological attention or relief wherever and however it seems to be available.

Another factor that can reduce a child's self-esteem can result from parental envy and jealousy of a growing child. Parents who feel that their own childhood was more difficult than their own child's and perhaps that their child is more "talented" in appearance, personality and ability may *unconsciously* resent this. The result is that the parent can subtly undermine their child in terms of its "talents", femaleness or maleness. The consequences are obvious to the child's sense of self-worth, femaleness or maleness - the child may seek a way of psychologically dealing with this in any way they can.

And so, children who have needed to grasp whatever comfort they can are particularly prone to latching onto and obtaining comfort from the Social Media. They may also have developed the habit of putting on a façade to try and please their parents and hence they are already adept at putting on a false face to the world - either directly to other people or via Social Media. Needing to present the self in a way other than it actually is, may be a prelude to taking on a transgender persona as using a façade has already been used as a way of psychologically coping by such children.

For young people, rebellion against parental values is an important part of being "different" to their parents and separating from them - so that everyone can get on with their own lives. If a child declares its transgender inclinations to its parents, the parents are very likely to experience a range of emotions including perplexity, discomfort and feeling generally unsettled. The parents may ask themselves if they have done something wrong. Given what is in the various Social Media about transgender children, the parents may feel conflicted as to what to do. Should they follow their instincts or should they follow what they may have learned from the Social Media about parents supporting transgender children's choices? By completely going along with their child's attempt to show some individual character and rewarding it, such parents are removing their child's point of adolescent kickback and this may then result in an increased extremity of transgender expression by the child in order to feel that they *are actually effectively* rebelling and differentiating. Clearly, at the point of teenage rebellion, the cool and "of the moment" transgender Social Media sites may strike a chord in a disaffected youth's mind.

Once a young person has had their need to be accepted, acknowledged and approved of satisfied by being part of online transgender groups it is exceptionally difficult for them to desist. Much is made of being loyal to the group, fellow group members having a shared experience and "being in it together". Failure to persist in a transgender lifestyle may result in online shaming. There is often a strong sense of, to use an old political phrase, "being with us or against us". When teenagers are "against" their parents, they are more likely to be "with" the group that *seems* to be on their side. Teenagers may become "against" their parents even if prior to puberty there had been a good and loving parent-child attachment with minimal feelings of abandonment, rejection and frustration of needs. Some teenagers just need that sense of rebellion that they can see "freaks out" their parents no matter what their upbringing was like, just as they now need peer approval.

HOW SOME PARENTS "MAKE" THEIR CHILDREN TRANSGENDER - BY CAUSING THEM TO HAVE UNCOMFORTABLE FEELINGS ABOUT THEIR GENDER

Some parents may have conscious and *unconscious* reasons for believing that their children are transgender and then use gender neutral or transgender supportive parenting. The reasons for this are complex and may include:

1. Parents who are *unconsciously* uncomfortable in their own gender or given the amount of current transgender publicity have actually come out as transgender themselves. It is very striking that parents with transgender feelings "just happen to have" transgender identifying children. YouTube has many examples.

2. Quite concerning are those parents who themselves enjoy the attention and approval they gain from being seen as progressive because of their gender neutral or transgender supporting parenting. Many Internet based gender neutral and transgender parenting Social Media entries appear to be more concerned with parental gratification than with their children's welfare. It begs to the question why any parent would make a point of filming their young son going to school in a pink dress and hair ribbons then posting the video on Social Media - worse still, including self-congratulatory statements made by the parents in the posting. This is exploitation of children or more accurately child abuse with a sexual component.

3. Equally concerning are the parents who enjoy the drama and prurience of being involved in medical procedures. This is a psychological equivalent of those who enjoy being an observer of medical procedures as demonstrated by the popularity of television medical programmes. The author painfully recalls when working in emergency departments the situation in which he wished to give his patient due confidentiality by asking relatives and "friends" to leave the room but who refused

to do so "because they wanted to 'support' the patient". The poor patient clearly wanted the privacy but felt very conflicted. It was all too obvious that the hangers-on were revelling in the drama.

4. Worse still are those who subject their young children to major medical transgender procedures as a vicarious way of obtaining psychological attention and prurient gratification for themselves - please do an Internet search on Munchausen's syndrome by proxy (now known as Factitious Disorder Imposed by Another).

Long before even getting to the stage of puberty blockers, cross-sex hormones and surgery, some parents may feel that gender neutral parenting is a good thing. Please be aware that social conditioning can only ever have a false masking and overwriting effect on biologically determined personality characteristics - gender-neutral parenting may nevertheless have very confusing and contradictory effects. Children are impressionable and when very young will go along with gender neutral or pro-transgender parenting as children tend to want to please their parents - there will of course, be the effect of children receiving conscious and *unconscious* positive reinforcement from their parents when they show any cross-gender behaviour. To summarise, this all becomes a self reinforcing process that may occur in the following stages:

1. A child is misdiagnosed by its parents (or a pro-gender transition practitioner) as being transgender.
2. The child is *unconsciously* and/or consciously encouraged to show cross-gender behaviour.
3. The child then actually shows more cross-gender behaviour - because they like the positive attention.
4. When noticing the child's cross-gender behaviour the parents think they are "correct" in their "diagnosis" and are *themselves* psychologically gratified.
5. The child continues to enjoy the parental approval.

6. The child is thus encouraged to show further cross-gender behaviour.
7. The parents are further psychologically gratified.

... The whole cycle or rather downward spiral continues.

A CAUTIONARY NOTE

It is worth noting that if a young pre-pubertal child is brought up using gender neutral parenting or in a transgender way this is bound to cause problems when puberty actually starts. It is very easy to bring up a child as gender neutral or transgender in the period before puberty - after all, the physical and psychological differences between young girls and boys are much, much less obvious than between women and men. Once the complex pubertal hormonal and brain maturation processes start matters are very different and things will almost certainly become very difficult.

A child brought up as its original gender is quite naturally being prepared for its entry into adulthood by consciously and *unconsciously* following its same sex role model and as a result of deliberate tuition by parents. For example:

To a daughter - "One day soon you will start growing breasts, but every girl develops them at a different time. Some girls have bigger breasts than others, but the size doesn't matter. You will also have something called a 'period' - this is when ... ".

To a son - "I see you are starting to grow some whiskers, when it's time for me to shave tomorrow we can shave together, and I can show you how to do it so you don't cut yourself with the razor. I will also talk to you about other things you need to know about being a man - and some things you need to know about girls and women so that you treat them respectfully. Women are to be loved, appreciated and respected too as to do that is part of being a real man".

This type of preparation is really excellent parenting and is something that parents and children can enjoy and all may benefit from an increased sense of family love and bonding. Such tuition chimes entirely with a child's natural and predestined pubertal development.

In worrying contrast please consider a child that has been brought up from a very young age as transgender or gender neutral. How can such a child be properly prepared for the puberty that relates to its birth sex? Once puberty and its natural processes start, the poor child will be terribly flummoxed as they will start to show psychological leanings towards their birth sex but this will not match the conditioning being given by its parents. The parents will be similarly conflicted and confused as to what then to do for the best. *This will all almost guarantee feelings of gender confusion, muddling and psychological discomfort* - which would doubtless then be diagnosed as "obvious gender dysphoria" by health care professionals. In this example, feelings of "gender dysphoria" have *actually been caused*. In this instance the response by gender identity clinics might be to give puberty blockers to "treat" what is *really artificially induced discomfort* about puberty. Please note the dangers here as to how a child can be denied the opportunity to revel in the excitement of being in and experiencing their natural birth sex.

(Parents of children who have genuine sex chromosome related or metabolic intersex problems are generally at pains to ensure their offspring are brought up as the sex that is most appropriate to their biology. This is clearly entirely commendable parenting in relation to sex and gender matters).

ARE SCHOOLS ACTUALLY UNDER INTENSE PRO-TRANSGENDER POLITICAL PRESSURE?

The adverse effects of some modern schooling styles have already been discussed but there is another area of concern. It would be hoped that schools would at least take a neutral political stance on the current tendency for children to adopt transgender choices. Alas not. Many schools are aiding and abetting it for fear of criticism and accusations of transphobia. They do not wish to be regarded as anything other than liberal, tolerant and progressive.

Whilst teachers are supposedly acting in *loco parentis* (in place of the parents), it is concerning that there are instances of children who are less than sixteen years of age and are expressing transgender behaviour although only at school and amongst friends - but their teachers are not informing parents of this. It is realised that teachers find themselves in a very delicate and difficult situation, but this denies parents the opportunity to prevent their children entering the potentially damaging psychological and physical processes of gender transitioning. As discussed earlier, if a mature adult makes a carefully considered decision to undergo hormonal and surgical transition and their life is improved by it in the long term, this can be regarded as a very good thing. However, children do not have the maturity and insight to sufficiently understand the potential psychological trauma later in life of not being able have their biologically own children. Nor do children have the capacity to understand the significance of the potential loss of orgasmic ability or other sexual functions and many of the other potential adverse effects of gender transition treatments. There is no comparison between the immature gratification of adolescent masturbation and the deep, sensual, romantically intertwined experience of adult sex, (whether this is transgender sex, lesbian sex, gay sex or cisheterosexual sex) - which can potentially be lost or impaired as a result of gender transition.

The question as to whether young children should be taught about the complex matters of transgender identity and non-cisheterosexual orientation at a time of their own sexual immaturity is very contentious. Perhaps it could be said that light reference could be made to these factors in order that children can avoid developing prejudice and intolerance towards LGBTQIA+ people *but that it should go no further than that.* Providing too much detail in schools about non-cisheterosexual matters can very easily add to any preexisting unsettled and muddled feelings that pre-pubertal and pubertal children may be experiencing about themselves as sexual beings - f*ar from being helpful, this might worsen their existing confusion.* Immature young minds need concrete facts as the ability to weigh up anything that is other than black and white takes quite a number of years to develop - children have to be well into their late teens before they can truly exercise critical thought. A young person's overall sexuality also takes a long time to develop and mature - therefore it is surely in their best interests that it is allowed do so in the fullness of time - without being exposed to modern gender theory, which can only serve to muddle their thoughts and identity. Children are very impressionable; they often seize upon things that seem a little curious and out of the ordinary. Schools teaching transgender matters to children are actually directly encouraging transgender behaviour even though the apparent and well-intentioned motive maybe educational.

Obviously, only a minority of school children believe they are transgender. Socially marginalised school children who are already in the "out group" and are trying to deal with their pre-existing psychological pain of being isolated by joining an online transgender forum and ACTING OUT as transgender will then find themselves *even more firmly placed* in the "out group" at school. This will merely serve to make them yet more of an outcast and at increased risk of bullying. Standing out or being seen as "odd" has *always* made someone a target for bullies. Quite rightly bullies should be disciplined but this may well result in the bullies resenting the transgender children for being punished. The problem is that in spite of punishment and attempted control of school bullies it is known that bullies will often still find a way of attacking their victim. Children are cruel and after all like their revenge. A concerning consequence is that the disciplining of "transgender bashing bullies" could actually reinforce their prejudice. Resentment of punishment is known to reinforce disdain. Ask any Police officer how this works.

Thus, what we appear to be seeing is children's welfare being sacrificed in order that teachers can avoid being seen as transphobic and outmoded. Schooling should be centred around and focussed on children's education, mental welfare and social development. After all teachers are paid and expected by society to put children's best interests first. However, in all fairness to teachers, they are often under intense pressure from education authorities to be pro-gender transition in their approach to children who seem to be adopting a transgender identity. The educational authorities themselves are in turn under incredible pressure to adopt a pro-gender transition approach from Government, which is itself under intense political pressure from pro-gender transition lobby groups. No teacher wishes to be reprimanded for not following their organisation's guidelines - everybody needs to keep their job and wishes to avoid complaints.

Nevertheless, in the United Kingdom educational authorities would be well advised to consider the Law as the legal position is quite clear. School lavatories and changing rooms have a particular legal status under the Equality Act - they must remain as same sex safe spaces for those under eighteen years of age. People under the age of eighteen cannot be legally given a Gender Recognition Certificate. Being mindful of this, the United Kingdom's Attorney General (at the time of writing, 2022) stated that schools do not have to regard a girl as anything other than a girl and a boy should be regarded as a boy. Furthermore, the Attorney General actually stated that, "Teachers should not pander to the whims of children".

MINDSET CHARACTERISTICS THAT MAY (IN SOME INSTANCES) BE ASSOCIATED WITH ADOPTING A TRANSGENDER LIFE MODE - HOW DIFFICULTIES CAN BE UNDERSTOOD AND HELPED

Factors that affect the development of a particular mindset have been touched upon in several sections of this book. Psychotherapists and psychiatrists who are consulted by transgender people have noticed that a particular mindset *may* be present in *some* of their patients.

There are many mindset characteristics that *all* people have to a greater or lesser degree. To state the very obvious, the "amount" of each separate characteristic that a person has determines their overall type of mindset.

If we are truthful with ourselves, we *all* know that we are a mixture of good and bad characteristics. Who hasn't noticed themselves at times being vain, arrogant, selfish, paranoid, aggressive, obsessional, impulsive and at risk of committing any of the Seven Deadly Sins? But if we are frank and honest, when we come across bad traits in others that we disapprove of, we know deep down that we suspect that we may have those characteristics in ourselves.

Certain mindset characteristics can lead to a lack of mental wellbeing and to the making of choices that are not for the best in the long run.

A person's mindset might make them struggle in life when they experience the following:

1. Deep and persistent problems of psychological experience that cause severe distress and discomfort in a social setting.
2. Ways of thinking about the self and others that are unhealthy and unhelpful.

3. Mood and emotional responses that may not be appropriate or proportionate to circumstances.
4. Behaviour that adversely affects social integration, employment and relationships. Impulsiveness and badly thought-out actions.
5. Use of unduly emotive verbal communication resulting from a reduced ability to first process strong emotions.
6. Problems that started in childhood or adolescence and have continued into adulthood.
7. Psychological problems 1 - 6 that cannot be explained by any other psychiatric disorder.

The various types of unhelpful mindsets include the rich array of characteristics of that complex and many varied thing we know as "human nature". To repeat, we *all* consciously or *unconsciously* know that have *some* of the features of 1 - 7 whether we are cisgender or transgender.

Some examples of how someone's mindset can affect their life in a major way:

Many top scientists have obsessive-compulsive characteristics.

Actors may have narcissistic and histrionic features. These features may actually help them to fully "get into their role". During acting it is temporarily "all about me", "how I present myself" and "I can be anything or anybody I want to be". Unfortunately, these traits can be unhelpful to the actor when off-stage in day-to-day life - these characteristics can make some actors appear self-centred and arrogant. They might also appear shallow and insincere.

CEOs of large corporations sometimes have antisocial features. Some may also have narcissistic features and it is of note that antisocial and narcissistic features often coexist in the same person.

The author will leave it to the reader as to the mindset of politicians.

It must be emphasised again that no one is immune from having at least some unhelpful mindset characteristics - but how we are as people is all a matter of degree. Most of us have made mistakes in the ways in which we approach life and other people - the author holds his hand up to a number of personal mistakes.

It is difficult to define what a "psychologically at ease and socially comfortable person" actually is, but this is something that is instinctively recognised. Such a person would be relatively free of unhelpful mindset characteristics - they would be as described in the literature about the "Five Factor Model of Mindset Structure" (please see the bibliography):

1.   Conscientious.
2.   Open to new experiences.
3.   Not neurotic.
4.   Slightly extroverted rather than introverted.
5.   Generally agreeable in nature.

What psychotherapists and psychiatrists have *sometimes* observed is that transgender young people show mindset features that could predispose them to making life choices that can be unhelpful in the long run. These features can be associated with a depressed mood, anxiety and poor self-esteem. People with depression sometimes try to manage their feelings of depression in a variety of ways. For some depressed and unhappy people, "new identity seeking", "novel experience seeking" and "group seeking" can be ways of coping with their troubling thoughts and feelings as a way of "lifting their mood". For some, adopting a transgender life-mode can be just that form of "new identity seeking", "novel experience seeking" and "group seeking". Seeking a "new identity" can be a way of leaving an unhappy self behind. Such   mental   processes   would   benefit   from   being psychotherapeutically explored before making any major decisions about gender transition.

MOST cisgender people and transgender people will recognise some unhelpful features in themselves!

Question 1. Why is this important to note this in young people?

Answer 1. If someone:

a. Has a certain mindset characteristics that increase their likelihood to have low self-esteem, poor confidence, guilt, worthlessness and is generally not happy with themselves as a person.
b. Already has uncomfortable feelings about their gender identity and sexual orientation as often naturally occurs during puberty.
c. Would "rather be someone else" in order to "have a better life".
d. Is on an extreme point on the "double curve sexual characteristics" graph - and inwardly does not feel properly female or male.
e. Is being influenced by transgender Social Media messages which seem to be a countermeasure to the psychological stresses described above.

… Factors a - e can very easily lead them to believe they are transgender or seek a "transgender transformation" as a way of dealing with their pain in life.

Question 2. It is really correct to automatically rush to treat such psychological matters in a young person with physical treatments such as puberty blockers, cross-sex hormones and surgery?

Answer 2. The answer to this is left to the reader - although for *some* mature adult transgender people hormonal and surgical gender transition can be an extremely helpful approach.

The decision about permanent treatments just has to be the correct one - please give the decision time and search the Internet and through this book to find various viewpoints about medical gender transition.

The other very, very important fact is that the origin of mindset characteristics is a mixture of childhood experiences plus a degree of genetic susceptibility to these experiences. When psychotherapists and psychiatrists identify certain troubling psychological symptoms in someone, they tend to find a history in early childhood of:

1. Feelings of abandonment.
2. Feelings of rejection.
3. Feelings of frustration of needs.
4. Poor emotional attachment to the main carer (usually the mother).
5. Possibly abuse (emotional, physical or sexual).

BUT as was emphasised before this is not necessarily an indication of bad parenting, *just that a particular child was especially susceptible to the effect of certain experiences.* Some people point to psychological features being "inherited". Of course, there are genetic factors in families, but mindset traits may of course, *seem* or *appear* to be "inherited" due to family characteristics being passed down the generations of the family simply by learning from example. (Epigenetic factors will also be a factor in inheritance but the subject is beyond the scope of this small book).

In addition to the 1 - 5 listed above a child may have the upbringing related factors 1 - 5 listed below (which were previously included in the sections on family factors):

1. Children are lavished with whatever material goods and personal freedoms they demand.
2. Children are protected from any sense of failure.
3. Children are not disciplined and firmly guided.
4. Children may be allowed to over-emote without being told to exercise self-control.
5. Children have an inability to tolerate delayed gratification.

These ten factors above put together predispose to the development of:

1. A self-hating individual.
2. A lack of the mental coping mechanisms and resilience that are required to cope with the real stresses of life.
3. A tendency to ACT OUT too forcefully.
4. An over-belief in "being right" and a lack of will to engage in detailed discussion - particularly if feels at risk of being wrong or being criticised.
5. A sense of not feeling right within the self and within wider society.

When psychologists and psychiatrists identify a certain mindset in a young person the most important things for them to do are:

NOT to simply give a psychiatric "label" as this can be felt to be insulting or stigmatising.

BUT instead to ask their patient the question, "What happened to you in your earlier life?"

THEN to explain how childhood experiences can affect the development of the mindset and how certain characteristics can lead to someone feeling uncomfortable about themselves and in society.

IMPORTANTLY to help the person understand that their parents did not deliberately do what they did. Parenting is the most difficult job in the world and there has never really been an ideal instruction book or manual available. Parents do not deliberately set out to negatively affect the development of their child. Parents are just trying to survive and get by in the world like everyone else. Please remember that parents generally do what was modelled to them by their own parents, or even try and make a better job of things.

EXPLAIN FURTHER how certain mindset characteristics actually developed in childhood as a way of emotionally handling:

1. Feelings of abandonment.
2. Feelings of rejection.
3. Feelings of frustrations of needs.
4. Difficulties with attachment to carers, particularly the mother.
5. Any abuse experienced.

To ASSIST the patient in identifying unhelpful MENTAL DEFENCES and providing the patient with techniques to deal with their unhelpful thoughts and feelings. It is a fairly widely held belief that being able to "unlock" buried memories and "retrieve" them from the *unconscious* can deal with certain psychological difficulties. In practice, it is making patients aware of unhelpful ways that they use counterproductive mental defences that is more important. It is often the unhelpful ways in which the mind uses mental defences that keeps certain memories buried. If a psychotherapist can help a patient to abandon the use of counterproductive mental defences and instead use more helpful defences, this can significantly improve mental wellbeing.

Some additional childhood factors are detailed:

It may have been necessary for a child to have minutely analysed its parent's mood for its own self-protection - this can make someone excessively sensitive to the moods and assumed intentions of others. This can then result in them being easily affected by other people's moods, opinions and judgements.

It may also have been necessary for a child to ACT OUT in order to get any parental attention whatsoever. Being made to feel "not worth the trouble to a parent" (e.g. father always on his smartphone or in the pub, mother always out partying etc.) makes a child feel worthless, develop feelings of self-hate and therefore be prone to self-punishment. These forms of approach to other people as survival behaviour can become lifelong habits.

Some children who have developed the above characteristics may be regarded as "difficult children". The reactions shown to them by their parents may make the child think and feel that "everything is wrong with me" and "everything I do is wrong". This again is harmful to their self-esteem and sets the child up to feel bad about themselves as a person in general.

Feeling bad about the type of person that you are, can contribute to the *feeling of wanting to be a different person altogether*. When self-esteem is low, a person may want to change their self-image to feel better about themselves by assuming a new identity. A way of achieving this is by becoming a "new and improved self" - in other words an *unconsciously* IDEALISED version of the self. The new self needs to eliminate or cancel the old self. It can therefore be understood how it can be very painful if a transgender person is referred to by the wrong pronoun (known as misgendering by transgender people) or is accidentally referred to by their previous name (referred to as dead-naming by transgender people). These reminders of the old self can be remarkably painful - this is entirely understandable. Cisgender people should therefore at all times do their very best to avoid doing this. Transgender people please remember that cisgender people are not perfect and will get it wrong at times - you may have to remind them several times.

Also, people who feel that "everything is wrong with them" can PROJECT these feelings outwards onto someone else as a way of trying to get rid of their uncomfortable feelings. You will know when you come across someone who is doing this because they give the impression that "everything you do for them is wrong", "everything about you is wrong" and "everything in the world is wrong". This PROJECTION of "wrongness" mindset is a surefire factor for relationship difficulties and of course, relationship problems lead to poor mental health.

Please be reminded that many childhood memories of bad experiences can be REPRESSED or SUPPRESSED and so it may not always be obvious where present psychological stresses originated.

And so, as painful as it may be to do so, it is far, far better to identify and acknowledge the presence of certain psychological stresses than to automatically assume that being in the body of the wrong sex is definitely the issue. *But the problem here is that young people rarely, if ever actually stop and think, "My problems in life and with other people are due to the way my mind developed".* Children and young people instead blame other people, circumstances or in the case of being transgender they explain things as a result of what they have read in the Social Media.

There are two pitfalls:

1. Young people are *misdiagnosing themselves as being transgender* when their underlying psychological discomfort results from their personal development and current life experiences plus the influence of Social Media.

2. Young people are often *being misdiagnosed <u>by healthcare professionals</u> as being transgender* when their underlying psychological discomfort results from their personal development and current life experiences plus the influence of Social Media.

Is it not better to at least consider dealing with mental wellbeing issues that result from the mindset and life stress related factors in the first instance? Surely this should be the initial response rather than to automatically resort to treating the body with puberty blockers, cross-sex hormones and gender transition surgery - for a problem that does not actually originate in the body.

It is not advisable for the first approach to a child or other young person to be to try and change who they are by changing their body with puberty blockers, cross-sex hormones and gender transition surgery. It can be even more confusing for an already muddled child during puberty to try and totally "change the inside" by "changing the outside". Having said that, for a mature adult, changing the body can help the person to remodel their life and how they see themselves - but there is no guarantee that this will be successful for everyone who undergoes hormonal and surgical gender transition. If it does work well, the person's life can of course, be improved.

Many of us will know of people who have troubling obsessive-compulsive symptoms and who like to check and double check things to ensure they are in order. What they are doing is trying to put the *outside* world in order as a way of putting their *inside* mental world in order so that they can feel safe and in control. Changing the physical *outside* of a young person cannot be guaranteed to put right their *inside* mental world.

When early bad experiences can be recalled, psychotherapy will help someone to understand where their tortured mindset originated. BUT *continually blaming* the past and *continually blaming* people in the past only entrenches psychological pain - it is best to try and understand that the problem came from the past *and then look to the future.*

When early bad experiences have been deeply REPRESSED into the *unconscious* quite extensive psychotherapy over a long period may be necessary to deal with them - but this can be very beneficial and liberating, particularly when the patient can also learn to use their mental defences more helpfully. *As just said and apologies for the repetition - focussing on the future is more important than focussing on the wrongs of the past - but understanding and coming to terms with the past can be key factors in healing and moving forward.* It is essential to *get through* the pain in order to heal. Many psychological techniques can be learnt to deal with unhelpful aspects of the mind - Harald Surströmming's book (mentioned in the bibliography) can be very helpful although it is slightly difficult to read. Also, by means of psychotherapy it is possible to use bad experiences in a positive way - by realising that bad times have been survived and how that was done can give confidence and increase resilience for the future. For some people, their relationship with a psychotherapist is the first truly trusting relationship they have ever had and this gives reassurance that other people can have integrity and care for them. To emphasise once again, for many people it is generally safer and preferable, at least initially to directly deal with matters of the mind rather than to alter the body with cross-sex hormones and gender transition surgery. Of course, a small number of people are best served by medical gender transition and find contentment through this but clearly this needs to be a decision that is extremely carefully made. It is unfortunately all too easy to be pulled along by the group-think phenomenon of transgender groups and Social Media. *The persuasive and emotional power of the group-think phenomenon should not be underestimated.*

A SUMMARY OF PSYCHOSOCIAL FACTORS THAT MIGHT LEAD SOMEONE TO CHOOSE THE TRANSGENDER SOLUTION IN SOME INSTANCES - IF YOU ARE CONSIDERING HORMONAL OR SURGICAL GENDER TRANSITION *PLEASE* READ THIS SECTION BEFORE YOU GO AHEAD

A number of factors and considerations that are relevant to transgender feelings and choices have already been referred to earlier in this book - they are summarised in this section and more are listed.

It is respectfully suggested that the following list is considered by anyone who is contemplating hormonal or surgical gender transition. As will be seen, this section is more applicable to the older age group than young children. Although this book is focussed on younger people it is only fair to include adults in the cautionary comments.

We are all constantly faced with minor and major decisions in life: which job to take, should a relationship become more committed and so forth. The list is endless. Sometimes the best decisions are made due to "that gut feeling" but it is always worth asking yourself, "Could I be wrong, is my heart ruling my head?" It is also valuable to discuss a dilemma with someone who doesn't have a vested interest or bias in the matter. If you ask a car salesman whether you should buy a car you are *un*likely to receive an *un*biased opinion.

Who would help you to have the least biased discussion about gender transition:

A practitioner in a commercial overseas gender identity clinic?

OR

An independent psychological or medical professional who is under the jurisdiction of an ethical body that guides their practice?

Very, very few people are completely happy with themselves in the way they are as people or how they think their body appears. Homophobia is fortunately decreasing in many societies but its effect on lesbian and gay people can still make them feel very disapproved of. For people who have such dissatisfaction with themselves and suffer from the effects of homophobia it is very tempting to wish to leave behind their persona, sexual orientation or a body they do not like. Humankind has always searched for answers to questions such as, "What is the meaning of life?" "Why are we here?" or "What is wrong with me and why do I hate myself so much?" "How could I change myself to be happier?" The third and fourth questions may seem to be explained by the belief of being in a body of the wrong sex but it is perhaps advisable if more questions are answered:

"Am I wrongly blaming my body for the pain in my mind? Am I PROJECTING my mental pain onto my body, when my pain is really due to my feelings as a person as a whole and how other people see me?"

"Do I somehow feel that I can control or change life by controlling and changing my body - but would this really work for the rest of my life?"

"Do I feel like changing myself or even punishing myself because I feel I am unattractive and that I am not a typical woman/man?"

"Could I be *unconsciously* responding to society's homophobia or my own internalised homophobia?"

The author profusely apologises that these questions might be uncomfortable to read as they may touch upon some very sensitive points, but they could possibly provide you with a "lightbulb moment" and you can think to yourself:

"Ah, I was considering medical gender transition due to my feelings of being a feminine man or masculine woman/my sexual orientation/my general feelings about myself as a person/my dissatisfaction with my body or other things that I couldn't explain or understand. I now see where it was all coming from, I will seek psychotherapy so that I can accept myself as I am and make the best of my life as I am".

Having read this section you may realise that *unconscious* use of mental processes may have led you towards transgender feelings and the option of hormonal and surgical gender transition. Perhaps you had DENIED to yourself the life difficulties that transition can cause, particularly if you make the wrong choice - *although of course, we must keep in mind that the correct decision can be life enhancing.* It is only human nature to seize upon apparent solutions to problems and to wishfully fail to see any problems in those solutions. We've all done it - many times.

If gender transition is right for you then it is hoped that it is a successful process, and your life is very much improved. However, before proceeding please consider if the following factors might contribute to your transgender feelings:

1. Polymorphous sexuality is a psychological factor that means that people can desire and enjoy sexuality that is not "mainstream" or cisheterosexual. Why not enjoy anything from the wide range of human sexuality? Gender transitioning hormones and surgery may not be necessary to enjoy this but for some people they can enhance their life in many ways - please, please just make the right choice.
2. Poor mental wellbeing, current mental stresses, certain mindsets, body dysmorphic disorder and counterproductive mental defences can all quite

understandably lead to you to choose transgender options that might be regretted latter. If you have ever thought to yourself or said to someone, "My mental health is really bad" it is particularly important to consider if this might be a contributory factor to seeking hormonal and surgical gender transition. Are you perhaps trying to leave an unhappy self behind by reinventing yourself? However, it can be immensely helpful for people who make the right decision.

3. Many people find that their previous sexual encounters of any type may have been less than satisfactory - they may have been awkward, embarrassing, uncomfortable, abusive, regretted and to cap it all did not end in full satisfaction. Becoming transgender may be an *unconscious* way of seeking satisfactory sex by satisfying underlying same sex attraction that has not been fully acknowledged. It might be a way of *unconsciously* "leaving behind" previous unsatisfying sex. It may also be an *unconscious* way of saying to the self, "It's not that I'm no good at sex or relationships, it's my gender that's wrong". But of course, many people *are* able to experience their best ever sex after hormonal and surgical gender transition - please choose wisely.

4. Being on a particular point of overlap on the "double curve sexual characteristics" graph may be a factor. If you are someone whose mind and body seem to be partly like the other sex, why not just be as you are and accept yourself in this increasingly diverse world?

5. Have you been over-influenced by Social Media? Have you been spending more time on Social Media than with real people? The transgender promoting influence of Social Media is well put together and very convincing. Sometimes people set themselves up as "experts" on Social Media but they may be far from authorities on their subject and will not be accountable or responsible to you if you make the wrong choice.

6. Early life trauma (particularly sexual abuse), poorly modelled sexual roles by parents, a lack of sexual skills

with a lack of social confidence, lack of sexual knowledge and experience can all lead to a lack of sexual confidence or general discomfort in the present gender identity. These factors can lead to holding onto what seems to be like a convincing solution as publicised in the Social Media.

7. Is it possible that membership of a transgender group and following its ideology became a source of social support, psychological comfort and solace in a lonely world? A transgender group may also have become a source of sexual satisfaction if the type of sex that is preferred is of any of the polymorphic types. It is only to be expected and quite natural that people are drawn to the sources of community feeling and sexual satisfaction that they prefer. As history has shown, it is very easy to be psychologically engulfed by a group as it is an entirely natural and human tendency to become attached to a group - humans quite naturally favour people in their own group. This tendency originated as a Cavewoman/Caveman psychological process that aided group survival in a hostile prehistoric environment. Although this psychological survival mindset is still programmed in the modern human brain, as modern humans it is best to ensure that we are inclusive as possible. Being emotionally pulled along by a group mindset can happen very easily and occurs in many areas of life such as politics and so forth. Group statements that seem to confirm our pre-existing thoughts, feelings and beliefs are more palatable and are therefore preferred. It is also more comfortable to go along with the group's beliefs than to challenge them, after all, who wants to be marginalised from their group? Humans evolved as group animals rather than herd animals for survival for reasons of efficiency of communication, social connection and distributing or sharing resources. Group behaviour favours the survival of the highly intelligent and emotion centred but relatively physically frail human animal. (Compare humans to less

intelligent and emotionally less complex but physically resilient animals who use herd behaviour as a survival tactic - consider wildebeest or migratory birds).

There are many other factors that may consciously or *unconsciously* pull someone towards transgender groups and transgender life solutions that may depend on whether the transition is female to male or male to female. Some factors are related to sexual preferences, but other factors are more related to mindset and self-view. (Non-LGBTQIA+ readers may not be familiar with some of the sexual desires and tastes referred to but a reference to widely available transgender porn will inform the reader as will a look at Internet shopping sites that cater for transgender people).

A number of important matters are now considered further:

THE FOLLOWING FACTORS MAY APPLY TO WOMEN WHO ARE CONSIDERING **FEMALE TO MALE** GENDER TRANSITION - *PLEASE CONSIDER THEM CAREFULLY BEFORE UNDERGOING HORMONAL AND SURGICAL GENDER TRANSITION*

Women who have found it difficult to be accepted as women due to their appearance and personality not being particularly feminine, perhaps tending towards the masculine. This may result in an over-identification with maleness. Masculine women can feel uncomfortable in a society that is unnecessarily and unjustifiably judging them.

Women who are concerned that the history of womankind has been one of misogyny and subjugation and no longer wish to remain a woman as men are felt to be in a stronger position. (Fortunately, some of these patriarchal social constraints and difficulties for women are being progressively reduced, particularly compared to a century ago. Long may this progress continue although there is still a long way to go. If men could honestly contemplate their role in their mistreatment of women, they would, or rather should hang their heads in shame. Dialogue between women and men about this issue in relation to the way forward would be preferable to berating men for the past. Men now are not responsible for the actions of men in the past although current men should absolutely learn from the past and keep these lessons in mind).

Women who feel uncomfortable being openly lesbian.

Being a bisexual woman and fantasising during sex about being a man who can penetrate or possibly taking on a male-type dominant role.

Women who feel that it seems easier to get on in the world as a man.

Women who have a feeling of hatred, envy or resentment towards men and wish to be on equal terms.

Women who have suffered extremes of various forms of physical, emotional and sexual abuse at the hands of men and would therefore feel safer as a man.

Women who wish to psychologically leave behind sexual abuse of their female body by surgically ridding themselves of physical reminders of their female form.

Women who feel that it is easier to become old as a man than as a woman.

Women who cross-sex dress as a way to psychologically leave the unsatisfactory and disappointing old self behind - even if only partially. There is also the effect of leaving life's worries and bad experiences in a gender role behind or being able to blank them out. Cross-sex dressing can therefore give more than a sense of relief - it can cause a sense of elation. Many cross-sex dressers say that they "become themselves" when they cross-sex dress by becoming an IDEALISED "someone else".

There may be any mixture of the above in one woman.

Many, many women will be painfully familiar with a particular phrase that may at times have gone through their mind:

"I hate being a woman".

Many women readers will know exactly what is meant by this. The cause of this thought is generally men and/or the roles that Nature has given to women.

None of the factors above necessarily mean that you "are really a man" or definitely need to undergo hormonal and surgical gender transition.

A brief footnote: Freud all too frequently referred to "penis envy" being experienced by girls and women but in actual fact this does not seem to be particularly relevant in most transmen. A surgically constructed neo-penis for a transman cannot have the full ejaculatory and orgasmic function of a male penis. Nor can it really be guaranteed to give the same sexual experience to either partner. Ciswomen can of course, envy the ease with which a cisman can have an orgasm during sex, even though it is not as intense and long lasting as the cisfemale orgasm. (However, cismen envy the intense and multiple orgasms that ciswomen can have and are certainly intrigued by them). Ciswomen may envy and fear the so-called "power" of cismen that is due to their greater physical strength, aggression and position in society - symbolised in some respects by the penis. In actual fact, remarkably few transmen wish to have genital surgery and so classical Freudian penis envy does not always seem particularly relevant to the female to male transgender mindset and transition process although of course, it might be the case in *some*.

THE FOLLOWING FACTORS MAY APPLY TO MEN WHO ARE CONSIDERING **MALE TO FEMALE** GENDER TRANSITION - *PLEASE CONSIDER THEM CAREFULLY BEFORE UNDERGOING HORMONAL AND SURGICAL GENDER TRANSITION*

There are some men who reject themselves as men and are struggling in the world as men - perhaps because they are less than "blokey" or "macho" physically and psychologically. They might feel that reinventing themselves as a woman will allow them to feel more confident and comfortable with themselves - of course, if this is the right choice and brings contentment then it is a good thing.

It is increasingly difficult for cismen to know how to act these days for fear of appearing to be showing "toxic masculinity" on the one hand and knowing how to be a "proper man" on the other. In any case, Western society seems to be producing far less masculine teenagers. A glance around United Kingdom town centres reveals a certain stereotype - skinny or flabby, muscularly underdeveloped, unkempt, long-haired teenagers and young men who slouch around dressed in black tee shirts emblazoned with superhero or computer game emblems. These young males, generally with smartphone in hand often seem very socially inept and certainly not "manly" in the traditional sense of the word. It is hard to imagine cisgirls or ciswomen being romantically impressed. Any resulting sexual rejection would only serve to undermine what little sense of masculine sexuality these young males had in the first place. Many such young males seem to be obsessed with warlike computer games in which they can attempt to satisfy some of their instinctive male drives in the safety of their bedroom where their sexual urges may (very likely) also be relieved by means of Internet pornography. As undesirable as it may be to stereotype and categorise people, it does seem that such androgynous and "geeky" young males, who are extremely under confident in their masculinity are of the type that can be drawn to a transgender life-mode as a way of dealing with their insecurities. In former generations young men were expected by society to "man up" or "grow a pair". "Manning up" is hard work and psychologically threatening due to the risk of failure but may actually be easier in the long run than following the difficult and complex gender transition processes *and* not feeling genuinely and honestly accepted by mainstream society.

Please consider the following groups of men who may contemplate hormonal and surgical gender transition. (As above transgender porn illustrates some of the sexual desires and preferences now referred to):

Gay men who want to sexually attract males but fear the social disapproval of being openly gay.

Men who may have had fantasies of having sex *as* a woman - either with a woman or with a man.

Being a bisexual man and fantasising during sex about being a woman who can be penetrated.

Middle aged men who have lost a female partner or other female loved one and may wish to "merge" with something womanly, to immerse themselves in femininity as a form of comfort and a reminiscence of the lost woman. (Having lost a wife in middle age is an example of this that is not uncommon).

Men who feel that as they get older they are becoming less sexually potent or less attractive and particularly if they have some feelings of same sex attraction may be drawn to gender transition. Some might seek to deal with these age changes by becoming an attractive younger looking transwoman by means of judicious use of makeup and/or plastic surgery.

Autogynaephilia as detailed earlier in the book is often a factor in choosing a transgender lifestyle. Sexual desire is an incredibly strong emotion and can be a powerful motivator to find a way of sexual release but one that may not always be approved of by mainstream society. If autogynaephilic desire is pulling someone towards hormonal or surgical gender transition it may be very helpful to consider the long-term consequences and also contemplate how this might be relevant to sexual desires in the future. Discussing things with other people in the same situation will obviously not necessarily provide an objective and unbiased opinion - it is pure human nature to justify your own plans or previous decisions.

Quite simply, some men feel intimidated by ciswomen and find it difficult to romantically and sexually approach them. They could feel that they can approach ciswomen for sex on equal terms as a transwoman. They may alternatively *unconsciously* feel that by cross-sex dressing and taking on a feminine form they no longer need a ciswoman for sex and can have sex with a man.

Males who have been anally raped and might consciously and *unconsciously* feel that they can psychologically leave their trauma behind by becoming a transwoman. (Tragically, in the opposite direction there was a particularly unfortunate situation in which a transwoman was raped by a man. They subsequently detransitioned as a way of dealing with their trauma).

Cross-sex dressing but without hormonal and surgical gender transition can help someone psychologically leave the unsatisfactory and disappointing old self behind - even if only partially. There can also be the effect of leaving life's worries and bad experiences in a gender role behind or being able to mentally blank them out. Cross-sex dressing can therefore give a sense of relief. Cross-sex dressing can also cause a sense of elation. Many cross-sex dressers say that they "become themselves" when they cross-sex dress but this is sometimes because they are becoming an idealised someone else even if only in fantasy. But why shouldn't they do this if it gives them pleasure? However, the elation can become addictive and can nevertheless be a strong motivation to undergo hormonal and surgical gender transition in the longer term for a number of cross-sex dressers.

FOR **EITHER SEX** CONSIDERING GENDER TRANSITION - IMPORTANT FACTORS THAT NEED TO BE DISCUSSED BETWEEN PATIENTS AND GENDER TRANSITION PRACTITIONERS:

1. If you are considering hormonal or surgical gender transition did your clinical practitioners fully warn you of the treatment side effects?
2. If you are a clinical practitioner in a gender identity clinic, did you comprehensively warn your patients of all foreseeable treatment side effects?
3. If you are considering hormonal or surgical gender transition have you discussed the possible side effects of treatment with several people in the transgender population who have undergone the treatments and have you done a thorough Internet search about the potential side effects? The vast majority of people who are to undergo emergency or routine general surgery for health issues are extremely concerned about the risks of failure or serious and dangerous side effects. In stark contrast it is often observed that many transgender people who are contemplating surgical gender transition seem to have an exceptionally great faith in the potential success of the procedure(s) and give little thought to the possibility of side effects or that the result may not be functionally good. This degree of certainty is definitely a cause for concern and may be due to a very strong DENIAL of the potential problems in relation to those hormonal and surgical gender treatments. This could lead to a

reluctance to fully consider the pros and cons and result in rushing into surgery.

4. Has the person who is considering hormonal and surgical gender transition had sufficient thinking time to ensure that they are making the correct decision? In the pioneering days of gender transition surgery there was generally an extremely long pre-operative waiting time. During this extended waiting period there was a significant drop out rate leaving only those who were extremely sure that they were making the correct decision on the waiting list. In *current* times, gender transition practitioners have the sincere and well-meant approach of very readily surgically affirming their patient's transgender feelings. In the *former* times, it was up to the patient to completely convince the practitioners of the need for gender transition. As a result of this and the long wait, there was very little post-gender transition regret. This contrasts concerningly with the present time in which it is remarkably easy to go overseas clinics to have almost any form of plastic or gender transition surgery performed immediately on demand. The main criterion for being accepted for surgery in such clinics is the ability to pay rather than having gone through a long decision period, ideally with psychotherapeutic exploration of transgender feelings.

5. Is the desire to undergo hormonal and surgical gender transition more related to: a. An actual long term fully thought through and unshakeable drive to change gender *or* b. Dissatisfaction with the self as a person and there is the wish that by changing gender it will change who you are as a person. (Please remember you can't be guaranteed to change the experience of the mind by changing the outside of the body - this could be MAGICAL THINKING) *or* c. A long history of poor mental wellbeing that could badly affect the way you view yourself and make judgments about yourself. If b or c could be the case, have you had in depth psychotherapy to help you improve your mental wellbeing and explore your deeper

reasons for wishing to undergo hormonal and surgical gender transition? It is best that major life decisions are not made when in a poor state of mental health. It must be said in relation to example a. there will be some people for whom changing the outside is actually the only way to satisfy the inside and they can go onto live extremely fulfilled lives that are doubtless better than what they would otherwise have had.

6. Is the desire to undergo hormonal and surgical gender transition in some way related to feelings of *unconscious* social discomfort resulting from being lesbian or gay? For those who are lesbian or gay, transgender surgery may actually be a form "conversion therapy" *unconsciously* imposed upon the self because of internalised homophobia. This complex, mind twisting notion is most definitely worth a precautionary thought.

7. Some transgender people have severe body dysmorphia as part of their transgender feelings, some have it to a minor degree and others have none. If someone does actually have a significant degree of body dysmorphia, they are particularly prone to finding fault with their body and as a result are more likely to find faults with the results of surgical gender transition. People who have body dysmorphic disorder are more prone than the average person of "just wanting one more surgical procedure to put things right". This is most definitely a matter that needs to be fully discussed with gender transition practitioners prior to surgery. It is also important to discuss the expectations of surgery with the surgeon. It is only natural to have huge expectations of surgery when so much hope has been invested in it but such expectations can be a prelude to profound disappointment if there had been overoptimism. There are limits to all forms of surgery that need to be discussed - as do the surgical complications and failures.

8. The risks of cancer were mentioned in the section about medication side effects - but fortunately the risk seems small. Hormonal and surgical gender transition will

obviously change the risks of sex-specific cancer in various ways depending on the direction of transition, how far transition has gone, and the duration of the gender transitioned state. It must also be borne in mind that undergoing gender transition and changing health record information may result in those undergoing gender transition not receiving the sex-specific cancer screening that they would usually receive from health screening "call-up" systems. Quite understandably, a transman who still has a cervix may be reluctant to have cervical smears. Transwomen may completely ignore the fact that they still have a prostate gland and even though they are at a reduced risk of developing prostate cancer if they are taking oestrogens - there is still a risk. As part of general health screening and giving health or lifestyle advice, the author has asked gender transitioned people if cancer screening has been advised by their gender transition specialists. The response has worryingly been universally negative. This of course, may not necessarily reflect badly on the author's colleagues as is would be quite understandable for those who have undergone gender transition to put such matters entirely out of their minds.

9. There is a certain phenomenon that the author calls in his mind, *"The everything will be OK when A or B happens phenomenon".* This is when we tell ourselves such things as, "Everything will be OK when I find a new job", "Everything will be OK when I fall deeply in love with the right person" or "Everything will be OK when I move to somewhere new". The reader can see what is meant and has probably also had such thoughts but also knows that life is rarely "All OK when" a certain thing happens. This is because we all continue to deal with life with the same old mental processes that we always have done and much of life around us remains just the same. Hormonal and surgical gender transition will not be guaranteed to change who you are and your situation. Full gender transition can of course help some people become the person they want to be and then be much, much happier.

However, it is all too easy to hope against hope that something might help when in an unhappy mindset. Once again, please make sure that major decisions are made in the best possible frame of mind.

PLEASE, PLEASE ANSWER THE ABOVE QUESTIONS BEFORE HORMONAL AND SURGICAL GENDER TRANSITION. (THERE WILL BE OTHER IMPORTANT QUESTIONS TO CONSIDER LATER IN THE BOOK).

*Please be aware: many people who have had full hormonal and surgical gender transition say that the underlying feelings that they originally put down to gender dysphoria **did not go away** after transitioning and that they have been left with a more complicated and difficult life. Of course, many people do manage to live their best possible life as a result of hormonal and surgical gender transition - it is therefore critically important to make the correct decision. Please make every possible attempt to consider all of the pros and cons.*

PSYCHOSOCIALLY CONTAGIOUS CONDITIONS - THEY START *UNCONSCIOUSLY* AND ARE THEN FOLLOWED BY COMPLEX CHANGES IN THE BRAIN THAT PERPETUATE THEM

As human beings we all consciously and *unconsciously* justify to ourselves doing things that are at first thought to be advantageous but may not be in our best interests in the long term.

There are a number of medical syndromes that appear to be psychologically based and are very socially contagious. Certain types of such conditions have become increasingly common in recent times, and they currently just seem to readily catch on and were not previously diagnosed as often by the medical profession. The Social Media have doubtless been a major factor in their "transmission". Being transgender is an example in some instances as is anorexia nervosa. There are also some psychosocially transmitted conditions that result in mostly physical symptoms, but these are not particularly relevant to this book.

Anorexia nervosa and self-harming behaviour have both increased in incidence and prevalence in recent times. Of course, eating disorders and self-harming behaviour have existed for many years but not in such large numbers as now and with so many similarities in each case. The Social Media have doubtless been a contributory factor to the copy-cat similarity and frequency of such cases. Nobody would logically say that anorexia nervosa is really only a physical condition, it is obviously psychological. Girls and young women are particularly predisposed to following certain types of online group behaviour just as boys and young men are prone to following gang and group "macho" behaviour. Peer group copy-cat behaviour is, of course, a feature of both young females and young males. For females emotions often tend to be *internally* directed and for males emotions often tend to be *externally* directed.

Without wishing to make generalisations and at the same time fully accepting that some people really are better off having cross-sex hormones and gender transition surgery, many people with transgender feelings have *unconsciously* picked up the transgender solution to their life's problems from Social Media as well as from their peers. The accounts they give to health care professionals can be remarkably similar and yet prior to the invention of Social Media there were exceptionally few cases of young people who believed that they were transgender. Before the invention of Social Media there were very few males who had symptoms suggestive of gender dysphoria and a much, much smaller number of females. In the past ten or so years, there has been a remarkable increase in the number females who are presenting to gender identity clinics. The overall rate of referral to gender identity clinics has increased astonishingly in the past few years and appears to mirror the ever-increasing use and influence of Social Media. It is also very usual to find a history of psychological, physical or sexual trauma and certain mindset factors in such young people. Some of these mindset factors are often related to the changes in society and styles of parenting as referred to elsewhere in this book.

CHARACTERISTICS OF PSYCHOSOCIALLY CONTAGIOUS CONDITIONS

The following are the characteristics of what the medical profession is increasingly realising are psychologically based and socially spread conditions:

1. Many of the symptoms and signs of the condition are impossible to deny or disprove.
2. The condition is believed to exist by the Media and the general population.

3. There is a degree of sympathy expressed for the condition.
4. There is some form of *unconscious* advantage to be gained by having the condition - certain benefits such as the AVOIDANCE of a task, role or anything else that is regarded as undesirable. Alternatively, there may be an *unconscious* motivation towards *gaining* something that might be otherwise unobtainable or unavailable.
5. There are organisations and individuals with a financial or political interest in the condition existing - charities, lawyers, psychotherapists, physiotherapists, physicians, psychiatrists, surgeons, politicians, activists and so forth or even the person themselves.
6. A certain degree of attention, approval, acceptance, acknowledgement or notoriety may be gained by having the condition.
7. The psychological symptoms of the condition may have been *unconsciously* DISPLACED from another deep psychological difficulty or trauma but of which the sufferer is *not* consciously aware. In other words...
8. The condition is actually a way of expressing or dealing with *unconscious* mental distress.
9. The condition may allow the sufferer to blame others or in other ways take blame away from the self. The advantage of being a victim is precisely that a problem is "someone else's fault" or that someone else "should be doing something about it".
10. The condition may allow the sufferer to control others. (People who tend to want to control others may have been subjected to over-control in their earlier life).
11. There are self-fulfilling processes in play. Psychiatrists are particularly aware that people "become" the label that is put on them, or even the label that they put on themselves if they have self-diagnosed.

So, what is going on?

Please do not think or say, "It is just in the mind" or "the person is deliberately putting it on". They *are* actually suffering. It is *totally real* to them. It must be emphasised that the mental processes originate in the *unconscious*.

To emphasise, the underlying mental process relates to a deep psychological pain that cannot be expressed in other ways that is *finding its way out in a set of psychological symptoms and in some instances in physical form.* In other words, a deep mental pain that is otherwise difficult to express is being "converted" into a psychological or physical form. These conditions are therefore known in medical circles as "conversion disorders". Transgender feelings can in some people be just such a conversion disorder - an outward expression of an inner pain that cannot be explained or expressed in any other way - and gender transition is felt to be the answer.

Once they have started, conversion disorders become "entrenched" in the mind. Please consider the following:

1. It is unusual for deep psychological pain or any *resulting* physical pain due to a conversion disorder to simply disappear.
2. Have you ever noticed how if you keep training at a sporting activity or reciting a song the brain learns and things become "entrenched" or "engrained" in the mind? This is because the brain's structure and chemistry actually change with repeated use of the same brain cell pathways. As memories are formed chemical changes occur in the brain and new physical connections are made between brain cells. This is known as Hebbian learning - "Braincells that fire together wire together". This is how "habits" are established in the brain and things are learnt. Shorter, "easier" and more direct pathways are created through the complex brain cell network. It could

be said that a sort of "habituation" and "short cutting" have occurred in the brain's functioning - this is "functional cerebral plasticity". During certain psychiatric conditions such as depression, schizophrenia or mania the unhealthy brain connection pathways and chemical changes that have occurred during an episode become well established. This is believed to be why it can sometimes be increasingly difficult to treat such conditions with every successive episode. People cannot therefore "just snap out of it". The brain's tendency to make these chemical and physical changes as the psychological condition develops can be referred to as "*dys*functional cerebral plasticity". This process of establishing new but unhelpful brain pathways also happens in psychosocially transmitted conditions. (This is in contrast to "regeneration cerebral plasticity" that can occur in very young children after a brain injury following which widespread physical changes and compensation can occur in the brain. This ability for significant change and "repair" is lost after the age of three to five). Neuroscientists and neuropsychiatrists often point to brain changes that may be seen on functional MRI and other forms of brain scan in certain psychological conditions. However, are these changes the *cause* of the psychological symptoms or are they the *result* of what is happening to the brain from the influences of the outside world? It's a very much a chicken and egg situation. (As an aside, it is fascinating to note that the quality of the attachment of a mother to a child or any psychological trauma that a child is exposed to can affect the way that its brain structure develops).

WHERE CAN UNDERLYING PSYCHOLOGICAL PAIN COME FROM?

There are three possible situations to consider:

1. There has been a clear history of major psychological trauma in the early years that *can* be recalled but hasn't been fully worked through psychologically.
2. There has been a history of major psychological trauma in the early years that *cannot* be recalled as it is too painful to do so - it has been REPRESSED into the *unconscious* and will require certain specific psychotherapeutic techniques to deal with it.
3. There is no obvious major serious trauma that occurred in early life but instead there have been many small events that were traumatic *to the particular individual* concerned. These will have been day-to-day occurrences that might seem to be unremarkable but happened to be psychologically painful *to the particular individual*. The most important factor for future good mental wellbeing is having had a good and loving psychological attachment to parents, particularly to the mother. The young infant or child needs to feel nurtured and protected at all times. Any experience of *perceived* abandonment, rejection or frustration of needs is psychologically traumatic. The child's reaction to these adverse factors may have been:
   a) Seeking attachment to the mother.
   b) Feelings of guilt.
   c) Rage/tantrums or expressions of psychological pain means of other forms of "bad" behaviour.
   d) An attempt to DENY to that there is a problem.
   e) The child may DISSOCIATE by going into its own mental world.

Many parents of transgender identifying children will say, "But they had the perfect childhood, they had everything they could possibly have wanted, we were always there for them, they were really happy". All true. But there will have been *seemingly harmless* occurrences that caused feelings of abandonment, rejection or frustration of needs *for a particular child*. In other words as individual events, some of these instances might have been traumatic for some children but not for others. As we all know, some people are more sensitive to bad events than others. Examples that might be painful for parents to read include a mother going to work to provide more for her family. A mother going off to work and leaving a toddler with a variety of child minders may be *perceived* as a daily abandonment by some particularly sensitive children but not felt as deeply by others. There are of course, numerous other possible examples. Parents should not feel guilty, it's just pure chance that their child was the one that was sensitive and affected. Even the arguments that parents may have in front of some sensitive children may make a particular child feel that their care and safety are being imperilled. Every one of us has had such micro-abandonments, micro-rejections, micro-frustrations and other micro-traumas. It must be said that one truly modern form of abandonment is parents being glued to their telephone or tablet screens when their child needs attention. Need more be said about modern IT devices? This also raises the question as to whether warring parents should divorce or stay together, to use an old phrase, "For the sake of the children" and to make every possible attempt to keep a united façade. Either option can be difficult for parents and for children.

Some transgender young people may have somewhere in their life history some feelings of:

1. Not being loved.
2. Not being good enough,
3. Not being wanted,
4. Not being "right" *as they are.*

These deep conscious and *unconscious* pains remain in someone as a feeling of not being "right" *as they are* and this can all too easily become blamed on being in the wrong body particularly when the Social Media are overflowing with messages about being trapped the wrong body.

In summary, transgender ideas have become very socially transmissible and have the characteristics of psychosocially contagious conditions in the list 1 - 11. This is why the author repeatedly recommends the need for safeguarding psychotherapy before seeking hormonal and surgical gender transition - especially in children and younger adults.

ARE TRANSGENDER FEELINGS A MATTER OF SEXUAL HEALTH *OR* MENTAL HEALTH *OR* BOTH? WE ARE OUR BODIES *AND* OUR MINDS - PLEASE REMEMBER THE TWO ARE COMPLETELY INTERRELATED

A number of LGBTQIA+ organisations have stated that gender dysphoria and transgender feelings are not related to underlying mental health matters but instead are purely disorders of sexual health. This is of course, an understandable point of view as transgender feelings are so obviously related to both gender and sex and it is only natural that a link with sexual health is made. However, this is a viewpoint that might benefit from further consideration in order that any required mental health care can be appropriately provided.

Transgender groups also tend to state that any mental health problems that transgender people experience are mostly due to transphobia and an insufficient availability of mental health services. Again, this is an understandable viewpoint, and these are highly important matters that are worthy of consideration. However, how many of us actually stop to think where our feelings, viewpoints, politics, wishes, beliefs and desires *really* come from? We just don't - they just seem to "be there" in our mind and in our life. They are our truths, our reality and our experience - but of course, because they come from the depths of our *unconscious* mind we cannot always consciously appreciate where they came from.

Unfortunately, to publicly state that transgender feelings are a purely a disorder of sexual health is potentially unhelpful as it can misdirect psychologically troubled transgender children and young people away from appropriate mental health assessment and management. It is vital that young transgender patients are properly assessed and managed in order to prevent the application of inappropriate and permanently damaging medical interventions, which may not help them in the longer term - *this is an important part of safeguarding in the younger age groups.* As mentioned earlier, many people who have undergone hormonal and surgical transgender treatments say that their dysphoric feelings are still there or are little changed after gender transition. The author has received personal correspondence from an academic authority in psychotherapeutic practice in which they stated that they had come across patients who had tried to change who they were by changing their body and generally failed in their endeavour - although please note the comments below as to how someone *can* remodel their persona.

Some children are treated more as bodies than as people with personalities and this can particularly apply to those who have been abused. This results in their body being over important in their sense of self and how they *unconsciously* chose to present themselves or act. Of course, the body does outwardly represent what is being experienced in the mind - we all instinctively know this, but it is helpful to keep in mind the two way connection between mind and body. The most obvious illustration of this is general appearance and body language - we consciously and *unconsciously* size people up by their facial expression and in fact how they move all of their body, how they gesticulate with their hands, how they walk and so forth. Someone's facial and even bodily type can give an indication of many things about them. How often have you heard it said, "He looks every bit a crook on that prison mugshot", "That person looks very nervous as if something terrible is going to happen to them", "That person appears really arrogant and self-important", "The boss has been under terrible stress in the workplace and at home, he is looking more and more haggard or "That person looks a nasty, dodgy piece of work".

Functional MRI scanning has revealed that when the emotional areas of the brain are active, signals are sent to the brain's areas that are involved with the control of the body. These signals not only go to the facial expression areas as you might expect but also to those that control many other parts of the body - they may produce virtually no movement at all or result in quite obvious movements. This explains the neurological mechanism behind body language involving the whole body, not just facial expression. The other fascinating brain fact is that when someone is observing *somebody else's* facial and bodily expression, brain cells called "mirror neurones" in the *observer's* brain fire off in the same areas of those that are firing in the *observed person's* motor control areas that are causing their bodily movements. Emotions are not confined to just one part of the brain that you might imagine would be called the "emotional area" of the brain. When emotions occur, signals are also sent to many parts of the brain that control a whole variety of internal bodily functions. It seems that huge areas of the brain are involved in emotional experience, this explains why when we have emotions that we might think are mostly in our minds we also have feelings in our gut or tension in our muscles - *in other words, our emotions are a total mind and body experience.* There is an inextricable link between emotional and bodily experience - one profoundly affects the other *in a two directional process.* There seems to be a feedback loop of mutual influence between body and mind. In other words the activity of the mind, particularly the emotions are expressed in bodily form and the body is used by the mind as an external "gauge" or "instrument" of inner experience. All of these mind and body mechanisms underlie how you can get an "instinctive feel" about someone from their appearance. The effectiveness of this wordless communication is very well seen where everything starts in life - that unspoken language between mother and infant. What the author is trying to say is that from an emotional point of view we are very much our bodies, and we communicate with all of our body. This can in turn lead to the very understandable idea that by changing the body it is *believed* that the self can be changed - and to an extent it can be. Changing the body can in many respects change self-image and self-expression. Someone can mentally metamorphose into being a "new person" and this can be remarkably effective in changing and improving the self. This mechanism of remodelling the personality can be very effective and has allowed many people to successfully make the best of their lives by means of hormonal and surgical gender transition - they really are able to develop a new persona as "functional cerebral plasticity" takes place - so they become a changed person. It is important to remember the cautionary words above - as this will not work for all people. For the right person full gender transition is life enhancing and for others it can be life destroying. Please, please just make the correct decision over a long, long period of reflection. Young children, adolescents and even young adults do not truly have the mental capacity and maturity to make such decisions with the accuracy of mature and life experienced adults who have extensively explored the deepest and most complex aspects of gender transition.

It is particularly important for those who have been subjected to early life psychological trauma to receive the correct type of exploratory psychotherapy if they are to avoid being psychologically imprisoned in a notion of being transgender and then being subjected to physical treatments for what actually started as mental trauma. However, it is only fair to say that people who are haunted by trauma can be helped to leave behind an unspeakably awful stage of their life by remodelling themselves. In common parlance this may be called "reinventing themselves".

Younger people who have transgender feelings will hopefully be able to achieve better mental, physical and sexual health by coming to accept themselves as they are within their current gender expression and sexual orientation having delved into their mind by means of psychotherapy and then as a result not require hormonal and surgical gender transition treatments. Psychotherapy can help to form and then establish new brain pathways by means of "functional cerebral plasticity" and this can help to maintain mental wellbeing. (A change in brain function and structure has been confirmed by functional MRI scanning once psychotherapy or psychoanalysis has successfully taken place).

To reiterate, some people's sexual and mental health can of course, actually be helped by hormonal and surgical transgender treatments, it may be the best way of helping them - but if gender transition is a mistake, their sexual health may be ruined forever and also their mental health may suffer irretrievably. Thus, it can be seen that sexual health and mental health are entirely interrelated and dependent upon on one another. They cannot be separated, and both can be improved together in the psychotherapeutic environment.

WHAT COULD PARENTS CONSIDER FOR THEIR CHILDREN WHO *SEEM* TO HAVE GENDER ISSUES?

FIRSTLY, PLEASE REMEMBER TO ASK YOURSELF IF YOUR CHILD IS JUST SUFFERING FROM SEVERE ANXIETY OR SEVERE UNHAPPINESS THAT IS BEING BLAMED ON OR RELABELLED AS GENDER DYSPHORIA AS A RESULT OF THE INFLUENCE OF SOCIAL MEDIA.

SECONDLY, PLEASE ALSO REMEMBER THAT A FEW CHILDLIKE FORMS OF CROSS-GENDER BEHAVIOUR OR A FEW CROSS-GENDER STATEMENTS DO NOT INDICATE THAT A CHILD HAS GENDER DYSPHORIA.

Please excuse the repetition, the first thing that parents of apparently transgender children could bear in mind is that their child is very likely to be experiencing "bog standard" emotional distress rather than an actual need for puberty blockers, cross-sex hormones or even surgical gender transition. The child may be struggling to put their distress into words as even adults find that putting their mental pain into words can be incredibly difficult.

It is important to emphasise to parents that if their transgender child is being assessed in a clinic, the staff will not be critical of their parenting or "think the worst" of the parents themselves.

Given all that is said in the Social Media about transgender matters in this day and age it may seem the modern thing for parents to do is to support children in their "transgender journey". It is only natural for parents to be extremely perturbed by statements made by well-meaning transgender spokespersons that children are at risk of suicide unless gender transition is supported. Some children may *already* be at risk of self-harm because of their actual pre-existing emotional distress that *makes* them latch onto the idea of being transgender in the first place. If suicidal, they need *conventional* suicide support from mental health services. Significant numbers of people identifying as transgender make suicidal gestures or actually attempt suicide *with or without* having undergone hormonal or surgical gender transition.

A most important point to emphasise is that anyone experiencing self-harming or suicidal thoughts and feelings should urgently obtain support and assistance.

Parents please be aware that some gender care professionals in some countries are all too ready to promote transgender treatments:

1. Because they are in private practice and make money from it although most professionals are earnest and ethical in their desire to help and profit is a secondary consideration.
2. Because medical professionals wish to avoid complaints from patients who don't get what they want.

Parents may or may not be aware that cautionary and safeguarding viewpoints regarding childhood gender transition have often been very successfully countered by the well-meaning and very politically effective pro-gender transition lobby. (This book was not intended to be influenced by political views as safeguarding was the one and only motive behind writing it. The author aims to be neither left wing or right wing and at all times tries to take a middle of the road approach to life).

Parents might consider reflecting on what might *seem* to be "*rapid* onset gender dysphoria" that children may *seem* to experience is likely to be due to the hormonal, emotional, sexual and identity roller coaster of puberty *rapidly* cropping up in young person. It almost always subsides. It may of course, ultimately mean that the child turns out to be lesbian, gay or bisexual - therefore no problem. Unfortunately, some parents wrongly feel shame if their children are showing signs of same sex attraction and are then tempted to believe that it is more socially acceptable to use a frequently quoted line, "To have a transgender daughter than a gay son or transgender son rather than a lesbian daughter". Being lesbian or gay is (or should be) perfectly socially acceptable. Going down a mistaken hormonal or surgical gender transition route can be permanently damaging as has been repeatedly cautioned about in this book.

Puberty blockers may be seen as a way to "buy time" or "give time" to a child to decide what to do about their "gender issues" - but please remember that "gender issues" may be just a way of expressing emotional difficulties that, to say it again, children may have difficulty expressing in other ways. They have consciously or *unconsciously* linked their distress of puberty or other teenage stresses to "gender issues" as a result of viewing Social Media - or simply because they are perturbed by their bodies changing in a "gendered way". (Parents please refer to the section near the beginning of the book - Possible Side Effects of Transgender Medication and Surgery and particularly the information about puberty blockers).

Unfortunately, it is not just a simple matter of saying to your child, "What is *really* bothering you?" If only it was that simple - but it is a good start even though it is often difficult for any of us to put into words what is *really* bothering us. This is why appropriate psychotherapeutic help is recommended from a Child and Adolescent Mental Health Service (CAMHS in the United Kingdom) in order to explore the complex factors that may underlie transgender feelings and also to provide healthy coping mechanisms to emotionally troubled children.

It is no criticism of parents to say that it is important to explore that the way everyone in the family relates as this is often a main concern - it is rarely "just the transgender child" that is the issue. An extremely useful book that explains how family factors are related to transgender feelings is - Gender Dysphoria, A Therapeutic Model for Working with Children, Adolescents and Young Adults by Susan and Marcus Evans - this book will be particularly appreciated by health care professionals.

JUST LET THE CHILD GET THROUGH PUBERTY

Given that puberty is a time of immense hormonal upheaval and that this is a normal part of the sometimes difficult journey from childhood to adulthood is it right to block a normal process with powerful medication rather than allow a child to pass through a difficult stage? After all, generations of humans have successfully managed to get through puberty in the past.

Physical treatments such as puberty blockers should therefore not necessarily be seen as the automatic solution to puberty related *emotional* problems. Dealing with significant emotional problems that constitute a significant mental disturbance is what the CAMHS is for. It should be remembered that for many young children and adolescents, gender confusion and same sex attraction are often just natural parts of the process of puberty and only by passing through puberty with support will these feelings generally pass - quite naturally.

In some countries medical transition is being considered for very young children for whom puberty is many years in the future. Should parents really allow their young child to make a decision regarding unproven and potentially life damaging treatments when they have such immature thought processes?

Puberty blockers may *appear* to relieve a difficulty even if only by *artificially* suppressing the pubertal hormonal and emotional roller coaster. Although the turmoil has really only been *medically* blocked, suppressed or masked it may lead parents to believe that the next "logical" step is to give cross-sex hormones. There is then the risk that children may possibly be chemically sterilised rather than being given a chance to grow out of any natural gender and sexual orientation ambivalence, which is so often a part of adolescence. Please recall the earlier comments about children's mental immaturity preventing them from perceiving reality as it truly is and how they cannot possibly have sufficient insight into the emotional experiences of later adult life. Who can be completely sure if they want children in their early twenties, let alone at sixteen or younger?

Adopting a transgender identity will tend to make a child become a social outcast and possibly the "odd one out" and therefore at increased risk of being bullied. The only group they will feel that they fit in with will be a transgender peer group in which the transgender thought processes will, of course, be encouraged and reinforced.

Parents would most likely find it best to provide a middle of the road, balanced and varied experience for their children in spite of any pressure to be modern and liberal. Love, acceptance, understanding, talking, listening and sharing life's simple pleasures are the most important factors. Some parents feel that they are showing love by frequently saying to their child, "I love you, I love you, I love you". Love is *shown*, love is *demonstrated* and love is *given*. It is given of the self, not just merely stated in the word "love" - words are cheap. The more emotionally connected time that parents can spend with their children the better - preferably in sport, exercise, learning practical skills together, art, dance, learning languages and particularly spending time in Nature. Note that in this list there was no recommendation of negative activities such as computer games. In spite of what many people might like to think, playing computer games with parents or anyone else is *not* a socially interactive activity because there is too much immersion in the screen image for any meaningful human to human contact to occur. A mother and father hiking with their daughter and son sharing Nature and having close quality time gives children a sense that their parents are interested in them *and have time for them* - something that is essential for good self-esteem. On a walk there is plenty of time to have educational and emotionally connected experiences without the deadening and isolating influence of IT screens. In an urban environment sport, keep fit, martial arts, skating, cycling, book clubs, dance groups and so forth are generally available for shared activities. Teenagers might initially appear sullen and resentful during these activities but the more they receive an adult to adult experience rather than a parent to child interaction the better the bond will be. The way that parents deal with day-to-day inevitable difficulties is important. Children should not be furiously disciplined for bad behaviour or other failings but instead the consequences of their action or inaction can be *explained* to them and they can be *encouraged* to find ways to put things right themselves. If parents deliberately model acts of kindness to their children it brings out further a child's natural human kindness and makes them more popular - the sullen, snarky and needy child is always less popular than the sunny, generous and kind adolescent. There is much useful information on these matters in Louis Weinstock's book. (Please refer to the bibliography). The number of disgruntled, aimless and generally troubled children seems to be rising very rapidly and this is where the principles of Weinstock's excellent book would be extremely helpful to parents. It has to be said that his book only makes the most minor and fleeting reference to transgender matters but his well-written advice is highly relevant to unhappy and dissatisfied children whether they are claiming to be transgender or not.

EDUCATE CHILDREN ABOUT THE IMPORTANCE OF THE EQUALITY OF THE SEXE

Also critically important is to educate children about the equality of the sexes - that the sexes don't actually have to be the same to have equality. One sex complements the other - it is their complementary nature and mutually equivalent contributions to humankind as a "team" that are essential, as all contributions are important. We live in a mostly man designed and manufactured material world but an exclusively woman birthed population. (For the sake of convention and clarity the previous sentence did not refer to transmen giving birth).

There has historically been much pro-male to male bias that has possibly been at least partly *unconscious* in its origin - "chaps together" being something that is a throwback to the Caveman tendency to form tight-knit male hunting groups. The fact that it may have been partly *unconscious* is absolutely no excuse whatsoever - it is important for men in modern society to be consciously aware of such behaviour. Positive discrimination has no place for either sex lest it appear that one sex can only get where it has by means of an artificial bias - all forms of bias and discrimination are unfair and always result in resentment in the end. The issue of balance of power and opportunity in the world between women and men is as complex as it is emotive. One sex being able to take on some of the traditional roles of the other and doing them well is often regarded as an indication of equality. This, however, is only a small part of the matter. Of course, some women can become highly successful CEOs of large organisations but as referred to in the section on mindsets, it is often the case that some CEOs have self-serving and insensitive traits although the latter is less common in women than in men. Some men can become outstanding midwives. Such people maybe outliers in their respective sex and are not necessarily representative of mainstream women and men. Men's historical power-based position that placed women in the "put down" position resulted from the following biological factors that are intrinsic to the XY testosterone driven male (please once again consider the Cavewoman/Caveman concept discussed earlier - we are still animals):

1. The male's greater physical strength.
2. The male's higher levels of aggression and disregard for injuries received or inflicted during physical conflict.
3. The male's increased tendency to form very hierarchical groups with a certain pecking order, which tends to maintain the position of the leader. (Of course, at a certain point there will be a challenge to the leader - this is also a natural process in male hierarchical groups).

Factors 1 - 3 have for time immemorial affected the relative situations of women and men in society. Factors 1 and 2 have put men in a position of being able to physically control, intimidate and put down women.

In terms of ambition, it is important for children to be what they realistically can become according to their innate capabilities rather than hankering after something else "traditionally" seen as the role of the other sex - or what parents want them to be. Of course, children can be advised that sometimes women can make a far better job of a traditional male task than a man or vice versa - it is quite reasonable to acknowledge this but to repeat, just doing what can be done based on natural abilities can be perfectly satisfying.

The ideal interaction between women and men would be one of reciprocity, mutual respect, mutual regard and appreciation of their respective abilities and characteristics. This interaction should not be characterised by men getting what they want by intimidation that is a result of their natural greater strength and aggressiveness. Unfortunately, what is often societally regarded as "success" or "status" relates to what has historically become the male bastion - monarchical, political and institutional leaders being obvious examples. Just as men have benefitted from the advantage of greater aggression and physical strength in order to achieve these positions, in the modern world women have suffered the distinct disadvantage of being psychologically pulled between the desire to have children and the desire for success in what have traditionally been male roles. This is an extraordinarily difficult inner emotional conflict and whilst men will of course, have some appreciation of women's difficulties in this respect, only women can truly know the extreme depth of such feelings.

Equality does not only relate to career opportunities. Cismen can never have the sense of deep satisfaction, achievement and fulfilment that comes from bearing another human life. Notwithstanding the emotional reward that comes from producing and nurturing children there are aspects of these roles that are an emotional and practical prison for women. Particularly in the days before modern appliances, readily available food and water, disposable nappies, formula milk and so forth a woman's entire life would have been centred around the numerous practical needs and demands of providing for babies and children. Women may now have been somewhat assisted by modern conveniences but the emotional pull towards their children's needs remains. All of these relative difficulties for women and men plus the complexities of the interaction between women and men are highly important matters for children to be educated about. For children to understand such important factors relating to equality might help to prevent them from *unconsciously* craving the role of the other sex or *unconsciously* trying to avoid the role of their own sex (AVOIDANCE).

EDUCATE CHILDREN ABOUT THE ACCEPTABILITY OF LESBIAN AND GAY RELATIONSHIPS

Children *unconsciously* pick up on the societal intolerance that can be shown towards lesbian and gay lovers as even in the present libero-diverse sexual revolution there are still unacceptable homophobic attitudes. Same sex attraction may first show itself during puberty - it may become lifelong or just be a temporary but entirely natural phase. If children haven't been educated about the acceptability of lesbian and gay relationships, they may feel uncomfortable about glimmers of any same sex attraction they experience during puberty and they may try and handle any shame by declaring themselves to be transgender. They should be able to be comfortable in being lesbian, gay or just exploring their feelings.

PROTECT CHILDREN AGAINST HARM AND HELP THEM WITH THEIR ANXIETY

Parents, please consider this. If as a parent, you went along with your child's hormonal and surgical gender transition but much later they regret that they will never be able to produce their own children - how would you feel? If your detransitioned daughter was unable to breast feed her child - how would she feel? If your child was unable to ever experience an orgasm - how would they feel? (Actually, they would feel nothing at all physically, but would suffer a lifetime of emotional impoverishment, sexual frustration and proportionate anger). Might you feel that you failed in your role as a parent to protect your child from harmful consequences that your child could not possibly understand at the time? Just as you protected your very young child against the dangers of heights, water and traffic, just as you advised your child against drugs of abuse when they entered their early teens. How would your child view you in the long term? If a child can't be relied upon to tidy their bedroom or get their homework done, how can they be relied upon to make such important life changing decisions?

IDENTIFY WHAT IS REALLY GOING ON DURING PUBERTY

Some transgender spokespersons and practitioners refer to the "terrible anxiety" caused by the appearance of secondary sexual characteristics such as pubic hair, breast development, menstruation, psychological changes and the dropping of voice and testicles etc. They recommend puberty blockers to stop these changes and therefore prevent this "terrible anxiety". If someone has "terrible anxiety" caused by large groups of people, is it not better for them to learn mental techniques and healthy coping mechanisms to deal with the "terrible anxiety" and to actually confront the issue of social anxiety? You can only harden up the mind to life events by gradual exposure and cope with life by learning life skills. Feelings of anxiety about the body, sex and sexual orientation are just normal parts of puberty. That's just how it is and always has been. Puberty hasn't in itself suddenly for some mysterious reason become worse than it has been for thousands of generations. In fact, in former times puberty meant hard physical labour or going to war for boys and for girls a lack of sanitary protection then forced marriage and forced sex aged twelve (in other words, child rape). Can Social Media *really* have made puberty seem that bad? It seems it has - particularly for a generation of children that is lacking in resilience and self-reliance partly as a result of overprotected childhoods and very much due to an overconsumption of screen-time. Modern psychosocial factors in upbringing have unfortunately made children less resilient to some of the unavoidable rigours of life such as puberty - but this is a matter of a general lack of psychological resilience, not truly a matter of gender identity.

REQUEST A REFERRAL FOR PSYCHOTHERAPY *OR* A REFERRAL TO A GENDER IDENTITY CLINIC? AN IMPORTANT DECISION

It has been somewhat overstated in the Social Media that children's emotional difficulties around the time of puberty are "likely" to be due to gender dysphoria and that such children are therefore transgender. Children who *seem* to have gender dysphoria are almost always suffering from general and *conventional* psychological difficulties that are being aggravated by the emotional difficulties that so often accompany puberty. They therefore almost without exception need *conventional* psychological help. Given the current climate of thought it is understandable that primary care doctors refer such children to gender identity clinics. The problem is that there is usually an extremely long wait to be seen and this is particularly the case in the United Kingdom. Being referred to a gender identity service reinforces in the child's mind *and* in the parents' minds the idea that "all of the problems" are due to gender matters - when they are most probably not. During the long wait for the gender identity clinic appointment, all of the focus will as a result be on gender identity and the belief that this is the problem rather than being due to *conventional* psychological suffering. Tragically during this wait there will be no professional attention being given to any *conventional* psychological suffering. Quite often, the sheer frustration of waiting worsens the distress - "Nobody is helping me!". The increasing psychological distress will again reinforce in the child's and the parents' mind the idea that all the issues are "due to" gender dysphoria rather than *conventional* psychological distress - and so the belief of having gender dysphoria becomes self-reinforcing. By the time the child is finally seen the psychological stress will doubtless have escalated considerably and any further wait for the wished for and assumed "cure" of puberty blockers or cross-sex hormones will make matters even more fraught. It can thus be seen how avoidable but desperate situations can so easily develop.

If only appropriate conventional psychological care could be provided in a timely manner matters could be far less troubling for young people.

So, to raise the issue again, is the time of maximal psychological and hormonal upheaval in a child's life the right point to be administering treatments that have not had their long-term effectiveness or safety evaluated? Please be aware that there are no accurate scientific surveys or research that confirm the long-term benefit of gender transition in young children. Some prestigious organisations have claimed benefit, but their methods of research have been somewhat flawed, and their reports based on impressions rather than accurate statistics.

LOOK CAREFULLY AT THE EVIDENCE OF THE EFFECTIVENESS OF PUBERTY BLOCKERS, CROSS-SEX HORMONES AND GENDER TRANSITION SURGERY IN YOUNG PEOPLE

One wonders what type of pressures that parents feel under when they allow their young children to be subjected to permanently life changing puberty blockers, cross-sex hormones or even transgender surgery. (Please note once again, it is worth revisiting the section earlier in the book - Possible Side Effects of Gender Transition Medication and Surgery).

Could it be simply that they have been pulled along by the tide of a well-meaning, highly effective and organised transgender publicity movement? It is very perturbing for a loving parent to hear from their child that s/he is transgender, feels suicidal and that s/he wishes to drastically change their body. It is an awful experience for parents to ask themselves if they had done something wrong in some way. They will also be perplexed as to where they can turn for impartial help, particularly as many services in the National Health Service in the United Kingdom are exceptionally keen to be seen as transgender friendly - but perhaps this is because of the pressure they are under from Government, which in turn is under pressure from powerful transgender lobbies. The transgender lobbies are of course well-intentioned but as in all aspects of life a middle of the road approach that takes into consideration all pros and cons of actions is preferable for most people in the long run.

These transgender lobbies may of course, be making admirable progress in the name of inclusivity, after all it is only right that LGBTQIA+ issues are dealt with in a nondiscriminatory fashion but what must not be overlooked is the fact that there is an immense difference between very young children and mature adults making permanently life changing decisions. In practical terms the child's parents become complicit in the decision making and consent process but often only as result of what their immature children say that they "need" and nothing more accurate, objective or informed than that. Adults may have the capacity and maturity to decide on LGBTQIA+ matters but minors *absolutely do not and cannot* - they cannot conceivably understand the complexities of adult life such as loss of fertility and mature adult sexual relationships. It is very difficult for a child to put into words the psychological upheaval that occurs during the period around puberty and of course, even earlier in childhood, particularly if there is family disharmony and as a result the child has become reticent to express its feelings directly. Children around the time of puberty are obviously reluctant to express their private thoughts and emotions to the very people they are trying to differentiate and separate themselves from. Children may believe that their parents couldn't possibly understand their "unique" situation as they fancifully believe - many of us as teenagers liked to feel a "special case" and "unique" after all.

If the medical services seem to parents to be too unquestionably pro-gender transition, balance can be provided by the following resources:

The websites www.transgendertrend and www.genspect.org are strongly recommended for their reference material and resources for parents, which can be remarkably informative. Likewise, viewing YouTube having searched under "transition regret" and "detransition" can be very helpful. For those who feel there is a need for expert psychological exploration of transgender feelings reference to the website www.genderexploratory.com (Gender Exploratory Therapy Association - GETA) can provide contact with psychotherapists who specialise in this area. For those who have same sex attraction and are considering gender transition a very useful website is www.genderhq.com (Gender Health Query). A very useful reference, which can also be especially illuminating is www4thwavenow.com. Very balanced and helpful viewpoints regarding the caution required with medical gender transition treatments for children, adolescents and young adults can be seen on YouTube and are being made by two particularly famous transgender people: Blaire White, a very attractive and articulate transwoman and Buck Angel, a very masculine and similarly articulate transmale who has been very successful in the film industry. Their discussions on YouTube are illuminating and intellectually very well considered - highly recommended.

VOLUNTARY AND INVOLUNTARY DETRANSITIONING - TROUBLE TO COME

There has been a headlong rush into hormonal and surgical gender transition as many young people have been psychologically "pulled along" by alluring and very professionally put together transgender websites that put out well-intentioned and convincing messages. The underlying feelings of those young people who opted for puberty blockers then hormonal and surgical gender transition were actually quite likely to have been related to:

1. Quite mundane and conventional forms of underlying mental distress.
2. Uncomfortable emerging feelings of same sex attraction that are often accompanied by feelings of gender non-conformity. All of these feelings can be a normal part of pubertal development.
3. A feeling of lacking sexual attractiveness in birth sex.
4. Not feeling fully female or male. As illustrated by the "double curve sexual characteristics" graph.
5. Convincing, "cool", trendy and even cult-like transgender influences in the Social Media.

The amount of gender transition regret and frequency of detransition can be expected to increase as more and more young people undergo hormonal and surgical gender transition and then more and more realise that transition has not solved their problems or even made their lives far more difficult and complicated.

In some studies, there has been just over one in a hundred regret and detransition rate *but in others it has been very significantly higher.* (Please don't take the author's word for it - a brief Internet search of "gender transition regret statistics" or "detransition statistics" will confirm this wide variation). This wide range of numbers indicates that we just do not have the most accurate of statistics at present - in fact some surveys have been remarkably flawed in the way in which data have been collected. It is therefore currently very difficult to come to any firm statistically based conclusions although it does seem that more people have been helped in various ways than harmed. It remains to be seen what happens in ten to twenty years' time to the ever-increasing number of young children and young adults currently attending gender identity clinics. There is a very concerning group of young people who are not attending formal clinics as they are buying cross-sex hormones on the Internet or are travelling overseas for "budget" gender transition surgery. With the latter two options, the risk of major medical mishaps is increased. Even if a decision to undergo gender transition was the correct one, it could be catastrophic side effects of medication or surgery that result in gender transition regret or lead to a need to detransition.

In view of the lack of accurate statistics, although it may only be crystal ball gazing, it is likely that there are some awful realisations yet to come for many children and young people who are undergoing hormonal and surgical gender transition. At the moment there is much mutual support within transgender groups and this is a sustaining factor for continuing in a transgender lifestyle. After all, it may have been a lack of a feeling of self-acceptance and acceptance within wider society that contributed to the desire of some young people to adopt a transgender lifestyle or fully transitioning in the first place - a feeling of societal acceptance was at last found amongst other transgender people. In the future it would be quite demoralising to see increasing dropout rates from transgender groups and this could perhaps become a self-perpetuating decline - as more people detransition the support within the group will diminish. This may represent the loss of the one and only support system in which some transgender people can have accurate and lived-experience based empathy. The author of course, hopes that transgender people will be able to feel increasingly comfortable in cisgender society as it becomes more accommodating. Transgender people will then be less reliant on transgender groups that may be somewhat insular and possibly over-focussed on gender transition as the way forward. If a practitioner asks a transgender patient if their transgender group has cautioned about side effects, the answer will invariably be no.

For some unfortunate transgender people, the emergence of side effects of cross-sex hormones such as metabolic abnormalities or cancer will result in the recommendation that the hormones are stopped leaving the individual in a physical state that could be described as a sexually intermediate or indeterminate. Late complications of surgery such as scar shrinkage and tissue distortion will also contribute to post-gender transition dissatisfaction as not all surgical complications can be corrected.

Just the effort of maintaining the appearance of the opposite gender will for some people become just too much trouble, particularly if they never felt that they comfortably fitted into wider society. Life does tend to throw things at us all and new mental stresses may occur and as a result there may be a worsening of the original psychological difficulties that contributed to transgender feelings in the first instance. The initial "high" and novelty of transitioning may just have been a distraction from the original psychological issues that had never been properly explored in the first place - this would present a real and continuing threat to future mental wellbeing. For those who just continue in their transgender lifestyle without psychotherapeutic help for their underlying psychological pain it may never, ever be properly explored and dealt with in the long term. Of course, the danger of eventually undergoing explorative psychotherapy *after* hormonal and surgical gender transition and *only then* coming to the conclusion that the feeling of being in the wrong body was in reality due to unresolved psychological matters would be a terrible situation.

A noteworthy example of gender transition regret is the now well-known courageous young woman who detransitioned and took the Tavistock Gender Identity Development Service to court. She realised that what she really required in the first instance was psychotherapeutic help and most certainly not gender transition. She had been given a puberty blocker aged 16, which was followed up with testosterone. She underwent mastectomy at 20. Now living as a woman, she is extremely troubled by having a deep voice, excess body hair and no breasts. Surely it is better to have psychotherapy *prior* to surgery as by undergoing such a psychological exploration it could be realised that trying to put life right using puberty blockers, cross-sex hormones and surgery in the case of young people may be nothing more than MAGICAL THINKING, in other words an illusion that by "putting right" the physical, the mind can be "put right". However, it must be said that for some people, hormonal and surgical gender transgender treatments *are* the best option to ease their psychological pain - but this must be very carefully considered after suitable psychological exploration. Such treatments would only be appropriate for psychologically mature people who are able to properly make such a decision.

Some people will continue their transgender lifestyle as it is difficult to admit to themselves that a mistake had been made and even more difficult to admit it to those around. Collection of detransitioning statistics will possibly be fraught with difficulties and inaccuracies as people will drop out of clinics and studies. Some might give inaccurate responses in surveys as it is normal for people to fudge their responses in questionnaires. Some will not necessarily appear in statistics due to travel outside their original survey area or country. Some loss to research follow up may sadly be due to suicide.

Some transgender people in part have a polymorphous sexuality-based motivation towards hormonal and surgical gender transition. The human sexual desire is exceptionally strong in the earlier part of adult life and it will generally be expressed in a way that depends where someone is on the "double curve sexual characteristics" graph, their particular mindset and sexual orientation. Sex drive usually decreases with ageing and with any decline of sexual excitement and need for satisfaction the likelihood of gender transition regret would be likely to increase.

In countries where it is necessary to pay for cross-sex hormones, complete loss of income may result in involuntary detransition. As detransition rates increase the doctors involved in gender transition treatments will almost certainly have to pay more for medical indemnity (insurance) and/or legal fees. This cost will unfortunately be passed onto their patients.

It can be predicted that there will be increasing numbers of transgender people for whom treatment cannot continue as they will not be able to take cross-sex hormones for the various reasons above. They will find in their now gender indeterminate state that they will be even more uncomfortable with themselves. To use a harrowing description from the First World War they will be in "No Man's Land" or of course, "No Woman's Land". The other concern for people in such a position is that in their desperate attempts to find acceptance and love they may experience repeated disappointment. It is all too easy when in a state of loneliness and longing to latch onto any form of relationship and to believe out of desperation that it is truly "love". Many, many people who have been in a state of longing have assumed that their feelings were actually love - but such feelings were far from real love. It is all too easy to confuse longing with love - many of us have been in that situation, whether we are cisgender or transgender.

On a potentially tragic note, those in a gender indeterminate state who need to enter transgender sex work as a way of earning money may be subject to abuse and humiliation. (The author has come across people in a similar situation it was absolutely heart-rending). This painful to read paragraph has described some truly awful situations that would be best avoided.

In society it is often cosily believed that "people in the same boat" have a mutual understanding of problems and a desire to help each other. However, when the chips are down, they don't - stressed and desperate people will almost always put themselves first.

Compared to the average population, there is sadly a much higher self-harm and suicide rate in the transgender population in *both* those who have and haven't undergone hormonal and or surgical gender transition. Regrettably, hormonal and surgical gender transition does not at the moment seem to have altered the overall rate of suicide in people who have transgender feelings. (Suicide is discussed further in a subsequent section).

A most important point to emphasise is that anyone experiencing self-harming or suicidal thoughts and feelings should urgently obtain support and assistance.

Anyone who decides to detransition will find very helpful advice and resources in the website www.post-trans.com (for female detransitioners), www.sexchangeregret.com and wwwtransback.org.

WHAT IS A WOMAN? A RELATED QUESTION - WHAT ACTUALLY IS A *DEFINITION*? SOME RELEVANT FEMINIST, GENERALIST AND SAFEGUARDING VIEWPOINTS TO CONSIDER. COULD WE PERHAPS COMPROMISE ON SOME IMPORTANT POINTS?

There is much current controversy as to whether a man can become a woman and in fact there is also much debate as how to define what a woman actually is.

This is important for three reasons:

1. It matters to cisfemales.
2. It matters to transwomen.
3. It may be relevant to young girls.

The author at first had absolutely no real wish to examine the highly controversial question, "What is a woman?"

However, cisfemale colleagues who were aware that the author was writing this book frequently mentioned to him two matters that concerned them:

1. One is the situation that ciswomen have sometimes been made to feel uncomfortable if they merely refer to themselves as women.
2. The second is that ciswomen and cisgirls can sometimes feel unsafe when a transwoman enters female safe spaces. (The ciswomen who expressed this viewpoint to the author stressed that they absolutely did not want in any way to be transphobic and wanted to be nondiscriminatory - but they could not help but naturally feel some uneasiness).

These two points prompted exploration of these extremely contentious matters. Some potential risks to the safety of cisfemales are explored further in the next chapter *and in the interests of equality and safety it is also important to bear in mind that similar feelings may be experienced by transwomen in certain situations.*

Any suggestion that a change of sex is not possible would be regarded by many in the transgender population as incorrect and transphobic. Alternatively, some members of the transgender population would openly say that although they have gone through hormonal and surgical gender transition they have not truly changed their biological sex. Buck Angel a very influential transman and Blaire White an equally influential transwoman who have both done very much for transgender people have publicly stated that transgender medical treatments do not technically change someone's biological sex. It can thus be seen that it is not only cisgender people who take such a viewpoint.

The difficulty for all concerned is that there will be many cisgender and transgender people who can just not agree on the matter of what defines a woman and whether changing sex is possible. This will therefore be an unfortunate cause of discomfort or argument and *the author sincerely wishes that there could be a resolution of this disagreement for the future harmony and mutual comfort of all parties. Perhaps a way forward would be to "agree to disagree" just as can happen in so many other aspects of life.* And so, we perhaps shouldn't argue unnecessarily - we would perhaps all be better off just making the best of our lives and stick to our own views and say, "To Hell with it if other people disagree - their opinion just doesn't matter to me that much. I'll just get on with my life and live and let live".

However, where opinions really do matter is when it comes to:

1. *Safeguarding children and anyone else who may be at risk of making a gender transition error.*
2. *Safeguarding safe spaces for cisfemales **and** transwomen.*

3. *Ensuring that ciswomen do not feel cancelled.*

In order to discuss the *definition* of what a woman actually is, it is firstly necessary to examine the term *definition* itself. Dictionaries indicate that a *definition* is:

"An exact description of the nature of something that is stated in precise, unambiguous and decisive terms".

Please note the following points about *definitions*:

1. *Definitions* are usually constructed as a result of a long-term consensus of opinion that can stand the test of time and an intellectual or evidence-based analysis.
2. Individual personal viewpoints cannot immediately change *definitions*. There is a form of "societal democracy" that applies to *definitions* - it generally seems that consensus rules and the majority viewpoint is the one that has the most weight.

When using scientific and biological principles a woman is *defined* as:

"A human adult female whose anatomy and function are focussed on and centred around the following functions: producing ova (eggs), becoming pregnant then carrying, giving birth to and nurturing children - all of which have a basis in XX chromosomal genetics".

However, it has to be said that if a ciswomen was born with an abnormality of the female reproductive system or develops a medical disorder, which prevents her producing children she is of course, still a woman.

Whilst on the subject of chromosomes, geneticists would say that if you have Y chromosomes throughout your body you are biologically a male. All male humans have a Y chromosome that is genetically related to a common ancestor who probably lived around 300,000 years ago.

The rare medical intersex conditions pose some difficult questions in relation to this matter. Although their opinion may be objected to, a genetic scientist would say that a transwoman is a biological male. But should that really matter if they are able to live their best life as a result of transition?

On grounds of acceptance and tolerance as a Straight LGBTQIA+ Ally the author would suggest that a transwoman should feel perfectly able to say that she is a woman or that they feel like a woman - but the author would quite rightly defer to the opinions of ciswomen on this matter. It is interesting that when asked what it actually *feels like* to be a woman, the author's cisfemale colleagues, friends and loved ones have stated that they don't actually know. Likewise, the author doesn't really know what it *feels like* to be a man. We all tend to indirectly try and describe what it *feels like* to be a woman or a man in terms of anatomy or "traditional" functions and roles in life. This is a perplexing and controversial area to put it mildly!

Therefore, by the principle of social acceptance, tolerance, understanding and indeed common courtesy it would be reasonable in society for a transwoman to be given appropriate respect for their chosen gender status by cisgender people by which is meant that cisgender people would do nothing to make a transgender person feel uncomfortable. If a transwoman referred to herself as a woman, this could be socially acknowledged.

Likewise, ciswomen should be able to refer to themselves as women without disapproval.

In the interests of future social harmony - transgender and cisgender parties could maintain their personal viewpoints on transgender matters whilst at the same time being polite and considerate to each other.

The following few paragraphs illustrate why there could be continued difficulties in discussion between some transwomen and some ciswomen regarding the matter as to what constitutes a woman and whether changing sex is possible.

The author will firstly quote some science-based viewpoints. Of course, in psychological and sociological terms there is much more to a woman than just a scientific or biological definition. The basis of what constitutes a woman is one of the most fundamental and considered topics of all time and this has been so over countless generations. A biological *definition* would not be changed by scientific organisations to fit in with subjective feelings or a political viewpoint - the sciences just do not function in that way. Whilst thoughts and feelings are vitally important in human experience, it is only by means of actual concrete *definitions* that communication between scientists can be meaningful, realistic, practical and unambiguous.

Feminists, biologists and scientists have stated that a man cannot possibly become a woman and instead of referring to "male to female transition" suggest we should refer to "male to transgender female" or potentially insultingly just "male to trans". Obviously, causing offence should be avoided at all cost - in all directions.

As stated, an unfortunate effect of the current climate in gender theory discussion has been that ciswomen can sometimes feel uncomfortable merely by referring to themselves as a woman and it has even been suggested by transgender groups that ciswomen should be referred to as:

1. "People who give birth".
2. "People who menstruate".
3. "People with a cervix".

To repeat, in the spirit of fairness and courtesy to all, if a transwoman is able to refer to themselves as a woman, it would be hoped that a ciswoman would be able to refer to herself as a woman without fear of disapproval. Some women have told the author that they have come to believe that they are almost having to give up their womanhood, which involves aspects that are particularly specific, special and wonderful. The human species relies upon the very essence and functions of womanhood for its survival. Women have been exposed to great difficulties and subjugation throughout history and it is only fair and reasonable for women to believe that they should not be "cancelled" and vilified regarding the *definition* of a woman. ***The*** most successful author of modern times has been roundly criticised for her views on what constitutes a woman. She has been sent rape and death threats. However, she has admirably and in a spirit of fairness to ciswomen stuck to her principles on their behalf - just as transgender spokespersons can stick to their views. As people of this world, we can all hold onto our views as a personal right - but threats of assault, rape or death remain disproportionate, unhelpful to either "side" and most certainly illegal.

It is quite reasonable to state that it is possible to very significantly alter gender *expression* although of course, there will be different degrees of gender expression ranging from a male cross-sex dresser who still has male genitalia through to someone who has undergone full male to female hormonal and surgical gender transition treatments. It is totally appreciated that a transwoman may truly feel in their personal experience that they are in fact a woman and the author would again suggest that they are completely at liberty to feel this way. As has been referred to elsewhere modified subjective experience can be habituated in the mind by "functional cerebral plasticity" and it is generally appreciated that people can extensively adapt themselves "into" a role and "become a new person". If someone can make the best of their life in that way, why shouldn't they? *As long as no one else is compromised as a result.*

It can be suggested that it is impossible for one sex to *completely and 100%* appreciate what the other sex experiences mentally or physically but that a great deal of cross-sex empathy is nevertheless possible. There has even been the interesting and tantalising suggestion made by some transwomen who have undergone full hormonal and surgical transition that they can have the advantage of enjoying the intense and multiple orgasms that ciswomen can achieve as opposed to the typically brief and genitally focussed orgasm generally experienced by cismen. Some transwomen do describe an orgasm that closely corresponds to what a ciswoman would refer to. Neurophysiologists and anatomists might comment on this matter by saying that surgically created female genitals are not connected *to* the brain in the exactly same way as they are in a ciswoman, nor are the related areas *within* the brain connected in the same way as in a ciswoman. A research question therefore remains as to whether this experienced change in orgasm is hormonally or psychologically based - or perhaps a mixture of both factors. Cismales do in fact have oestrogen receptors on their brain cells that react to that hormone. However, certain cismale tissues react differently to oestrogen than the equivalent tissues of ciswomen. At the current state of research, we just don't know enough but future sex hormone research with functional MRI scan studies may eventually shed light on this and many other matters. There are many significant unknowns in the complexity of the *unconscious* psychological and the physical physiological processes relating to each sex.

Feminists have pointed out that some male cross-sex dressers and transwomen tend to use exceptionally exaggerated female stereotypes - they overdress, apply extremes of makeup and use overstated feminised mannerisms. Of course, they are just enjoying a particular way of expressing themselves in feminine form and why shouldn't they? There's no law against it and it is celebrated in a well-known television based competition in a main television series. However, Feminists have made the valid observation that such overtly feminised stereotypes are casting women in a sex-object role and this is therefore something that is worthy of further discussion for the benefit of all concerned. However, on balance it could be pointed out that some cisfemale Media "personalities" flaunt their female sexuality in very short skirts, plunging necklines and see-through clothing. They are more than happy to appear in extremely skimpy bikinis. Feminists might understandably take a dim view of this also. Perhaps in some instances, flamboyantly cross-sex dressing men may have an *unconscious* desire to be "better at being a woman" than a ciswoman, perhaps in some cases as a compensation for some feeling of missing something in their life as a man - but even if that is the case, is it of any serious consequence? They are making the best of their life and so long as they are not truly imperilling ciswomen this surely does not matter - although once again the male author would defer to ciswomen on this view.

Some male cross-sex dressers and transwomen may have unresolved painful psychological wounds from women as a result of traumatic events in an earlier period of their life for example due to a mother who was abandoning, rejecting, and frustrating of their child's needs or was abusive in other ways. Becoming a woman symbolically gives a feeling of control over the womanhood that their mother represented. There may also be an *unconscious* desire to be more of a woman than their mother was. As they may be trying to get over an *unconscious* trauma, a compassionate and understanding viewpoint should be taken. However, if these male cross-sex dressers and transwomen feel their life is being improved then this is all to the good but the author again makes two requests:

1. That male cross-sex dressers and transwomen are treated without prejudice or hostility by the cisgender populace and that their rights are respected.
2. The rights of cisgender women are likewise not compromised and they also receive the respect they deserve.

When discussing sex and gender, the question is whether you are referring to biological sex or a particular psychosocial way of expressing gender and the associated feelings. It is all too easy to end up discussing matters at cross-purposes with some people using scientific principles and definitions while others are referring to subjective experiences. This once again is unfortunately a recipe for disharmonious discussion. Perhaps discourse would be aided if everyone stated their position as being scientifically evidenced based or relating to personal experience but with an acknowledgement that everyone is entitled to take their own viewpoint. If someone disagrees with the other, it is merely an alternative viewpoint and if they wish to hold it, why shouldn't they? Every one of us holds at least some viewpoints that are debatable - but life goes on.

There appear to be some definitions and statements made during discussions about transgender matters that are difficult for cisgender people to understand, an example is the now fairly well known statement:

"Not all people who menstruate are women".

This quote relates to a transman who identifies as male and has the outward appearance of a male but still has a womb and can menstruate. As menstruation had occurred it is assumed that he was not taking testosterone at the time and thus was possibly not in his most masculine state.

Scientists might say that there are attempts to ignore the absolute truths of the binary sexual principles of Nature that date back into the mists of Time itself. Admittedly some species are hermaphrodites but even in these, sex is still actually binary - it is just that one organism possesses both female and male sexual organs. Some species can change from one sex to the other under certain conditions but of course, humans cannot make such changes in response to environmental conditions.

Considering matters in an entirely theoretical way for a moment, in the future, it might be technically possible to transplant a vagina and a womb from a ciswoman into a transwoman. There is probably a surgeon somewhere who is rash enough to consider attempting it. (In a more conventional manner there have been instances of ciswomen receiving a womb transplant from a deceased donor and successfully bearing children having had in vitro fertilisation).

Gender theorists might raise some unusual questions about a transwoman receiving a womb implant:

1. Would they then be a biological woman if they identified as one?
2. Would they be a man if although they could (artificially) become pregnant they identified as a male?

This mind-boggling notion raises the question of, "Just because something may be possible, should it necessarily be done?" It also reminds us of the point that how gender and sex are being designated is becoming somewhat removed from XX and XY chromosomes and personal experiences are being given priority and being valued above conventional biological definitions. But, once again, if a transwoman inwardly feels that they are living as a woman, this is their personal experience and the emotional reality of their personal existence - where is there a problem with that? Just so long as ciswomen aren't being compromised in some way, just so long as ciswomen aren't being devalued and just so long as ciswomen are fully respected.

For both sexes there is a certain allure and mystery of the other - there is a special "wonder". Indeed, women and men may sometimes ask themselves the question as to what it is like to be the other sex. Having said that, there are some studies which suggest that some transwomen have some similarities in brain activity to those seen in scans of ciswomen.

The vast majority of the cisfemale population is tolerant, middle-of-the-road and adopts a "live and let live approach" to other people. However, even such accommodating ciswomen might be irritated by what they might regard as overly vocal transwomen denigrating mainstream ciswomen. The unfortunate result of this is that feelings of irritation might be felt against transwomen *in general* when the feelings of annoyance should really be directed to only those taking the strongest viewpoints that offend ciswomen. The majority of transwomen are just quietly trying to get on with their lives. In other words, the more extreme transfemale activists could be regarded as making life more uncomfortable for the average transwoman.

In summary:

The author hopes in the areas of transgender psychology, medicine and societal courtesy that a position can be reached where:

1. People who are best helped by hormonal and surgical gender transition can undergo this and feel comfortable in the world - but the need for extremely careful decision making should not be overlooked.
2. Those who are mistakenly considering gender transition and have poor mental health resulting from complex psychosocial factors can be helped towards better mental wellbeing. As a result they will be able to make the correct decision about hormonal and surgical gender transition.

3. Ciswomen can comfortably refer to themselves as "women".

4. A compromise is reached regarding the terms "woman" and "man" for transgender persons. Most cisgender people would doubtless extend the courtesy to a transwoman or transman of using the terms woman or man according to the preference of the transgender person. Those extending this courtesy would know in their deepest mind that they are demonstrating politeness but at the same time being aware of the biological background of the transgender person concerned. Cisgender people would prefer to put the need for courtesy and social harmony above any political considerations - as would transgender people. It could be considered that it does not seem particularly democratic that ciswoman are not "allowed" to be referred to as "women" but transwomen can be "allowed" to be referred to as "women".

5. Ciswomen's safe spaces are in fact safe. There is of course, a simple but expensive and space consuming solution to the problem of communal changing facilities - this is to have only single occupancy cubicles in which there is no shared area in which mingling is possible.

Two final thoughts on this matter:

1. It is of note that it is ciswomen who take most of the flak for making statements about what constitutes being a woman. Cismen do not seem to receive as much flak from transmen.

2. Cismen and transwomen could check themselves to ensure that they are not acting in ways that are harmful to ciswomen and to most certainly keep in mind the sacrosanct nature of cisfemale safe spaces - just as the safety and comfort of transwomen are also highly important.

THE RISKS OF VIOLENCE TO AND FROM TRANSGENDER PEOPLE

RISKS *FROM* TRANSWOMEN

As mentioned before, an **extremely small number** of transwomen may be a risk to ciswomen. It has to be emphasised again that this statement most definitely only applies to the smallest minority of transwomen and although it may not be a statistically high risk - a risk it is. Just as "general" criminals will use any amount of cunning to achieve their aims, then so will those with sexually predatory motives. A male with sexual motives may choose to identify as a woman in some countries where social and legal guidelines allow them to enter female lavatories, changing rooms, women's refuges and so forth. They only have to try to pass as a transwoman and/or identify as a woman to enter these female formerly safe havens and other areas in which it is vital that the privacy of cisgirls and ciswomen is not invaded. This may result in the incredibly small number of transwomen (or "fake transwomen") who have sexual motives being a risk to cisfemales. There have been some notorious but very rare cases of ciswomen being raped in female prisons by a transwoman (or "fake transwoman").

Examples of areas where it is vital that cisfemales are free from such intrusion are as follows:

1. Where intimate searches are required for legal and security reasons.
2. Specific female medical procedures such as breast examination, taking cervical smears, other gynaecological examinations or procedures and indeed any medical process that could make a cisfemale feel overexposed or vulnerable.
3. Assessment and examination after sexual or other assault on a ciswoman.

4. Female psychiatric facilities.
5. As required by religion.

To repeat, we are dealing with a real and major area of concern for vulnerable ciswomen and cisgirls, yes a potential risk to defenceless children - predatory individuals could easily use a transgender cover to gain access to young cisgirls. However, it must be yet again clearly stated that the vast majority of transwomen are in no way implicated in such behaviour, they are instead just seeking personal happiness and contentment by living as a woman.

It must be borne in mind that predatory males who are pretending to be women in order to invade female safe spaces are also a risk to transwomen who are politely utilising female only areas without posing any threat to cisfemales or other transwomen.

Feminists who are sceptical regarding the status of transwomen are not being transphobic and they are not "hating" when they are expressing concern regarding their safety in ciswomen's spaces. An excellent website that explores the of difficulties that may occur between cisgender and transgender people in general and does so with particular emphasis on the position of ciswomen is www.sex-matters.org.

In addition to factors 1 - 5 in the list above, there is an important group of cisgirls and ciswomen for whom it is particularly important to keep safe spaces - those who have been subjected to male on female emotional, physical or sexual abuse and have or are at risk developing post traumatic stress disorder (PTSD). Even vague similarities to their previous trauma can bring on PTSD symptoms. For those who are not acquainted with the symptoms of PTSD, it is characterised by the following features:

1. Recurrent and intrusive recollections of the original trauma in the form of images, thoughts and feelings.
2. Feeling as if the trauma is happening in the present moment.
3. Extreme discomfort on coming across a reminder of the trauma.
4. Avoidance of anything similar to the original trauma.
5. Recurrent distressing nightmares of or related to the trauma.
6. Feelings of guilt regarding their feelings.
7. DISSOCIATION or a feeling as if the surroundings or the sufferer themselves are not real.
8. Hyperarousal - feeling "on edge", particularly when the victim is reminded directly or indirectly of the trauma.
9. Inability to remember important or significant parts of the trauma (REPRESSION).
10. Decreased interest in major aspects of life.
11. Emotionally distant and possible loss of empathy with others.
12. Restricted range of emotions.
13. A sense that their future is somehow limited.

RISKS *TO* TRANSWOMEN

Being a transwoman puts her at risk of being sexually assaulted by a cismale if passing well as a sexually attractive woman. Some transwomen dress in a flamboyant and a very sexually female way, which could be something that entices a would-be rapist. Rape could very conceivably result in damage to their neo-vagina. (It is often the case that transwomen need to use an artificial vaginal lubricant for neo-vaginal sex).

Given that we all potentially have deep within us a degree of polymorphous sexuality, some of us might be prone to having sexual desires about which we are not comfortable. What we are not comfortable about within ourselves we sometimes criticise or attack in others due to PROJECTION. For example, men who are ashamed of glimmers of homosexuality in themselves might assault those whom they suspect of being gay. Some men equate male to female transgender life-modes to being gay and this puts transwomen at risk of "homophobic assault". Similarly, men who are uncomfortable with their gender and have transgender leanings that they are uncomfortable about may possibly attack a transgender transwoman as a way of handling their uncomfortable feelings.

Anal rape could unfortunately be inflicted on transwomen if and when the attacker finds their victim's only orifice available for sexual satisfaction or conquest is the anus. The attacker may justify anal sex as a way of punishing his victim but equally he could perhaps even be justifying the anal rape to himself.

The reader will of course, be aware that cismen finding transmen in their lavatory will have an entirely different psychological experience to ciswomen finding a transwoman in their lavatory.

RISKS TO TRANSGENDER CHILDREN

No matter which society or culture that is being considered, there is always a sense of conformity and uniformity. Consider an elderly church congregation in England - if someone didn't wear their Sunday best and comport themselves well there would be titters of disapproval. The solitary man wearing a Manchester United football shirt in the Liverpool end of a football stadium is likely to be made to feel "just a little" out of place.

So, please consider the only transgender child in a school classroom. In spite of the orders from the teachers to the contrary, the transgender child *will* at some stage be made to feel uncomfortable and possibly badly bullied. The other pupils are children after all rather than liberal intellectuals who would be more accommodating and nuanced in their thinking or actions. The risk of psychologically excluding behaviour and bullying is another reason for parents to be cautious about rushing headlong into supporting transgender behaviour.

A CONCLUSION IN RELATION TO SAFE SPACES FOR CISFEMALES

The criteria for what actually allows a male to enter female safe areas should be subject to continued scrutiny and robust legislature. **It must surely, without doubt be a cisfemale's right to have potential sexual predators excluded from their personal space when they require it.** Again, the website www.sex-matters.org is an excellent resource and one which explores important relevant legal matters.

IN THE INTERESTS OF EQUALITY AND SAFETY OF TRANSWOMEN AND TRANSMEN

It must also be emphasised that a transwoman or a transman should be able to choose the sex or gender expression of a person that may need to enter their personal space and that this personal space is kept safe.

What the author would ultimately like to see is cisgender people being not just polite to transgender people but becoming more relaxed during their interaction - just as is becoming increasingly the case for lesbian and gay people. Throughout the successive generations (birth years in order): Baby boomers 1946-64, Generation X 1965-80, Generation Y 1981-98, Generation Z 1997-2012 there has been a progressive increase in identification as LGBTQIA+ and so it can be expected that it will become increasingly comfortable for transgender people in society - but cisfemale's safe spaces should still be sacrosanct. There is currently a drive within transgender movements to support "self-identification of gender", in other words it is only necessary for someone to declare their gender and that is all that is required to legally "change gender". This means a man only needs to say that he is a woman and need not have undergone hormonal and surgical gender transition to refer to himself as a woman. This self-identification process potentially has very dangerous effect on ciswomen's safe spaces in a small number of instances.

THE IMPORTANCE OF DEEP AND FULL DISCUSSION. ARE UNIVERSITIES FAILING IN THEIR ROLE IN PROMOTING INTELLECTUAL DEVELOPMENT OF THEIR STUDENTS?

Even though there have been many positive changes for sexually diverse groups it is still possible that discussing transgender matters will continue to be fraught or simply blocked if the nature of some university debates is any indication. The function of a university is not merely to provide an education in a particular subject, after all someone can become knowledgeable to degree level by moderately intense solitary private study.

A highly important role of a university is to equip young people with the ability, confidence, resilience, open mindedness and tolerance to discuss difficult matters. University was traditionally somewhere for young people to enhance their own critical thought and also improve their ability to intellectually consider other people's viewpoints - no matter how uncomfortable or unpalatable those opinions may be. This is a very important attribute for young people to develop and it is painfully obvious when they haven't managed to - whenever they are confronted with a view that they feel they strongly disagree with or it brings up *unconscious* doubts, conflicts and insecurities they might then act defensively or offensively. Being able to be reflective and contemplative about a point of view rather than be overly reactive is an attribute that has to be learned and university used to be the place where many young people acquired this ability. Perhaps the world would have suffered less bloodshed if extreme opposing viewpoints had *all* been subject to rigorous and critical debate without one side shutting down the other by means of extreme violence, oppression or worse still, war - after all, *a middle of the road and compromised view of things is generally the best for all.* Reaching a position of compromise and harmonious coexistence is an aim of this book - it was not intended to be only about reducing the risk of gender transition regret.

A much larger proportion of young people go to university than in the author's youth but there now seems to be less of an opportunity to robustly debate sensitive subjects in universities. University debating groups now increasingly resort to no-platforming established intellectuals they disagree with rather than engaging in interesting discussion. There is a current tendency to simply disengage from or avoid the discussion of difficult but important topics altogether. Universities are thus failing and short-changing their undergraduates who after all are paying handsomely for their education. Students thus lose the opportunity to develop the confidence and mental toughness that are necessary in the rough and tumble of the real working world that can only come from the experience of engaging in difficult and uncomfortable debate. At a more basic and emotional level, modern students are missing out on the fun and exhilaration of lively and interesting discussion.

How would a psychologist explain why the nature of debate at modern universities has changed in a generation? Once again, love him or hate him, Freud has described many psychological principles that help us to understand matters relating to the human mind that may be relevant. It was mentioned very early in this book that every interaction that we have with people in the present will have "echoes from the past". This is due to the persistence of *unconscious* memories of encounters with significant figures in our early lives - our parents. There will always but always be some negative *unconscious* memories from the vulnerable and dependent time of childhood. This is because even in apparently happy childhoods every single child will have had at least some feelings of rejection, abandonment and frustration of needs. Some children may have been emotionally, physically or sexually abused. Therefore, we all have hidden (REPRESSED) painful memories and emotions from childhood. Reference has also been made to Freud's concept of "repetition compulsion" in which we *unconsciously* get ourselves into situations from the past - they may seem like "new creations" but they are not. (We may of course, just by chance happen to get into situations that have echoes from the past - but we will still react in the same way).

We *unconsciously* recreate situations from the past for two reasons:

1. This is because this gives us a sense of familiarity.
2. We hope that this time around things will work out better - but they often don't because we tend to do things in the same old way, with the same old mind habits.

In relation to REPRESSED memories, Freud famously said, "What we can't remember, we are destined to repeat". When we deal in the present with matters that have similarities to *unconscious* memories of painful old conflicts and arguments from the past this can bring up extremely powerful emotions. It will not be obvious to us where these emotions are *truly* coming from - we blame the situation in the present, but the origin of the emotion is in the past. This is particularly the case when the matter in question relates to our beliefs or our identity. Also, being seen as right or wrong can be an emotive issue. If our opinion is rejected, this has *unconscious* echoes of being a child in the wrong or being the inferior and dependent child. The modern generation of students has had a more emotionally sheltered existence and a "longer childhood" than previous generations. Modern students may also have spent too much time in front of IT screens and smartphones in their lives as opposed to dealing with real people and being able to develop the psychological resilience that is required for the intellectual rough and tumble of mature academic debate. Deep emotions seem to readily emerge and take priority and cloud logic.

It can be helpful for every one of us to examine our own personal reactions during discussions - and be mindful of Freud's principles above. It is the most accommodating approach to be able to completely oppose someone's viewpoint but to acknowledge and respect their right to hold such a view - and to still feel able to go for a drink with them afterwards without rancour. (Perhaps that was just the experience of this book's ageing author who often enjoyed a friendly pint of beer with someone after a heated discussion with them in what now seems like a different age altogether). Alas, open debate on many subjects does seem to have become increasingly rare in universities and other arenas where debate can and should occur. If someone was to hold a reprehensible and socially unacceptable viewpoint this could and should be roundly defeated by a superior intellectual and moral argument - *and so all topics should be on the debating table*. Shouting, over-emoting and talking over people seems to have become a substitute for holding a valid intellectual viewpoint and it could sometimes be said that such tactics often *actually* indicate the lack of an effective logical counter argument.

A particularly modern trend is to claim that hearing a certain "hurtful" viewpoint in a debate "damages someone's mental health". This can only be regarded as a less than academic response and a way of trying to use emotional blackmail to counter someone's alternative opinion by shutting them up. This cannot be regarded the most academically respectable approach in a university environment. It is clearly somewhat of an exaggeration to describe what is merely the irritation of hearing a different viewpoint as "damaging to mental health." It would surely merely have been briefly unpleasant or annoying to hear it at the time - but nothing more than that.

No-platforming speakers can perhaps also be seen as an indication that the no-platforming side lacks a reasonable counter argument, as if it did, it would surely welcome the chance to put it forward to win the argument. Being completely unable to acknowledge that there may be some validity in someone else's viewpoint can sometimes indicate an extreme overuse of mental defences to protect the self from painful truths.

The most successful current author and a world-famous intellectual Feminist, both of whom have valid views on the question of "What is a woman?" have been no-platformed by universities. This either illustrates that university administrators are:

1. Cowardly and craven in the extreme.
2. Personally biased.
3. Failing in their duty to their students to give them experience in the art of mature debate - and value for their extortionate tuition fees.

... Or all three.

It is not the place of a university administration to take sides in a subject that should quite rightly be subject to open discussion. It is only by reasoned, open and mutually respectful debate that an improved mutual understanding of transgender and cisgender people can come about. It would have been hoped that university chancellors on salaries of up to £300k per year would regard ensuring proper intellectual debate in their university as something they should be concerned about, unless preserving their salary by keeping their heads down is their true priority.

Politeness, a willingness to listen and openness to discussion are the most important factors that need to be maintained - intellectual correctness rather than political correctness.

To summarise - in order to obtain the best for all, particularly in the fraught subject of transgender matters, open discussion with open minds would be most helpful - but with the maximum of mutual respect and politeness during the discourse. Almost everything and anything can be challenged in life - very few things can be exempt from being critically examined. It is always but always an intellectual "red flag" when someone acts as if their viewpoint should not be subject to scrutiny.

PSYCHOTHERAPY - WHAT CAN PREVENT IT FROM TAKING PLACE EFFECTIVELY? SOME RELATED ETHICAL CONSIDERATIONS.

Sometimes patients who feel that they are transgender maybe given testosterone or oestrogen after just one session with a psychotherapist and even top surgery (breast tissue removal) can be carried out on patients in their early teens or early twenties following minimal psychological examination. This is an example of where some practitioners are seeming to focus on physical matters as a way of dealing with mental and sexual matters as if there are no deep and complex *unconscious* psychosexual and non-psychosexual processes taking place in their patient's mind that need to be explored. It as if they believe that manipulating the body can be regarded as the first and best approach to helping their transgender patients. Of course, gender transition surgery can help in many instances, but it is not as simple as surgically changing healthy body parts if the patient is struggling terribly with self-hatred and other incredibly complex buried *unconscious* mental phenomena that involve gender expression and sexual orientation. There is far more to a person than just their physical sexuality.

It is quite often the case that during routine clinical practice one becomes aware of people undergoing gender transitioning treatment who have had little or no psychological assessment other than that which vaguely ticks a box so that they can move on to hormonal and surgical gender transition treatments. It seems that it is sometimes just too easy for young people to obtain hormonal and surgical gender transition treatments. Young people who are considering undergoing medical gender transition are, let's face it, medical lay people and may not know or do not wish to know of the possible adverse consequences. Is this not against one of the most fundamental treatment principles of, "Primum non nocere" = "First do no harm"? Is this not the basis of medical ethics? (Further ethical considerations that relate to hormonal and surgical transgender treatments are discussed later in the book).

As in the example above, undue medical haste might be giving a young woman testosterone after just one consultation during which there was very little psychological evaluation. Testosterone tends to give a definite but artificial "feel good" factor to cisgirls and ciswomen. The unfortunate misleading result of this is that it makes them *feel*, "This is the right thing for me". Therein lies another trap, its bait being the gratifying disappearance of fat from "those places" (hips and thighs) and also a feeling of assertiveness. Feeling good in these ways may make the young patient think that they do not need psychotherapy to explore what is *really* going on as they believe that they have found the answer - or so they think. They quite understandably *feel* that they are on the right pathway and the next "logical" step is breast removal. Alas, the testosterone may have adverse effects on their uterine lining, which may result in intolerable pain for which the solution is hysterectomy (removal of the womb). If, as happens with many women when they reach a particular age, they would like to have their biologically own children but of course, now they can't. Now where are they in life? Now where are they psychologically? This abject tragedy could have perhaps been prevented by means of psychotherapy, which could have addressed any complex underlying psychological factors that made her unhappy with her deeper self, rather than a misleading idea of being transgender. Underlying non-gender related factors such as poor self-esteem and self-hatred together with sexual insecurity and uncertainty are often the truths of the matter whereas the idea of solving problems by means of gender transition may be nothing more than MAGICAL THINKING - which is in reality a dangerous deception of the self. Transgender people can end up suffering terribly from this type of self-deception purely because the hormonal and surgical gender transition treatments can be life destroying if unwisely chosen.

The author can think of no one he has ever come across who has not at some time been prey to self-deception - himself included. The more that the underlying truth is faced, the less suffering there will be from the self-deception. Please remember the saying, "The further we are from the truth, the more complicated and painful our lives become".

Poor mental wellbeing is all too often not really due to one single "seemingly apparent" problem such as "being in the body of the wrong sex" - which could in some cases be more accurately translated as:

1. "Being in a body or personality that I am embarrassed by or uncomfortable with".
2. Discomfort regarding sexual orientation.
3. Various other factors that have led to self-hate and poor self-esteem.

Self-hate leads to self-rejection and this can lead to rejection and DENIAL of gender identity given that gender is such an intrinsically important part of a person's identity and sense of self.

Mental wellbeing matters are invariably extremely complex and the cause of difficulties is often not apparent to the conscious mind.

The concern is that some psychotherapists who work in gender clinics may be a little too pro-gender transition and resultantly, even if unwittingly, not fully explore the mental processes that underlie transgender psychological processes such as DENIAL and RATIONALISATION, which can lead to a decision to undergo ACTING OUT in the form of undergoing hormonal or surgical gender transition. There has to be a high psychological price to pay if a transgender person eventually comes to feel that they are living a lie in the pretence of being the other gender and living in a constructed identity.

A psychotherapist working in a gender identity clinic would be recommended to COMPARTMENTALISE their own views out of the consultation in order to see the reality of their patient's true psychological state. The therapist could then empathically reflect back to their patient the patient's own actual deeper viewpoint, which might otherwise have been submerged in their patient's *unconscious*. The patient is then able to see their own situation more objectively. In other words the patient's true insight into the situation will be coming from within their own mind with the assistance of the psychotherapist.

During psychiatric consultation with transgender patients, the author generally found a wound to self-respect, self-confidence and self-image. It is almost invariable to unearth a history in the patient's earlier years of feelings of rejection, abandonment, frustration of needs. They very frequently gave an account of poor maternal attachment. There may have been a history of emotional, physical or sexual abuse. Instead of exploring these factors, some pro-gender transition psychotherapists may be excessively keen to focus on and support the transgender leanings of their patient rather than explore their underlying complex psychology. *In other words, physically "affirming" rather than psychologically "exploring".*

At present there are no infallible protocols or other guidelines that could guarantee that post-gender transition regret will not occur. It would be absurd to hope that any guidelines in any medical let alone a psychological area could be 100% accurate, particularly in the case of gender identity medicine due to the complex and sometimes unfathomable underlying *unconscious* mental processes. Psychological assessments are sometimes based on little more than *assuming* what is going on in another person's deepest mind. Being only human, patients will always have the tendency to adjust their responses to what they feel is required in the moment to gain what they need.

Practitioners working in transgender psychology and medicine are sometimes people pleasers and *unconsciously* may err on the side of conniving or colluding with a patient to support the provision of hormonal and surgical transgender treatments that their patient has *already decided* that they want. This is an entirely understandable aspect of human nature - in both the patient and the practitioner. It is because of these all too human factors in patient *and* practitioner that caution is the watchword for anyone considering hormonal and surgical gender transition - they would both be recommended to give sufficient time to focussed reflection. It should not be the role of a practitioner in the psychological disciplines to "rubber stamp" a patient's self-diagnosis, which may have merely been made following "consultations" with YouTube and transgender Social Media presenters, it is instead essential to explore the psyche.

Please consider someone who has diagnosed themselves as having a heart problem after looking up their symptoms on the Internet. Would a cardiac specialist hand over powerful cardiac medications without thorough investigation and let a patient take them unsupervised? Is this not an equivalent to what is happening in *some* gender identity clinics in *some* countries? Such clinics in certain countries may be financially or even politically motivated. Some clinic staff may be psychologically motivated because of their own gender transitioned state and are perhaps therefore *unconsciously* swayed by their own transgender situation. This is, after all, an understandable aspect of human nature. If these factors do not apply to practitioners who are running clinics, then this is for the best.
A function of a psychotherapeutic encounter is to give a patient and understanding of their own mind. The psychotherapist's role is also to help the patient in achieving self-acceptance and to help the patient be aware when they are using unhelpful mental defences. This can all help to foster the realisation that the idea of being in a body of the wrong sex is maybe an illusion. Surely it is not advisable for

a practitioner to collude with a patient's illusory ideas, it is preferable to psychotherapeutically unravel delusory thoughts and analyse deep psychological pain. It is clearly also preferable for a psychotherapist to help someone be able to accept themselves as they are. As human beings we are all imperfect and sometimes cling to a wished for and constructed "improved image" of ourselves as a way of solving emotional problems - but this can sometimes be nothing more than MAGICAL THINKING.

It is a common misconception that psychotherapists can "repair" their patient's mind. Psychotherapists have no "trick phrases" or "psychological quick fixes" but they can help their patient to see how their mental defences have led to unrealistic hopes and solutions or false images of the self. They can help their patient to see how unhelpful use of mental defences can cloud the mind and prevent reality from being seen. Please remember that "*reality is relative*" for every one of us, our own reality *seems* to us to be real but is actually distorted by our *unconscious* mental defences. The more unhealthy the mental state - the greater the likelihood of making unhealthy life choices. "Desire clouds perception" to paraphrase Celenza.

Transgender spokespersons have often referred to the fact that transgender people are often not well served by the mental health services. The author would fully agree that they are entirely correct in this as many generalist United Kingdom National Health Service staff are not sufficiently familiar with transgender people's specific requirements. (This would doubtless also apply to many other countries).

There are many risks associated with gender transitioning hormones and surgery but far fewer risks with psychotherapy. Of course, psychotherapy can bring up inner conflicts and painful memories, which can sometimes lead to suicidal thoughts. This in no way suggests that psychotherapy is actually causing suicidal ideas, as in reality, those thoughts and feelings would probably emerge at a later date in any case. Suggesting that psychotherapy causes problems such as suicidal thoughts is akin to simplistically saying that lingerie advertisements cause anorexia nervosa - they obviously don't. It is rather the *pre-existing* effects of psychological trauma and current psychological stresses that are usually the causes. Psychotherapy provides an opportunity to explore suicidal thoughts and deal with them. The immediate provision of puberty blockers, cross-sex hormones and surgery does nothing to deal with any deep underlying mental conflict but instead acts as a distraction from psychological pain - it may only *appear* to be providing a solution.

A most important point to emphasise is that anyone experiencing self-harming or suicidal thoughts and feelings should urgently obtain support and assistance.

Psychotherapy can always be repeated should psychological symptoms re-emerge. It is impossible to reverse the effects of gender transition surgery. A psychotherapist should not just be used by a patient to "tick a box" in order to obtain hormonal or surgical gender transition treatments, nor should the psychotherapist feel that this is their role unless they and their patient can conclude after much time spent in consultation that hormonal and surgical gender transition are the best treatments and can have a good chance of helping the patient rather than harming them.

How many people have you come across with false beliefs of any type but have absolutely no idea of the inaccuracy of their beliefs?

Would if not be more helpful for a psychotherapist to assist someone to come to accept their gender expression, sexual orientation and personality characteristics and also gain an insight into any inaccurate beliefs that they might have? Helping someone to explore their deepest thoughts and feelings about their gender and sexuality during psychotherapy is NOT conversion therapy. Too often launching into the use of cross-sex hormones and gender transition surgery avoids the psychotherapeutic process because the patient *feels* that something positive is being done to help them and "put their life right" but the underlying *unconscious* psychological conflicts remain both unchecked and unresolved. This psychological pain is therefore highly likely to re-emerge if gender transition treatments fail to "put life right". As has been mentioned before, so many people who have undergone full hormonal and surgical gender transition say that their feelings of gender dysphoria and other psychological distress have not gone away. One of those psychological discomforts may have been nothing more than commonly experienced self-hate - meaning that the person just did not like themselves as they were and it was actually nothing to do with being in a body of the wrong sex. In fact, many fully gender transitioned people say that their life has just been made more difficult and complex by hormonal and surgical gender transition treatments.

It often happens that fully transitioned transgender people coach those at earlier stages of gender transition as to what to say to practitioners in order to get what they want, be that cross-sex hormones or gender transition surgery or both. There are complex ethical and moral matters associated with encouraging someone to lie to obtain medical treatments. The transgender journey is tough and often filled with self-doubt and it may be that some of those practitioners who have fully transitioned are possibly *unconsciously* justifying their own decisions to themselves as it is reassuring to see other people make similar choices. It is clearly inappropriate for a practitioner to collude and assist their patients in achieving physical aims that take origin in a traumatised and troubled mind.

One of the most persuasive mechanisms to obtain transgender treatments is the threat of suicide, "If you don't give me Testosterone, I will feel more suicidal" or "If I can't have my breasts removed I'm going to kill myself". Here also, it would be beneficial for psychological practitioners to explore what really underlies such an expression of deep emotional pain - for that's what it is most likely to be. If someone is using the emotionally loaded word, "suicide" this could be a way of giving vent to complex inner conflict, self-hate, poor self-image, anxiety and other forms of severe distress deep within the mind.

The above paragraphs may sound reasonable to a cisgender person but may be regarded as nonsense by a transgender person contemplating hormonal and surgical gender transition. As stated, some transgender people merely regard psychotherapy as a stage to go through to tick the box so that they can proceed to hormonal and surgical gender transition. Psychological exploration of a transgender identity may be experienced as an attack on the very transgender identity that gives comfort. As has also been discussed some transgender people have suffered deep feelings of rejection as a result of childhood experiences and they might feel that attempts to explore these feelings would be excessively uncomfortable. Feeling that someone is exploring their transgender solution might be felt by a patient as a rejection, just as they may have felt rejected in earlier life. Sometimes, transgender people can turn their own deep feelings of rejection back onto the therapist and then forcefully reject the psychotherapist's attempts at care (PROJECTION). Transgender people who as children felt marginalised and as if "everything was wrong with them in their parent's eyes" may also turn this around by PROJECTION onto the therapist so that "everything is wrong with the psychotherapist" - again, the only thing that seems right is the comforting notion of a transgender life solution as convincingly portrayed in the Social Media. The problem for psychotherapists is that the aforementioned processes occur very deeply in the *unconscious* and it may take a very long time to build the required therapeutic relationship that enables the patient and psychotherapist to begin to have access to *unconscious* material in the mind and for the patient to realise that the psychotherapist is caring for them, not attacking them.

Conversion therapy was briefly mentioned previously but to repeat, psychotherapists and psychiatrists should absolutely not try and "convert" their patient to being cisgender. The aim of psychotherapy is purely to deal with mental pain and to help the patient explore the factors underlying their transgender feelings *and come to their own conclusions*.

Many transgender patients feel judged by cisgender practitioners in the psychological disciplines, just as they felt judged in their earlier life - this then results in the patient also turning this around to adversely judge the therapist and possibly stop their psychotherapy. (Just as in the paragraph above, this is also PROJECTION). Quite understandably, some transgender people may both resent and envy their psychotherapist as someone whom they might assume by PROJECTION has a happy, contented cisheterosexual life and this maybe an obstacle to building a therapeutic relationship. But this is an obstacle that clearly needs to be overcome.

It well known that people in their teens and early twenties are at the stage of life in which they are most likely to be an active supporter of what they believe is an important social cause as an "activist" - human rights, animal rights, climate change and so forth are well known examples. These are of course, all exceedingly important matters but for some young people being involved in such activism is *unconsciously* motivated by the need to feel good about themselves, to feel significant, to feel adult, to feel powerful and to feel virtuous - but deep down the young person may feel just the opposite and is compensating for their negative feelings. Some young activists give the impression that they are trying to "find a problem with the world" in order to give their own life some form of meaning and purpose. Of course, having a sense of common purpose also gives a young protestor a sense of belonging to a group, which is a very strong human need. However, for most people the protest phase of life tends to end when the less exciting aspects of life such as a routine job, mortgage and parenthood consume most of their available time and energy.

LGBTQIA+ rights are of course, extremely important and activists are quite rightly improving matters for members of the transgender population. Unfortunately, a psychotherapist may be viewed as someone who is directly challenging and rejecting strongly held transgender principles and politics. This is hardly a position that is conducive to effective psychotherapy. It is important to note that one of the core principles of psychotherapeutic practice is to not judge and to be neutral in matters of opinion.

COULD PSYCHOTHERAPISTS REALLY HAVE OVERLOOKED TRANSGENDER FEELINGS FOR MORE THAN A HUNDRED YEARS IN SO MANY PEOPLE? THE NEED TO KEEP POLITICS AWAY FROM DISCUSSIONS

As previously mentioned, Freud (born 1856) revolutionised the understanding of the mind and developed new approaches for dealing with psychological pain that originates from complex *unconscious* processes. Having opened up such approaches, psychotherapists and psychoanalysts have been able to develop a wide variety of ways of exploring their patient's mind in order to help them:

1. Avoid using unhelpful and counterproductive mental defences.
2. Come to terms with previous psychological trauma.
3. Understand why they are as they are and be self-reflective.
4. Accept themselves as they are.
5. Learn helpful "mind tools" to deal with unpleasant thoughts and feelings.

In "classical psychoanalysis" as started by Freud patients will consult their psychoanalyst several times per week often for several years. This enables a very involved and deep trusting therapeutic relationship to be built up in which the patient is able to divulge their deepest, most painful and embarrassing factors about themselves. Those people who cannot afford the considerable expense of classical psychoanalysis may instead undergo more standard psychotherapy in which far fewer sessions take place but even in this type of therapy incredibly personal details may be divulged. It is often sexual desires and fantasies that are the most difficult to divulge but after doing so and finding that they are not harshly judged by their therapist most patients generally feel relieved to have talked about them. Obviously, in the hundred or so years of the practice of psychoanalysis and psychotherapy its practitioners have encountered much sexual detail and have heard very many accounts of cross-sex desires and fantasies. What is striking is that it *is only is the past ten to twenty years* that psychotherapists have noted a sudden and massive increase in the number of patients with transgender feelings. The psychoanalytic and psychotherapeutic environments have *always* been *the* situation that is most conducive for patients to feel able to talk about non-cisheterosexual and transgender matters - so why the recent sudden huge increase in patients presenting with such issues? It surely cannot be that the very nature of human sexual desire has only just changed in very recent times. Could psychotherapists really have totally "missed the point" for the last hundred years and not identified numerous transgender people? The author will leave the reader to ponder how the influence of the Social Media plus other societal changes have resulted in the sudden huge increase in the reporting of transgender feelings *in only the past ten to twenty years*.

It has to be acknowledged however, that in some instances the mindset that underlies some people's transgender desires will not be altered by psychotherapy. Furthermore, their body type also makes such people very amenable to full hormonal and surgical gender transition. The most helpful course of action for them *is* therefore full medical gender transition and they can live far more contentedly than they would otherwise have done so. However, such people are exceptionally rare. The author has been gratified to see such people as patients. More famously, April Ashley MBE (1935 - 2021) readily comes to mind in this respect - she made much of her life having transitioned and is an excellent example of successful male to female gender transition. The early years of her life and transition were incredibly difficult and it is of course, hoped that in the modern world a transgender journey would be far, far less traumatic.

It is sometimes said by commentators in the Media that pro-gender transition politics are the province of the political left and anti-transgender views are the stance of the political right. It should be remembered that history records some right *and* some left-wing governments have been exceptionally brutal and intolerant. Neither the left nor the right has the moral high ground. Both have been absolutely and abhorrently wrong in so many ways. Modern political movements may have the tendency to over-focus on mistakes of the past about which nothing can now be done *although it is vital to be mindful of these errors to prevent a repetition.* Some political movements also appear to be over-focussed on making accusations of the other side rather than trying to come up with a practical, conciliatory or humane way forward. The critical issue is that left or right wing politics should be irrelevant and that a person should be able to make the best possible decision regarding gender transition. For the welfare of patients, it would be best if politics were not brought into the consulting room or into the committees running hospitals and clinics - the greatest focus absolutely must be on ethics and evidence-based practice in order to give the best possible care to patients. The next section discusses an area that is often not openly considered but is something that is decreasing the United Kingdom's National Health Service ability to treat the patients under its care.

PLEASE BE AWARE OF A SCANDALOUS WASTE OF THE UNITED KINGDOM'S NATIONAL HEALTH SERVICE RESOURCES

The United Kingdom's National Health Service is too sick itself to provide adequate levels of mental wellbeing care to everyone requiring it - whether they are cisgender, transgender or a detransitioner. Reference is often made in the Media to the fact that the NHS is overloaded by demand - and it most certainly is. The other area in which the NHS is overloaded is with ever-increasing numbers of managers and dysfunctional modern management processes. (The ways in which modern parents have to suffer dysfunctional "management" processes in their day to day working lives were referred to earlier).

Hands-on staff in the NHS often feel that the NHS is being mis-managed into oblivion - if you don't believe the author, just ask a random member of hands-on clinical staff - the majority will agree.

When the author was a junior doctor forty years ago hospitals *were managed well* by a very small team: the matron, senior consultants, a small personnel department, secretaries, a small number of administrators and heads of supporting departments. Of course, scientific and medical advances have made treatments more complicated and the clinical demands on the NHS have increased tremendously, particularly in the last quarter of a century.

*But what was **actually** required was simply a **proportionate** increase of the hands-on clinical staff, support staff and administrators that were **already managing well** forty years ago - **not** an ever-growing NHS management monster.*

In certain recent periods actual hospital bed numbers have been *decreasing* at the same time as the numbers of NHS inpatient managers have been *increasing*. If there are fewer beds, what are they managing exactly?

If a car factory wished to increase its production, it would install more manufacturing machinery and employ people to operate them. A disproportionate increase in managers would not get more cars rolling off the production line.

Millions upon millions of pounds of the NHS annual budget are actually spent on the "NHS internal market" in which subsections of the NHS buy and sell services from and to each other. This "NHS internal market" was introduced in the 1990s with the idea that if the NHS was run on business lines the subsections could be given their own budget to manage and if they ran things frugally and efficiently, they could "keep the profit". *Real* businesses as run by the self-employed, limited companies and corporations have to run things efficiently and prudently as otherwise they go bankrupt. The NHS was never ever run like this, precisely because it was never ever a proper business.

Various governments have just kept throwing more and more money into more and more administrative and management "internal market" systems. This money would *obviously* have been better spent on hands-on clinical personnel and patient treatment facilities. As governments changed, they claimed that they had got rid of the "internal market" but in reality just had changed its name and continued to increase spending on it. The NHS now has in "internal bureaucratic monster". The monster has an insatiable appetite for money that, to say it again, should be spent on patient care but instead is spent on flashy offices for managers while the hands-on staff are often treated like second-class citizens and have to slum it. Once again, if you don't believe the author, just ask a random member of hands-on clinical staff - the majority will agree - if they dare.

Stressed, demoralised and exhausted hands-on clinical NHS staff notice that the often 0905 to 1630hrs, Monday to Friday managers have a far less stressful working life and to add insult to injury the managers often have higher salaries. Senior managers are sometimes known as "leaders" but are generally invisible and unknown to hands-on clinical staff — it is more a case of headmanship than leadership. Their mugshots (smugshots) appear in glossy NHS magazines, posters and websites but that is the only time the hands-on staff see their self-satisfied faces.

The management is rarely actually held to account for its failings when there is a scandalous rise in hospital death rates or other unacceptable situations occur. It is far easier to target and blame individual hands-on clinical practitioners than to point the finger of blame at the multi-person decision making management process that spreads and dilutes the accountability. To add insult to injury, senior clinical consultants often find that the "leaders" are on much, much higher salaries. More importantly, it is often the case that sound advice and opinions from senior clinical staff are overruled by non-clinical financially motivated "leaders".

In a proper industrial business such as a car factory or perhaps a building site if someone was seriously injured the local foreman would have to answer some serious questions. However, the Health and Safety Executive in the United Kingdom would ensure that all levels of the management chain would be fully investigated and held to account. This is in stark contrast to the NHS in which management coverups are common.

The British Medical Association encourages whistleblowing when hands-on staff identify any factors that imperil patient care. Clinical staff sometimes dare to raise concerns regarding poor management and management coverups. Unfortunately, whistleblowers are often bullied or hounded out of a job - the author knows former colleagues who have been in this situation. The interested reader only needs to put, "NHS Whistleblower Tribunal" into an Internet search engine to obtain innumerable interesting articles - some are quite shocking.

The author has come across many earnest and experienced hospital doctors and other hands-on clinical staff who have been mentally ground down by extraordinarily complex and dysfunctional management processes and just can't wait to retire. Rather than ensure that hands-on clinical staff are content in their work, feel supported and have good morale the management focusses on productivity - in spite of a shortage of hands-on clinical staff. Rather than ask the hands-on clinical staff what is required to get the job done and provide such necessities, the management focusses on imposing targets. The targeting processes effectively put the blame on hands-on staff and can be a form of bullying. Targets also cynically take the spotlight off of mismanagement and its misspending. Such targets are often accompanied by yet more counterproductive, time consuming and bureaucratic procedures. Hands-on clinical staff are therefore having to increasingly battle against yet more badly thought-out administrative systems (often on outdated and unintegrated IT systems) to try and get their patients treated. It is hardly surprising that the term "toxic targets" is commonly used. In fact, the word toxic is often applicable to management systems and processes.

The author is at pains to point out that it is not just hands-on clinical staff who face such treatment from management - many other essential NHS staff members are similarly badly treated. This will clearly also have a significant adverse effect on patient care.

However, it may soon be the case that particular managers and "leaders" in certain gender identity services in the NHS will discover that they cannot hide behind a multi-person management decision making smokescreen.

Why does this situation so obviously matter to the author? Well, because it ultimately means that money and mental energy that should be devoted to patient care are being lost - and this is very obviously so in the case of mental health services.

Please put this *very recent* newspaper heading in an Internet search engine:

"Number of NHS executives earning £250,000 or more rises by 50% in a year".

Given the parlous state of the NHS - is there any actual evidence that this is money well spent? For each of these "executives" sacked several psychiatric nurses, psychotherapists, support staff and doctors could be employed in the mental health services. It is nurses, doctors and the other hands-on staff who actually get patients through treatment processes. "Executives" having "meetings about meetings" do not treat patients. These "executives" may be jolly good at "moving the deckchairs on the Titanic" - but patients are suffering. The author recalls a senior clinical consultant's exasperation following an invitation to an "executive" meeting. Afterwards he could only describe it as, "Emperor's new clothes management". This was due to the extraordinary detachment from clinical reality and the incredible degree of stifling, pointless and inefficient micromanagement that was part of the "thinking" processes. None of the "executives" had the common sense or insight to realise how they were just making matters worse *and* far more expensive and bureaucratic. The senior clinical staff present at the meeting were reluctant to comment as experience had shown them the risk to their career should they point out the the "emperor's lack of clothes". It seemed that the high levels of egotism and sheer hubris shown by the executives were significant factors in the way in which the meeting was run. It is surely high time that NHS money is no longer be *wasted* on administratively "moving those deckchairs on the Titanic" and instead, *investing* in hands-on clinical staff. As one professor of health policy and management complained, there is no point having yet another, "Evidence poor redisorganisation of the NHS". (Please refer to the reference by Smith, Walshe and Hunter in the bibliography).

The 1950s were a time when UK industries and the NHS were less afflicted by a dysfunctional bureaucratic management monster and the country's economy was improving rather than precipitously declining as it is now. Recent governments have effectively sold off public utilities and watched while the UK's industries were sold to overseas countries - they have "sold the goose that lays the golden egg". The UK no longer has the machinery, or the highly skilled workforce needed for manufacture - all have withered and diminished. A sustainable economy mainly comes from manufacture as China and India are currently proving. Various UK governments have effectively made the country a "financial vassal state of everywhere else" - no wonder the NHS can no longer be afforded. From this former period comes a polar opposite management process in the form of J. A. C. Brown's "The Social Psychology of Industry" - avoid micromanagement, avoid over-bureaucratisation and look after the morale of the staff. This will invariably give better results than punitive toxic targets.

The author painfully recalls working in a 24/7 NHS unit which was "underperforming" because it wasn't reaching its toxic targets. How could it? The *reality* was that it was understaffed and under-equipped because it was underfunded. Needless to say, the unit in question had no shortage of 0905hrs to 1630hrs, Monday to Friday or part time managers. The author is aware of two day per week managers who work from home earning more than specialty doctors who work in a hospital full time.

*Apologies for the repetition - but what was **actually** required in the NHS was simply a **proportionate increase** of the clinical staff, support staff and administrators that were **already managing well** forty years ago and **not** a bureaucratic monster whose only function is to move taxpayers' money around the NHS.*

The author is at pains to point out that the above comments cannot be applied to all NHS managers, some are quite good but the overall effect of NHS mismanagement and misspending is appalling.

In the absence of adequate NHS psychotherapy, for those who can afford private psychotherapy reference to www.genderexploratory.com (Gender Exploratory Therapy Association - GETA) will help someone to find a psychotherapist who has experience in exploring transgender thoughts and feelings. Indeed, please be aware that many detransitioners would say that they were sure that they didn't need to explore their deeper feelings before hormonal and surgical gender transition but have come to regret it.

VARIOUS FORMS OF DISCOMFORT EXPERIENCED BY TRANSGENDER PEOPLE IN CISGENDER SOCIETY - IS IT ALL DUE TO "TRANSPHOBIC HATE"? WHAT IS A "PHOBIA"? WHAT ACTUALLY IS "TRANSPHOBIA"? AND WHAT IS A "BIGOT"?

It is often said by transgender people that "transphobic hate" is a major reason for any poor mental health that they may suffer. It can be completely understood why this view is taken. The term "transphobic hate" conjures up unpleasant thoughts of someone shouting at a transgender person an exceptionally rude and obnoxious insult that makes reference to them being transgender and was deliberately intended to be hurtful and insulting. This would of course, be a totally unacceptable way of behaving towards transgender people. However, what is sometimes being labelled as "transphobia" by transgender people who are uncomfortable in a mostly cisgender society results from feelings that may come as much from *within* the transgender person as from the *outside* world.

WHAT IS A PHOBIA?

The word "phobia" is a psychiatric term that *actually* means a severe, overwhelming and debilitating anxiety due to an extreme or *irrational* fear of an object or situation. A phobia is worse than just proportionate fear.

If a cisgender person inadvertently upsets a transgender person during discussion of transgender matters, to respond by calling the cisgender person transphobic is technically an incorrect use of the word "phobia". Phobia, remember is a diagnosable psychiatric illness. The cisgender person was merely trying to discuss a point, not having a mental breakdown. But the cisgender person would be well advised to apologise as offence is offence even if accidental - but in all fairness in many areas of life it is sometimes impossible to second guess who might be offended and by what.

For practical purposes during writing, the author will continue to use the word transphobia. Even though it may be technically incorrect to do so, it is a word whose meaning is generally understood.

A mental skill that is easily taken for granted and overlooked is the ability for humans to minutely and accurately *unconsciously* assess each other within microseconds. Some transgender people are quickly recognised as being transgender in society although some transgender people are indistinguishable from cisgender people. However, some transwomen and male cross-sex dressers are not so subtle, their styling may be far more flagrantly and overstatedly feminine than most ciswomen would display in a similar social situation. Cisgender people may therefore realise that there is a male cross-sex dresser or transwoman in front of them. Cisgender people may ask themselves why a transwoman or male cross-sex dresser would dress in a way that might result in criticism but of course, in a sense, the transwoman or male cross-sex dresser has unwittingly given themselves a sense of control of a social situation by perhaps *unconsciously* (or even consciously) using shock of those around them as a way of being noticed or gaining some form of social power and influence. Feminists would be justified in making the point that the overt and exaggerated femaleness portrayed by transwomen or male cross-sex dressers reinforces the position of women as sex objects that could be sexually objectified. However, an alternative viewpoint is that the male cross-sex dresser or transwoman is just making the best of their life. This is a matter that clearly requires discussion between parties to reach an understanding.

Humans have always responded to each other according to the sex of the other person. This is a fundamental, hardwired and evolved part of human behaviour - there is a deep and innate desire to respond in a specific way depending on the sex the other person. There is therefore an automatic wish to know the sex of the other person. Responding in a conventional female to male or male to female way has for countless years of human history helped to ensure that everyone knows how to interact and can feel comfortable. Therefore, if a cisgender person is interacting with someone who appears female but it is believed that they were born as a male, the cisgender person may feel a degree of instinctive mental dissonance - "It doesn't feel usual". This isn't "transphobic hate" - it is really just a natural unsettling feeling of confusion as the cisgender person will be consciously and *unconsciously* conflicted as to how to act and feel. The transgender person would doubtless pick up on the cisgender person's instinctive reaction and then also feel some discomfort. It is of course, understood how a transgender person might feel this is transphobia and how frequently experiencing this would be detrimental to mental wellbeing - but this is *not* transphobia or transphobic hate, it is an involuntary reaction being shown by a cisgender person.

Please consider the following two scenarios. The first is an example from personal experience (in the author's younger years) and the second is based on what a colleague divulged to the author:

1. A straight cismale in his twenties meets a similarly aged and attractive straight cisfemale. They were consciously and *unconsciously* sizing each other up sexually and in terms of personality and even status. He was consciously thinking, "Hmmm, good looking. We seem compatible, we might be OK as partners, nice body, quite sexy, I would like to ...".
2. A straight cismale in his twenties met a similarly aged and attractive looking transwoman. The author's cismale colleague thought, "Mmm, if they were a woman, I would find them very attractive but I'm pretty sure they are not a woman. Oh, this feels uncomfortable, how do I act?

Should I give the impression I think she is female and compliment her in some polite but PC way? Blimey, I mustn't do anything that might be interpreted as being transphobic as I will be reported to HR and they will f*ck everything up as usual. Now she is playing with her hair - I read this is a sign of sexual interest. Oh no, this is really difficult". This is not deliberate transphobia, to repeat, this is unfortunately how many cisgender people might react as sexual human beings. The colleague who told the author example 2 said that it was very obvious that both parties felt very uncomfortable. It would be hoped that on subsequent meetings things might be easier for these two people but next time the transwoman meets a different straight cisman the whole process might repeat, then again with many other but hopefully not all interactions. This will be a source of incredible psychological strain for the transwoman and a detriment to her mental wellbeing. An equivalent situation could obviously possibly occur to a transman on meeting a ciswoman.

An often overlooked conscious and *unconscious* cause of social discomfort between transgender people and cisgender people follows and relates to noticing other people's styles of thought. Even though some transwomen can pass remarkably well, they may still demonstrate male type thought processes - "thing or object orientated" thinking or a transmale may still demonstrate female type thinking - "person and emotion orientated" thinking. This is a throwback to our Cavewoman/Caveman days and remains hardwired in our brains. This may be a very subtle phenomenon and one only noticed by the more interpersonally sensitive cisgender person but this will nevertheless give them a sense of inner perplexity and confusion - the transgender person might unfortunately sense that the cisgender person is experiencing confused feelings.

The world has, for the most part always but always been incredibly polarised into strictly female and strictly male identities. It is of note that even many languages are structured so that they have female or male general nouns as well as proper nouns - this again illustrates the inbuilt tendency of humans to involve sex and gender in communication. Transgender people who are strongly identifying with what they feel is their natural gender will find it easier to fit in with the mostly binary nature of society than those who identify as agender, gender non-conforming or gender fluid. The situation could be particularly difficult and involuntarily unsettling for a cisgender person meeting an agender, gender non-conforming or gender fluid person. Again, the question arises, how do they act to ensure maximum social comfort for all? Consider a cisgender person meeting someone who is gender fluid - they will almost certainly not know how to act and will feel a different type of discomfort on each meeting depending on the gender expression at the time. Such agender, gender non-conforming and gender fluid people will unfortunately often be given an additional quizzical "look" from a cisgender person and of course, even from other transgender people who will, after all be sizing each other up in terms of gender expression.

To use a basic comparison, many people are familiar with that uncomfortable feeling of being out of place when in another country whether on holiday or working (the author certainly recalls this when working overseas). No matter how hard you try to fit in by learning the language, following cultural rules, abiding by customs and so forth there may be a sense of not really being part of the culture - in spite of being welcomed. Unfortunately, transgender people can feel a similar discomfort.

This is why it would be helpful for transgender people and cisgender people to appreciate that each other will at times get the interaction wrong.

It can only be hoped that mutual comfort and accommodation will eventually increase with increasing interaction between cisgender and transgender people but even if the situation improves, for many transwomen and transmen there will be a sense of being an "imposter" within the members of the gender they are identifying with. This is similar to the "imposter syndrome" as is well described in psychiatric literature. The imposter syndrome as identified by psychiatrists has the following features:

1. Feeling a fraud.
2. Not feeling "qualified" to be in a role.
3. Fearing being found out.

It has to be said that the general public cannot always be blamed for a transgender person's feeling of being an "imposter" as this is very much within the subjective experience of the transgender person. It is a situation that is quite difficult to deal with psychotherapeutically particularly if there has already been a long-term feeling of poor self-esteem and not fitting in earlier in life. There will also be lifelong physical reminders as gender transition surgery does not always produce a body that is totally authentic, even though current techniques are very good and will doubtless improve.

It is quite possible that the main social world that transgender people will have in which they can be most comfortable in is their own groups due to the aforementioned factors. However, to repeat, it is sincerely hoped that continuing mixing and coexistence of transgender people and cisgender people in the longer term will result in everyone feeling more at ease and society can appreciate the value of diversity. A factor that may impair progress towards this preferable situation is unwarranted accusations of transphobia when there has been none. It is completely understood that such accusations may be made when a transgender person truly feels as it they have been deliberately hurt or deliberately made to feel uncomfortable. However, it sometimes seems that accusations of transphobia are made when a transgender person is experiencing an inner conflict about what is being said.

A cisgender person may think that accusations of them being transphobic are a way to tell them "To shut the f*ck up" - and of course, this could actually be the case during a tense discussion. But in reality it would be better to discuss matters because engaging with other people breaks down barriers and then better relationships and understandings can come about. Even if people only agree to disagree so that everyone can get on with their lives the best way that they can - this would be advantageous for both transgender people and cisgender people. Overly frequent accusations of transphobia when there has actually been no prejudice or intolerance shown by the cisgender person may unfortunately worsen feelings of alienation between cisgender and transgender people - *when we all really need to get on*.

WHAT IS A BIGOT?

When it comes to discussing transgender matters it is sincerely hoped that bigotry can be avoided by people who hold *either* viewpoint, but what actually is a bigot?

A bigot is defined in dictionaries as:

1. An intolerant, obstinate and narrow-minded person whose belief in something is completely inflexible.
2. Someone unwilling or unable to contemplate and discuss an alternative viewpoint to their own.
3. A person who is also apt to being overly influenced by strong emotions rather than being able to objectively accept the truth of long established fact.

Tolerance of diversity of opinion and the ability to politely listen to another person's viewpoint are markers of a tolerant and civilised society - these are the factors that are essential to a comfortable coexistence. The use of any accusations and insults as a form of power-play is counterproductive and not helpful in reaching the situation where transgender people and cisgender people can have a mutually comfortable experience with each other in society. Please recall the earlier quote, "Transgender is here to stay" and therefore we *must* all get on as well as possible.

Both "sides" would be best served if *all concerned* were able to make a point of contemplating rather than automatically dismissing the other "side's" point of view. It would be helpful for both "sides" to look inwards as to where either could perhaps give more thought to their point of view and not allow feelings to get in the way of progressive discussion. It would hinder progress if cisgender people started making accusations of cisphobia. For the mutual benefit of both transgender people and cisgender people an overly forceful approach could be avoided by *both* parties at all cost. *We must adopt and approach that is best for all.*

A WORD TO BE UTTERLY AND COMPLETELY AVOIDED IN DISCUSSION ABOUT TRANSGENDER MATTERS

Fortunately, in society there is now an increasing understanding and accommodation of transgender people but there is a long way to go and further progress would be most desirable - in fact, it is regarded as essential by transgender groups and anybody else who takes a compassionate viewpoint. To remind the reader of what was said earlier - there are over 60 countries in the world where people can be arrested for being LGBTQIA+.

Extremely unfortunately, some people have referred to transgender people as "perverts". The author most definitely did not even want to even write the word in this book *and only did so in order to dismiss it totally*. The author has been horrified to hear of transgender people being referred to as p******** in a public house conversation. **This is totally unacceptable and there is absolutely no place or justification whatsoever for the use of such a word in relation to a transgender person.**

Spokespersons from the transgender population have been at pains to make their point that there is no connection between a lack of mental wellbeing and becoming transgender. They have strongly stated that people from this population often have poor outcomes from care given by mental health services. They have further stated that transphobia has a deleterious effect on mental wellbeing.

The appalling word p****** has been replaced by the term "paraphilia" in matters of psychological terminology and the Law in relation to sexual predation and abuse that could result in physical or psychological harm. A combination of dictionary entries and excerpts from psychological and legal sources would describe paraphilia as having the following components:

1. Sexual arousal and sexual activity that includes desires towards certain people, situations, objects and body parts that are not regarded as mainstream. *Many cisgender and transgender people harmlessly have such desires but to be a troublesome paraphilia any or all of 2 - 4 are also required.*
2. There may be psychological components of domination, violence, triumph, submission, compulsion, guilt, humiliation, degradation with an erotic focus on non-genital or non-human factors.
3. The sexual act may in some instances take place between people of a different generation.
4. There is an absence of full consent. Total domination or total submission may be features - the lack of mutuality is a key feature of the definition.
5. Occurrence of harm to the self or to others.
6. It is an act rather than a relationship - in fact the act may be a way to block the development of a relationship.

Certain psychological conditions that are clinically recognised by psychiatrists as being a paraphilia or associated them are listed in the two main internationally recognised psychiatric classification systems:

1. The International Classification of Diseases (ICD-10).
2. The Diagnostic and Statistical Manual of Mental Disorders (DSM-5).

The interested reader is referred to the dispassionate and entirely practical and academic reference in the bibliography - the Oxford (Pocket) Handbook of Psychiatry. Alternatively, ICD-10 or DSM-5 can be researched using an Internet search engine.

If taking part in paraphiliac sex, deception of others is sometimes necessary due to the fear of societal disapproval and its potential illegality - depending on its type. Some people who take part in paraphiliac sexual activity may carry out many aspects of their life in an extremely dysfunctional way. However, others seem perfectly able to conduct the remainder of their life in an apparently unremarkable way due to the use of the mental defence of SPLITTING by which such sexual behaviour is separated and COMPARTMENTALISED from other aspects of their life.

Throughout society behind closed bedroom doors many cisheterosexual partners enjoy the excitement and tantalising feelings that can accompany mild sex-play, which may technically be a mild paraphilia - but so long as it is mutually acceptable and enjoyable without causing harm it can be a positive and exhilarating experience. Such cisheterosexual paraphilic thrills have been found to be remarkably popular judging by the viewing figures of the Fifty Shades of Grey film series. (Many people enjoyed the titillation seen but it is important to be aware that the film series actually portrays an extraordinarily coercive, controlling and abusive relationship). Sometimes such experiences occur outside the confines of private bedrooms as shown by the popularity of various cisgender Internet dating and sexual meeting sites. Many transgender people of course also take part in such mildly paraphiliac sexual activity. No matter what the gender expression or sexual orientation of lovers, it is vital that relationships are not abusive. So long as there is no psychological or physical harm being done, there is no reason why people shouldn't enjoy a frisson of sexual excitement.

Those who indulge in illegal paraphiliac sexual acts whether they are cisgender or transgender tend to have unhealthy personality characteristics.

It is important to completely distinguish the average cisgender or transgender person from paraphiliacs as they are fully *consenting* to sex.

It is generally the case that men and women* who partake in brutal, sadistic, coercive and controlling sexual activity have themselves been subject to sexual, physical and emotional abuse during their formative years. They are in a sense trying to "expel" intolerable *unconscious* pain by ACTING OUT - they are *unconsciously* recreating a situation they suffered in their earlier years in order to try and symbolically gain control over it and the associated emotions. Some maybe *unconsciously* IDENTIFYING WITH THE AGGRESSOR who made them suffer as a child - this may give them a sense of power and control as a compensation for deeper feelings of vulnerability - as they will have felt as a child. There may also be a sense of "getting revenge" for previous hurt.

When childhood sexual abuse occurs it is generally at the hands of an adult male and the child's mother may be powerless to prevent it although sometimes women will be co-abusers. This is *unconsciously* perceived by the child as both abandonment by the mother and her "giving permission" for the abuse to take place as she did not (or could not) do anything to prevent it. This *unconscious* "mental echo of permission" makes the victim *unconsciously* believe that such abuse across generational boundaries is permitted.

*Sometimes the general public takes the view that it is only men who subject others to sexual and other forms of severe physical abuse and that women do not. This is partly because of society's IDEALISATION of mothers - as was said earlier, a child particularly needs to IDEALISE its mother in order to feel fully safe and nurtured. Such IDEALISATION of mothers consciously and *unconsciously* stays with us in later years. When women ACT OUT in order to deal with their *unconscious* pain they may sometimes direct it to their own bodies (by cutting for example) or on the produce of their own bodies (their offspring). This has been very eloquently described by Welldon.

To emphasise once again, this form of personality type and sexual activity is not seen in most transgender people. There will be some such people in the transgender population who indulge just as there will be some within the cisgender population.

A REVISIT OF FACTORS RELATING TO THE RISKS OF SELF-HARM AND SUICIDE IN TRANSGENDER PEOPLE - FULL DISCUSSION OF TRANSGENDER MATTERS MAY HELP TO REDUCE THE RISKS

A most important point to emphasise is that anyone experiencing self-harming or suicidal thoughts and feelings should urgently obtain support and assistance.

Before someone undergoes full hormonal and surgical gender transition it would be advisable to ask themselves if the risk of experiencing the many problems detailed in this cautionary safeguarding book are worth taking. It is also worth asking the question if not being able to have children is going to be problematic at some stage in life. Ova (eggs) and sperm can be frozen for future use during in vitro fertilisation but there is sadly no guarantee these processes will work. Another significant matter is that gender transition surgery can go horribly wrong with the loss of orgasmic ability. These are all very significant psychological stressors, which can worsen any pre-existing poor mental wellbeing or suicidal thoughts.

Practitioners in gender identity clinics point out that they have noted a reduction of the amount of suicidal thought in young people who have undergone gender transitioning treatments. So far, studies have only been short term and in the more distant future we could conceivably observe worsening suicide statistics. The moral onus is really on practitioners in gender identity clinics to provide scientifically valid statistics regarding the *long-term* reduction in suicidal thought or actual suicide.

Young people undergoing gender transition treatments are getting their own way, receiving attention and feeling a sense of power over adults and this is surely likely to make them "feel better" at least in the short term - but what about in the longer term when these feel-good factors no longer apply?

It is often *pre-existing* underlying psychological pain that may tragically cause transgender people to have a suicide rate 10-20 times the average depending on which research is read. It is often said by LGBTQIA+ groups that this high suicide rate is due to transphobia and a lack of suitable access to mental health services. As already discussed, what may be called "transphobia" against transgender people is not always a one directional psychological matter, it is not necessarily a one directional issue of prejudice or intolerance alone. It can be described as a mix of the psychological confusion experienced by a cisgender person in the presence of a transgender person plus the understandable discomfort felt by a transgender person due to the cisgender person's *unconscious* display of discomfort and perplexity. Nobody would deny that cisgender people can actually be directly transphobic, and this is totally unacceptable - it is hoped that conciliatory discussions between transgender and cisgender people will ultimately help to reduce this occurrence. Unfortunately, feelings of being an imposter in an adopted gender and the sheer practical difficulties of maintaining a cross-gender appearance together with all the medical complexities can sadly have a very negative effect on mental wellbeing.

Whilst transgender treatments are not particularly new, the statistical scale of gender transition is becoming ever greater and the techniques yet more complex. People who hate themselves sometimes believe that other people hate them due to the psychological process of PROJECTION. Some transgender people may state that transphobia is their main problem in life, but they may be shielded by their very own mental defences as to the *true* cause of their mental pain. To put it another way, transphobia is unlikely to be their only problem as there may be a conscious and *unconscious* gnawing dissatisfaction with themselves and other effects of *pre-existing* underlying psychological pain. In fact, living as another gender can actually be very hard work although after extensive and long IDENTIFICATION with an alternative gender, it does to a great extent become automatic and well incorporated into the personna.

The author obviously strongly condemns *any* actual prejudice being shown to transgender people. Sometimes what comes across *as* "prejudice" is in reality more of an unfamiliarity with something that is out of the mainstream or what is consciously or *unconsciously* not expected.

Very unfortunately, *nobody* can completely avoid feeling certain forms of *unconscious* discomfort with other people or even prejudice in certain of aspects of life. Anybody who claims that they don't feel any prejudice about anything or anybody, is deluding themselves or perhaps merely trying to give the impression to others that they are the better person. As previously mentioned, since Cavewoman/Caveman times humans have instinctively formed groups as a matter of survival. Humans were originally hunter-gatherers and there is an optimum size for the efficiency of a hunter-gatherer group and as a result there is an instinctive in-group loyalty *and* a feeling of hostility to the out-group. This out-group hostility is as hardwired in the brain as the sexual instinct - both are exceptionally powerful drives and emotions. Just as it is necessary to hold off sexual activity until is it is socially appropriate, showing inner feelings to another group also needs to be subject to self-control. Clearly, no one should actually *show* any deliberate negativity or rudeness to another group such as transgender people or anyone else for that matter, full stop. No one has the right to actually act in prejudicial ways, we can all have our own views and politely discuss them but not in a way that is deliberately designed to wound - not least because a person on the receiving end could be made to suffer a worsening of their mental wellbeing if they are repeatedly subjected to uncomfortable situations.

The freedom to express views is the mark of a mature society as is the freedom to politely disagree - but with strenuous attempts not to cause or indeed deliberately take offence. The author would most definitely defend the right of transgender people to express their views but as a matter of democracy, those with trans-sceptic, trans-cautionary, trans-explanatory or trans-safeguarding views also have the right to express theirs. All that those involved in trans-safeguarding are earnestly trying to do is to warn against misjudged use of puberty blockers, cross-sex hormones and surgical gender transition treatments - in young people. We are all allowed to be wrong in our opinions and the author himself tries to be open to other people's viewpoints. There was the intention to completely avoid any transphobia when writing this book and merely the wish to pen some trans-cautionary comments to reduce the risk of post-transition regret. The author's intentions were primarily focussed on safeguarding young people.

Avoiding gender transition regret is an important factor in reducing suicidal risk in transgender people.

Also, minimising the experience of actual or assumed transphobia is important in reducing the suicidal risk for transgender people. Part of this is ensuring that transgender people appreciate that cisgender people are generally not deliberately being transphobic but they might just accidentally come across this way. It is of course most important that cisgender people are self-aware to minimise any comments that might appear to be deliberately transphobic. Deliberate transphobic comments are utterly and totally unacceptable.

The author's heart goes out to the parents of young children and teenagers who are expressing suicidal ideation in relation to apparent transgender feelings. Parents are in a double bind. They may not agree with their children undergoing cross-gender treatments but are totally horrified when confronted with statements from gender identity clinic professionals who suggest that without cross-gender treatments the risk of suicide is high. Some children will of course, have consciously and *unconsciously* realised that threats of suicide provide them with considerable amounts of attention, not to mention control over their parents. This is a nightmare situation for all concerned but as with any suicidal feelings, *conventional* mental health care should be urgently requested from the psychiatric services. This is because children who say that they are transgender generally have what can be described as "classical" psychological difficulties *underlying* their apparent transgender feelings.

One particularly awful situation was mentioned previously in which some transgender people are no longer able to take cross-sex hormones for medical reasons or they have had botched surgery or surgical complications that result in them in having neither female or male genitalia. Their bodies are scarred and disfigured. Their bodies are not particularly female or particularly male. They may not be able have an orgasm. They may feel that they are unattractive to people of any gender expression or sexual orientation. "Orgasm inequality" could become a relationship stress between such transgender sexual partners although of course, this is something that can affect all relationships whether they are lesbian, gay or cisheterosexual. Bringing attention to the awfulness of experiencing this sexually indeterminate situation was another of the safeguarding motivations behind writing this book.

As more and more people undergo transitioning procedures it can only be expected that post-gender transition regret will tragically increase, and the suicide rate will sadly worsen in proportion.

EXCELLENT PROGRESS HAS BEEN MADE BY THE PRIDE MOVEMENT. THE NEED FOR TALKING AND LISTENING WITH MUTUAL RESPECT FOR THE BENEFIT OF ALL. GENDER TRANSITION IS TOO IMPORTANT A SUBJECT FOR DISCUSSION TO BE BLOCKED.

It is essential that the pros and cons of hormonal and surgical gender transition are fully discussed between all of those who have a personal or professional interest. It is a statement of the obvious that discussions about transgender matters can unfortunately become very heated and even break down entirely.

There is too much at stake for discussion to be blocked.

Hormonal and surgical gender transition can be very helpful when treatment decisions are carefully made but sometimes there can be very severe side effects and gender transition regret is a terrible tragedy. In this section the background to how open speech and dialogue can unfortunately be blocked will be explored further.

We are all people of the world, every person has a right to free speech - or should do, no matter how contentious their viewpoint. Obviously, nobody should deliberately aim to give offence, be prejudicial or incite violence and law breaking. It is all too easily to overlook the possible consequences of our actions to other people in the heat of the moment when the mind is powerfully driven by personal or political matters. During debates about transgender matters it is not unusual for people who feel that they have been offended to respond with what amounts to threats to inflict actual violence - as **the** most successful author of modern times found out. She has been subjected to rape and death threats - this is nothing but hate. Even if there are not threats of actual physical violence, career sabotage can occur. Some of the authors in this book's bibliography/source material list have experienced abuse.

Such actions and unfortunate disproportionate response only serve to paint protesters in a bad light and lose wider support for their movement.

The majority of people in society are not transgender and most of this majority would not have a particularly good understanding of complex transgender issues. Some would feel inherently perplexed and confused about the idea of someone being transgender. Please bear in mind two considerations:

1. It would be completely wrong for the cisgender majority to try to shut down the voice of the minority transgender population.
2. It would likewise be unhelpful for transgender spokespersons to try to shut down the voice of the majority cisgender population as this would potentially cause feelings of resentment that would not help the transgender cause overall.

Taking the example of governmental politics, it is normal that people can disagree on major and minor points. It is not reasonable for one side to call the other's viewpoint bigoted whilst actually taking a totally rigid view itself. Functional disagreement can be seen to take place in the parliaments of democratic countries although an outside observer may feel that at times there is a similarity to a children's playground (particularly in the United Kingdom's Parliament). At least matters can be fully discussed in the United Kingdom's Parliament, and this is due to the fact that there are rules and courtesies that *must* be observed - if they are not, sanctions can be imposed by a politically neutral arbiter or referee. In the United Kingdom's Parliament this person is the Speaker and whilst she or he may have a political allegiance under no circumstances should this be shown. The Speaker at all times must be impartial. The Speaker herself or himself would be sanctioned if they failed to be impartial.

It is the function of a free and mature society to allow the majority viewpoint to prevail but at the same time protecting the vulnerable or minorities and allowing all viewpoints to be heard and considered.

During the discussion of personal matters, as important as they may be, it is probably most helpful to adopt an approach that deals with the whole person, in order to take a holistic approach rather than focus on just one aspect of them. As important as gender may be, it is only part of an individual person.

It is of note that *both* pro-gender transition practitioners *and* trans-cautionary practitioners have been subject to aggressive protest. All such forms of abuse are unacceptable. Please consider the following methods that might be used for the shutting down of free speech and matters that are not wanted to be heard:

1. The use of *directly* aggressive means - actual or threats of physical violence, forcefully shouting down or physically no-platforming. Unfortunately, words have become weaponised in transgender debates and even used in electronic messaging systems to make death and rape threats.
2. The use of *passive* aggressive means - "taking offence" or no-platforming by administrative means. Taking offence can be an emotionally loaded way of saying, "Shut the f*ck up". It can be a tactic in a debate, and it does seem that in some political debates people give the appearance of actively or deliberately trying to take offence in anything they can. It is generally very obvious if someone is deliberately trying to actually *cause* offence by way of their wording, intonation and body language. During debates it is also clear if someone is merely trying

to make a polite and reasoned statement judging by their body language - but they might still be told by a listener that they are offended. If taking offence is accompanied by deliberate over-emoting, it can be regarded as using emotions purely for effect and is therefore a form of emotional blackmail. Such obviously insincere over-emoting can give an indication that taking offence is being used "tactically" in the discussion. *To repeat, it is generally obvious to an impartial observer if offence is being deliberately given or taken.* It sometimes even appears that some people actually appear to relish taking offence as it puts the person accused of giving the offence on the back foot and the person taking offence therefore gains a sense of one-upmanship in a discussion. At the end of the day, being preoccupied by claiming to be offended is counterproductive in many ways.

3. There are various reasons why someone may actually feel or just claim to feel offended:

    a) Because a statement relates to a highly private and/or sensitive personal matter.
    b) Because there is more than a grain of truth in what is being said.
    c) Because the recipient's self-respect has been damaged or their identity has been insulted.
    d) Because their claim to be offended is a defence of a deep emotional pain.
    e) Because someone has received a deliberate insult.
    f) Because they just want to shut someone up.

If a doctor suggests to a severely overweight patient that they should lose weight for the sake of their health, the patient will likely feel offended due to reasons a, b and c . The patient may "hit back" by "being offended" because of d - but that is not the best response and in fact is probably an indication that the patient inwardly knows the doctor has a point and that the doctor has touched on an area about which the patient has some inner conflict. The doctor was not giving a deliberate insult (e). But the patient may not wish to hear any more on the topic and may wish to stop the doctor exploring a topic about which the patient is uncomfortable (f).

4. It should be remembered that just because someone is "offended" does not mean they are necessarily correct in their viewpoint - their emotional reaction of taking offence may sometimes be due to a conscious or *unconscious* inner conflict about the viewpoint in question. Please remember that someone is likely to feel "hated" or to feel "disrespected" when they already have *unconscious* feelings of self-hate and they do not respect themselves. They may then PROJECT their self-hate onto someone else and accuse them of being the hater. Trans-cautionary commentators have been accused of being "haters" when all they have been doing is trying to prevent harm to young children or young adults. The *actual* hate is regrettably being shown by the activists who are making any hate-filled threats. We often have an *unconscious* knowledge of our faults and weaknesses that we don't want to see and we deal with them by means of DENIAL or PROJECTION. *Our true inner deep feelings are often those that we PROJECT onto others.* It is of course, important for a distinction to be made between aggressive political activists and peaceable transgender people who are quietly working on behalf of the transgender population. History has shown that activism isn't always particularly successful. Generally speaking, only peaceful and dispassionate talks between influential stakeholders produce effective results. Mahatma Gandhi is a shining example of using truth and peaceful means to make progress for the many.

5. In all fairness, transgender activists may, with a good heart *believe* that they are acting for "the cause" but they are sometimes unfortunately alienating mainstream cisgender people who may then become less

accommodating to transgender people in general due to the human tendency to tar everyone with the same brush. In most peaceable democratic countries human rights for all are enshrined in the Law. In the United Kingdom the Equality Act covers the needs of those who have undergone hormonal and surgical gender transition remarkably well. The Gender Recognition Act has likewise been helpful. If it is felt that a change to the Acts is required then an approach to local Members of Parliament could be effective. It is very pleasing to note that in the year of writing (2022) we celebrate the 50th anniversary of London Pride. This is an exception to some other protest movements inasmuch as it has ultimately achieved a huge amount for LGBTQIA+ people. There is surely much more that it can achieve in the next fifty years and it is hoped that life can be made easier for transgender people as a result. For those whose life can be improved by hormonal and surgical gender transition this will be very welcome indeed. Credit must naturally also be given to Pride groups throughout the world.

It is worth thinking about the notion that restricting freedom of expression ultimately hurts everyone as disagreements are therefore unresolved and the subject becomes a festering sore in society. For the overall benefit of all, loaded words could perhaps best be avoided and more conciliatory words tried instead in order to promote healing and understanding of other people's viewpoints. It may be unrealistic to expect everyone to agree but hopefully people can "agree to disagree" and to co-exist with mutual respect.

In any dispute, each side generally believes it is right but rather than embark on a competition for who is "right" and who is going to "win" it is surely better for collaboration to take place that may lead to at least some understanding of each other's differing viewpoints. After all, different types of people and differing points of view add to the richness of human existence.

Merely making a comment such as the suggestion that a lack of mental wellbeing might be related to some transgender people's mental processes is not transphobia and is surely something that could and indeed should be the subject of detailed discussion - if only so that those who are in definite need of psychological care can receive it, particularly in the case of troubled children.

Of course, strong protest can indicate that there is a valid need to deal with injustice and certainly that was the case in in early days of London Pride. In current times the majority of the general population will already be well aware of the desirability of having a comfortable coexistence with all minority groups and most will be aware that there are quite rightly laws against bad treatment of such groups.

There are two directly opposing viewpoints regarding mental wellbeing in relation to transgender young people:

1. Many references are understandably made by transgender spokespersons to the effect that mental health will only improve once full gender transition has been carried out. Of course, *some* people *will* be much more content with life and within themselves when full gender transition has been carried out - as long as the correct decision has been made. BUT please remember
   ...
2. It would be unhelpful to ignore the possibility that for many people it may well be the other way round. Dissatisfaction with the self and poor mental health, particularly in young people, maybe the factors *underlying* transgender feelings and that their mental wellbeing will only improve when psychotherapy is in progress and that full gender transition is not the answer as trying to treat only the

physical to treat the psychological will not be guaranteed to help.

It would be advisable to not overlook the fact that some transgender people find that even if full hormonal and surgical gender transition have taken place, their general and gender dysphoric feelings persist. In some unfortunate instances, their lives have just been made far more complicated and in the worst of situations - they come to suffer bitter post-gender transition regret. It must be repeated of course, that gender transition can be of great benefit to some - it is the best way of helping them. It is obviously critically important to make the correct decision. It would be best for all if these important pros and cons are fully and openly discussed. The author knows all too well from personal experience how easy it is to make mistakes in life choices when young.

The complexities of transgender matters indicate a need for open discussion - *we all have to do our best to get this right.*

Some transgender spokespersons and experts may quite understandably self-appoint because of their "lived experience". Lived experience of anything is of course, very valuable and no one would deny that a transgender spokesperson has a deeper and more profound experience of being transgender than a non-transgender person, but this is something that is very much based on *feelings* rather than a deep professional understanding of psychological processes. Admittedly they will in the course of their transgender journey have learnt as much as any lay person can about medical processes but a true expert is someone who has both an incredibly deep and holistic academic knowledge and understanding of their subject.

There are consultants working in transgender psychiatry, endocrinology (hormone therapy) and surgery - they are clearly experts in their own specialties. However, it is probably only in the future that they will perhaps be better able to predict who will benefit most from transgender medical treatments and who will be harmed - but their predictions could never be 100% accurate just as in other medical specialties. There is so much subjectivity involved in the assessment of the psyche - in fact, a psychiatrist's own mind can get in the way. This is illustrated by psychiatrists being at times unable to accurately assess whether a patient is no longer suicidal and can safely be discharged from a psychiatric ward - there have been tragic examples of this. Certain conventional medical specialties can be more scientifically evaluated than others as to which patients will be best served by which treatment. Doctors in conventional medical areas can give a somewhat more accurate prediction than a transgender specialist where there is a particular lack of concrete evidence at the present state of resesrch. This again points to the need for caution, safeguarding and the fullest open discussion between all interested parties - which is one of the main requests made in this book. The fullest discussion between pro-gender transition practitioners and trans-cautionary medical practitioners with the results of long-term clinical studies available will enable the safest treatment protocols to be developed.

Sometimes Social Media transgender spokespersons glamourise the use of cross-sex hormones and surgery rather than emphasise the side effects and possible complications. Some transgender spokespersons use YouTube and various forms of Social Media to put across their message - in fact being influencers and YouTube performers may actually be their source of income. In some instances, their only qualification is their opinion and lived experience rather than them possessing any professional diplomas or degrees in psychological and medical subjects. They therefore might have a conscious and *unconscious* vested interest in ensuring they remain in the Social Media. Some might be motivated by:

1. Financial incentives.
2. Justifying their stance to others and themselves.
3. Political advancement of the transgender cause. They might block those who oppose them on Social Media. They might do their best to no-platform any opposition, no matter what their academic status - indeed, established academics have lost their jobs for raising trans-cautionary issues. Discussion sometimes does not seem possible, there just seems to be little room for dispassionate intellectual discourse, hence the need for this chapter in which a plea for progressive dialogue is made.

Some transgender spokespersons say that non-transgender people are generally ignorant of transgender matters and of course, they would very often be correct to say this. There is therefore the suggestion that the cisgender population needs "education" on transgender matters. This again is a reasonable point of view and it would doubtless be helpful if cisgender people were more understanding of and educated about transgender matters as this would aid a more comfortable coexistence. Unfortunately, it does occasionally come across that when transgender spokespersons refer to "educating" cisgender people it can regrettably come across as, "You must accept and believe our viewpoint". In a democratic society, everyone must be able to come to their own conclusions. Less than 1% of the population cannot really expect the 99+% to automatically agree. Free and friendly discussion will result in the best passage of essential information to cisgender people.

It would be hoped that most cisgender people would not wish to give offence in any way to transgender people. It is very easy for a cisgender person to unintentionally cause offence to a transgender person when their gender is not obvious. After a lifetime of habit it would be entirely natural to refer to a person with a beard as "he" whilst perhaps momentarily forgetting that they had previously stated that their preferred pronoun was "she". Understandable verbal accidents like this should not stop essential discussion from taking place.

Transgender people sometimes strongly challenge cisgender people who they feel are questioning the validity their preferred gender. Why is this? As mentioned earlier, gender is one of the key elements of someone's identity and so we can sympathetically understand the transgender person's concern. As also previously mentioned, some transgender people suffer low self-esteem due to childhood experiences. Anything which is felt to be an attack on someone's very identity would be extremely painful and understandably reacted to very powerfully - particularly in a public debate. A transgender person has often done their best to leave behind an identity that they were unhappy in or was associated with bad memories and it can therefore be understood how reminders of these factors would be most unwelcome. There may therefore be an accusation that such disrespect or using a previous gender or name was affecting their mental health. Fortunately, they can be reassured that a one-off experience of perceived disrespect would not have a long-term bad effect on mental health - it would just have been an unpleasant experience at the time. Obviously, repeated experiences over a considerable time could be detrimental to mental wellbeing.

Raj Pathagoerer

PLEASE BEWARE OF THE POSSIBILITY OF THE PLACEBO EFFECT IN TRANSGENDER MEDICAL AND SURGICAL TREATMENTS - THIS MAYBE A PRELUDE TO DISAPPOINTMENT

One factor that is not widely discussed in the literature regarding the apparent effectiveness of hormonal and surgical gender transition is the possibility of the "placebo effect" being involved.

First of all, please let me describe the placebo effect:

If a medical treatment is *strongly believed* to be effective, then for many patients *it will actually have a positive effect*. A fairly well known but basic example of the placebo effect is the administration of chalk tablets or injections containing only a salt solution to a patient in pain having told them that they are receiving painkillers. This can be remarkably effective in giving *actual* pain relief. You may ask yourself how this effect comes about. Scientific experiments have shown that psychological processes can have surprising and astonishing effects within the brain and on bodily experience. Almost unbelievably, mental mechanisms can also alter bodily hormone secretion, the chemistry of the blood and can even influence the immune system. Functional brain scanning (fMRI) has shown activity in the brain that is similar for both placebo and actual painkillers. Many "herbal" or "alternative medicines" produce their effect by means of the placebo effect - although it is only correct and fair to say that some plant based remedies do actually have a genuine pharmacological effect, just as they may also have actual toxic effects in the same way as any prescription medicine. If a treatment seems sophisticated and scientific and the prescriber and patient have a great belief in it then it works much better - whether it is a placebo or a genuine medicine.

For some people undergoing hormonal and surgical gender transition at least some of the apparent benefits may well be

310

due the belief and hope that the treatments will work. These feelings of hope and optimism can enhance the effectiveness of treatment due to the placebo phenomenon. Factors that give a sense of control over life and an ability to change social image or identity can feel very beneficial. This positive effect is noted in people who undergo general plastic surgery or have other body modifications. Of course, for some people hormonal and surgical gender transition can be of great long-term benefit and it is genuinely a good thing for them - if chosen appropriately. However, for other people, hormonal and surgical gender transition only gives temporary relief due to the placebo effect and the temporary sense of control and relief that the idea of gender transition had given them. Unfortunately, for some people the placebo effect and the sense of control will *possibly* diminish with time as the personality and psychological state of the transitioner will unlikely to have been permanently changed. As important as the body is in relation to the world and the experience of the world, it is the interaction of the personality with the world that is actually the most important.

On balance, it is only fair and reasonable to say that even if part of the initial good effects of hormonal and surgical gender transition are due to the placebo effect, once the person fully enters into their gender transitioned life and the changes become incorporated into their personality and bodily structure, a definite long term benefit can still be gained. This is because the person is remaking themselves psychologically and the new personality characteristics are incorporated into the brain by "functional cerebral plasticity".

From a safeguarding point of view the author is merely trying to assist the process of fully informed consent regarding medical gender transition treatments and of course, leaves it to the person considering medical gender transition treatments to discuss matters thoroughly with their practitioners. The main effects of treatment are, of course, directly as a result of the hormonal and surgical gender transition treatments themselves but there is a considerable psychological component as well - but if the combined process is helpful, that is all to the good.

DETRANSITION AND ITS DISCONTENTS. WHERE ARE THE SUPPORT AND PSYCHOTHERAPY FOR DETRANSITIONERS?

Doubtless with a genuine and good heart members of the transgender population state that they are there to support transgender people. This may all change when someone decides to abandon their transgender identity and then desists or detransitions. The desister or detransitioner may suddenly find themselves blocked from Social Media, possibly having been pilloried first. The poor desister or detransitioner then finds themselves without a major source of support. They may turn to the United Kingdom's National Health Service where they hope against hope that they will get help. They may see fancy shiny posters in clinics of psychiatry units stating how LGBTQIA+ friendly they are. However, that's just the window dressing and they will be most unlikely to find any suggestion that the psychiatry trust is actively planning to provide specific support to detransitioners.

It is of course, an extremely good thing that the rights and needs of transgender people and indeed the entirety of the LGBTQIA+ population have been put into the public eye. It is only right and proper that LGBTQIA+ people are treated with respect and given appropriate provisions - as given to the rest of society. However, there is relatively little detransition support in the health services compared to the support given to the pro-gender transition aspect. In many respects the life of a detransitioner can be particularly difficult and in some instances, more difficult than for an actively transgender person. The detransitioner will face several types of withdrawal and loss:

1. Withdrawal from hormones - this has very specific problems and difficulties. We could use the term,

"transopause". (Hormone withdrawal should be supervised by a medical professional).

2. Withdrawal of support from the gender identity service being used.
3. Withdrawal of support from the transgender population.
4. A form of withdrawal of support from family, friends and colleagues. These supporting people may have been approving of the transition or at least partly approving. The changing direction of transition so to speak may at first result in a strained or even strange interaction between the detransitioner and others.
5. Withdrawal of the "right" to speak out about detransitioning due to the strong disapproval shown about detransitioners by transgender groups. Of course, the right to speak out is actually still there in principle. Indeed, the detransitioner point of view *should* be heard. It probably won't happen, but on grounds of compassion and equal treatment, LGBTQIA+ could be restyled as LGBTQIA+**D**. Understandably, the LGBTQIA+ lobby appears to mainly focus on identity matters and the words' "identity" and "rights" are generally used far more than "welfare" in debates. The author can of course, understand that approach given the degree of historical prejudice experienced by transgender people. The **D** would probably be felt to contradict the pro-gender transition stance of the overall LGBTQIA+ message. It is extremely unfortunate that transgender people sometimes feel hated by cisgender people, but the other side of the coin is that detransitioners can feel hated by transgender people.
6. Loss of previous dreams of a happy and contented life and a lifestyle that was felt to be "the answer".
7. Loss of self-respect. It is incredibly difficult to admit to others and particularly to the self that a major mistake has been made. This can be very damaging to self-respect although to give due credit, it does take an incredible amount of courage to admit to making a mistake and coming out as a detransitioner. Coming out as LGBTQIA+

is difficult in the first place and for detransitioners this is a *second coming out* and may be particularly painful. The gender transitioned state may have only been carried on for a while to avoid losing face.

8. Loss of physical identity. The detransitioner may feel bereft and mentally dislocated, particularly if they now look like a masculinised woman or a feminised man. There will therefore also be a form of loss or withdrawal from the former gender identity that had been experienced since the earliest years of life and is now gone forever depending on how far transition had proceeded. This will require a long and difficult period of mourning and readjustment.

9. Loss of the emotional and sexual satisfaction experienced with a former partner - depending on detransition status and how it affects the relationship.

10. Loss of mental wellbeing as factors 1 - 9 are cause for a depressed mindset and deteriorating overall mental health.

In the United Kingdom both transgender people and detransitioners hoping for any psychological support will have a long wait to see a Community Psychiatric Nurse (CPN) or a psychiatrist in the National Health Service (NHS), neither of whom will necessarily feel sufficiently well prepared to deal with transgender matters as so few have been on relevant training courses - they may feel particularly unprepared to assist detransitioners. Of course, NHS staff are inevitably gaining some experience due to the ever-increasing influx into the service by troubled transgender people and the same will apply to detransitioners. Hopefully the NHS staff will realise that a detransitioner's *underlying* psychological difficulties are often actually much like they see on a day-to-day basis in other patients - but with an added dimension. (This book aims to provide a helpful and practical understanding of transgender psychology for practitioners in the psychological services and to emphasise the need for psychotherapy for those who feel that they are experiencing gender related psychological problems). The hard truth is that in some NHS psychiatry trusts patients will wait up to a year to have formal psychotherapy although very many patients referred to psychologists by CPNs or psychiatrists don't "officially qualify" for this. Many *do actually* clinically "qualify" but the financially motivated gatekeeping systems result in psychotherapy referrals being rejected. If NHS organisations reject referrals, it saves them money. Rejecting referrals also keeps down waiting list numbers and therefore NHS organisations cannot be criticised for having long waiting lists - cynical but true. The author has frequently had this bitter experience with his general psychiatry patients. Resultantly, he has referred patients to private psychotherapists as the only way of providing psychotherapeutic support and in some instances, this has clearly been lifesaving.

So, now what happens for many patients in NHS mental health units? Ah, yes, a handful of Cognitive Behavioural Therapy sessions and they're "done and discharged". If you are in crisis, then it's the Crisis Team for you, except that the Crisis Teams are in crisis themselves as they are so overstretched and under resourced. It is not the role of Crisis Teams to provide long term care and so the poor patient is then passed back to the waiting lists of the aforementioned CPN and psychiatrist - and the whole sorry referral cycle repeats itself.

The author therefore makes a heartfelt plea for increased availability of psychological health care services to deal with the needs of those who are:

1. Considering adopting a transgender lifestyle.
2. Actually, undergoing hormonal and surgical transgender treatments.
3. Post-hormonal and surgical gender transition.
4. Thinking of or are actually detransitioning.

A further difficulty that may be experienced by detransitioners who decide that they had made a mistake and now wish to have their biologically own children. Depending how far the transition had progressed, some will find that they are unable to. Many transgender people have not been advised to harvest and store ova (eggs) or sperm prior to treatments that would remove their fertility. Even transgender patients who were advised to preserve ova or sperm often did not do so as they wanted to proceed without delay to hormonal and surgical gender transition. They couldn't face lingering in their former gender identity any longer and/or did not like the idea of the medical manoeuvres required for the harvesting - this is because being able to produce ova or sperm may require a period of reverting to the previous gender due to to the medication changes that are required. Very young people who were prescribed puberty blockers then cross-sex hormones may possibly not have been able to produce ova and sperm to harvest and store in the first place as they could have been chemically sterilised depending on the timing of puberty blockers and cross-sex hormones.

There are potential difficulties regarding the nature of the romantic relationship the detransitioner will be able to have with a cisgender person or a transgender person in the future. According to some of the author's patients there may be a niggling doubt in the mind of a new sexual partner as to whether the relationship is emotionally and sexually genuine - even if it actually is.

You may now have detected a major contradiction. The author has repeatedly stated the importance of psychotherapy but is also stating it may be impossible to see an NHS psychotherapist within a reasonable time (if at all) - due to the limitation of funds and availability of psychotherapists the NHS. So what now?

Simple. (It isn't of course, but here goes). An absolute fortune has been spent by London's Tavistock Gender Identity

Development Service (GIDS) handing out unlicensed puberty blockers and cross-sex hormones to children and young adults then referring such patients for surgery - only to be taken to court for their trouble. Other gender identity clinics across the land have similarly been consuming scarce NHS resources. The author recalls an experienced psychiatrist he met at a meeting in London saying that "It appeared as if the Tavistock GIDS was making up as it went along" - the word "development" seemed very appropriate to him. However, a sizeable number of Tavistock GIDS staff members who have felt that they could not ethically continue have resigned and then written extensively about their experiences (Please do an Internet search on this subject). The Tavistock GIDS has treated several thousand patients but one of its senior psychiatrists publicly criticised this *psychological* organisation for its lack of attention to the true underlying *psychological* and sociological basis of some its transgender patients' choices. (By sociological is meant peer pressure, Social Media and home situation). Surely but surely some of the money would have been better spent in the various gender clinics across the land by providing more conventional *psychological* care - obviously not to "convert" but rather to explore their young patients' *psychological* distress that will have been almost invariably *not initially* due to gender issues but instead connected to non-gender related *psychological* difficulties. Such assumed gender issues in many young people had actually been a way of expressing their conventional *psychological* pain. The author feels sure that those who have been the subject of the very well publicised legal cases against the Tavistock GIDS would agree. It is quite conceivable that the Tavistock will be subject to much litigation in the future. In the past NHS "leaders" and "directors" have been able to avoid taking *personal* blame in legal cases surrounding notable failures in NHS care. In the case of the Tavistock GIDS, litigants and lawyers will be able to obtain the testimonies from various aggrieved psychotherapists and psychiatrists who resigned in protest when their trans-cautionary clinical opinions were run over in a roughshod manner by "leaders" and "directors". The "leaders" and "directors" will have nowhere to hide.

Many desisters/detransitioners have had to fund their own private psychotherapy and as expensive as this may be, it is certainly money wisely spent.

Anyone who decides to detransition will find very helpful advice and resources on the website www.post-trans.com (for female detransitioners) www.transback.org and www.sexchangeregret.com.

TOUCHING FURTHER UPON THE SUBJECT OF PROFESSIONAL ETHICS AND MEDICAL RESEARCH. MEDICAL LAWSUITS PERHAPS PENDING

Many psychological and medical professionals are just too uncomfortable about becoming involved in the argument as to how far sex can be changed. In truth, some are wary of openly opposing what seems to them to be a dangerous trend even though many secretly have the concern that hormonal and surgical gender transition can result in very serious harm to some of their patients - particularly in the younger age groups. There can be few medical staff who have not been swayed by the demands of patients to do certain things for them. There is a very human tendency to want to please others, even if only *unconsciously*. Psychological and medical professionals are only human and may wish to avoid complaints because they had refused to comply with a patient's wishes, particularly as too many complaints would damage their career and then affect their ability to maintain their income and support their family. Psychological and medical professionals understandably feel that they have to look after their own and their family needs and any necessary "financial survival hypocrisy" would be uncomfortably borne.

There can be little doubt that transgender matters are "big business" for pharmaceutical companies and private health care providers - who might take a dim view of a trans-cautionary and trans-safeguarding book. The author merely wishes that those with transgender feelings can make the very best decision for themselves in the much longer term as well as the short term. The author has lived most of his life and is now concerned that younger people are able to make the best of their lives no matter how they might express their gender and sexual orientation preferences - transgender or cisgender.

320

Whatever happens, the medico-legal profession is poised to swoop - sooner or later.

There are some gender identity care professionals who are earnest in their desire to help and are exceptionally pro-gender transition for quite understandable conscious and *unconscious* reasons. Possible examples include:

1. Their own transgender status.
2. They have set themselves up as transgender experts and their academic and personal status depend upon it.
3. They fear criticism from gender care colleagues should they appear to be less than supportive of the idea of gender transition.
4. Quite simply, their income depends upon it.

The author has discussed ethical matters with a number of practitioners working in United Kingdom gender identity clinics and it was abundantly clear that they were doing their very best for their patients. They were very genuine in their desire to help those under their care. Let's face it, the very same points apply to most practitioners.

However, an earnest desire may not be enough. Practising modern medicine is now, or should ideally be, mostly based on evidence available from good quality clinical trials and other forms of rigorous research. Although invidious to compare, it appears that transgender medicine is one of the most lacking in robust supporting evidence for its long-term effectiveness. Transgender medical practice often appears to be based on feelings, opinion or faith rather than statistically valid research. Given that the current treatment processes for children and young people are often based on the relatively recent "Dutch Protocol" - we most definitely do not have very long-term clinical study results available to us. How could we? The Dutch Protocol was only published in 2006. At the time of writing (2022) it is far too early to determine the effects of loss of fertility regret and sexual relationship difficulties in the much longer term. In the absence of such statistically valid long-term research, certain aspects of hormonal and surgical gender transition treatments can, in some instances, be regarded as medical experimentation.

It is very concerning that due to the ever-increasing pressure on gender identity services in the United Kingdom it was decided that the degree of psychological assessment prior to the administration of puberty blockers and cross-sex hormones would be reduced in one particular gender identity disorder service. There was no evidence that this was a safe change in practice.

It must be remembered that transgender treatments are for some people given for "lifestyle" choices or in relation to polymorphous sexual desire even though such treatment is being regarded as being for gender dysphoria. Of course, if transgender treatments *really* and *truly* are required to prevent suicide then they can be justified if sufficient detailed and in-depth clinical assessment has confirmed that this is the case. This would of course, only relate to the older group of transgender patients who are better able to give fully informed consent. In younger patient's care would almost invariably best confined to management of their suicidal mindset rather than rushing into using physical treatments. *It would be advisable for young patients to make decisions about gender transition in the best possible state of mind - rather than using gender transition treatments to try and "put" them into a better mental situation.*

It is concerning that in some countries there are surgeons who will conduct the most extreme forms of surgery of any type requested. If the patient wants it and is prepared to pay, the job will be done with little or no regard of the need for prior psychological assessment or post operative follow up. However, just because something "can" be done, most definitely does not always mean that it should. For many forms of overseas "budget" transgender surgery the burden of aftercare falls to the United Kingdom's National Health Service (NHS). It would be helpful to potential patients if overseas surgeons are honest about what really can and cannot be achieved by means of surgical procedures and also to be particularly explicit about the risks. The same frank honesty is also required from endocrine (hormone treatment) specialists. Surgery that is unable to give a functional result provides no more than helping a transgender person to partially ACT OUT the role of the other gender. But in this instance, it can be RATIONALISED by the patient that it is the surgeon's fault, not that of the individual if they cannot fully function in the preferred gender identity - but this is sadly unlikely to be much of a compensation in the longer term. Failed surgery is likely to lead to gender transition regret.

It is perhaps reasonable to suggest on safety and ethical grounds that gender transition treatments should *only* be carried out in the setting of controlled clinical trials with the most stringent and careful long term follow up. Thorough analyses of data relating to satisfaction or dissatisfaction would assist in determining how best to help transgender people in the future. It is only in this way that the safety of treatment and long-term welfare of transgender people can be optimised (as much as it can in any medical intervention).

As already suggested, it is quite possible that those practising in the transgender psychological, medical and surgical areas might receive increasing numbers of legal cases being brought against them in the future. They are practising in a developing and incredibly complex specialty in which there is a high risk of making an extremely serious error. The ever-shortening period between a patient's request for hormonal and surgical gender transition and these treatments being carried out will doubtless be a factor in an increase in lawsuits against practitioners.

REQUESTS TO PRACTITIONERS IN GENDER IDENTITY SERVICES AND THE WIDER TRANSGENDER POPULATION. SOME CONCLUDING THOUGHTS

The author's lifetime in medical practice has taught him some painful and some useful things about being wrong. For a doctor it is a truly terrible thing to get things wrong and harm a patient as the sense of guilt is exceptionally and acutely painful. It is of course, much worse for the poor patient. All doctors get things wrong at times. Sometimes in certain clinical situations even with modern technology it is absolutely impossible to be completely sure what is best for a patient. In spite of the advances in modern medicine a doctor sometimes still has to take a chance for a patient in the hope it will help rather than harm as a result of an unfortunate occurrence or totally unforeseeable side effects. That is the awful burden of being a doctor. Many doctors say that only another doctor can understand this. It is a burden of course, also shouldered by doctors working in gender identity clinics - they are doing what they personally feel is right and it will only be in the future that it will be known how much good and how much harm has been caused by gender transition medical treatments. But the least the doctor can do is warn the patient of any and every known side effect or even that a treatment is experimental and that there may be totally unforeseen problems.

However, to an extent, embarking on gender transition treatments is much the same situation as just described - sometimes a chance is being taken in the hope of helping but there is no way of completely accurately predicting whether it actually will help. There is no way of predicting who will suffer side effects of medications. There is no way of predicting if surgery will go wrong or how badly, even in the best of clinics. To state the very obvious, the risk of a disaster is likely to be greater in certain lower priced overseas clinics. There is currently no way of being absolutely sure who will and who will not suffer the most awful post-gender transition regret.

The other thing regarding being wrong about something is a certain satisfaction in being put right - satisfying because if makes you a better doctor and sometimes even a better person - if you can admit that you were wrong. Being able to show humility as well as humanity is important for all of those involved in discussion about gender transition matters. It is unfortunate that those who are pro-gender transition are described as being on a different "side" to those who are extremely cautious or even sceptical about gender transition treatments.

As war zones painfully illustrate, being on opposing "sides" is a recipe for carnage and tragedy but as the era after the Second World War has shown - reconciliation by means of "sides" working together in a sense of cooperation, mutual understanding and respect is the best way.

Neither "side" should shout down or no-platform the other - after all everybody should have the right to put forward their viewpoint when the future welfare of young people is at stake. In a calm and considered environment it will become obvious who is taking an intellectual and balanced approach as opposed to who is not. If either "side" adopts overly heavy-handed tactics progress will be impeded and lives avoidably ruined for those on opposing "sides" and most importantly for their patients. Neither "side" necessarily has all the answers and all of the truths. Someone who feels that they are completely and utterly right in their belief without the slightest hint of self-doubt may well be actually desperately hanging onto such a viewpoint as a compensation for profound and painful *unconscious* doubts and insecurities.

Perhaps the term "sides" should therefore be avoided and the terms "parties" or "opinion groups" be used instead.

In his attempts to make cautionary and safeguarding statements the author will obviously appear to have a different view on transgender matters to those of the committed transgender population. Other than feelings, intuition and present lived experience there is little to go on as to who will be wrong and who will be right in the area of medical gender transition in the much longer term. We will only have a better idea of the rights and wrongs of gender transition in a good number of years' time, assuming suitable statistics have been collected.

The number of people undergoing hormonal and surgical gender transition is increasing astonishingly rapidly. In the period 2010-11 the Tavistock Gender Identity Development Service in the United Kingdom received 138 referrals for young people and in the period 2020-21 it received 2383. It would be a terrible tragedy, say in several years' time if it becomes apparent that a very significant number of young people have come to suffer terrible gender transition regret and their lives have been irreversibly ruined. At the time of writing (2022) the United Kingdom's gender identity services are under review. The author predicts a wholesale change, particularly to the Tavistock Gender Identity Development Service.

It would be best to avoid a situation in the future when, with the benefit of hindsight that statisticians or medico-legal practitioners might say, "What on earth was the reasoning or justification for doing this to young people?"

Whilst this book may be criticised, hopefully its cautionary principles speak for themselves, it is hoped that it will help to prevent at least some transition regret *but* at the same time those who can make the best of their life by means of hormonal and surgical gender transition will continue to do so.

The author is always most happy to hear of good outcomes for anyone who has successfully gone through hormonal and surgical gender transition procedures. The message of this book is primarily one of safeguarding, to urge caution and recommend that someone has the fullest possible psychotherapeutic assessment prior to gender transition medication and surgery. There's no immediate rush. People have the rest of their lives to enjoy life, hopefully without regret.

Please bear in mind:

Hormonal and surgical gender transition can change someone's previous life so that they can lead their best possible life.

But on the other hand:

Mistaken hormonal and surgical gender transition can change someone's previous life to their worst possible life.

It is the author's earnest hope that there will be a full range of services for both those who can be helped by gender transition and those who are detransitioning. There is unfortunately a woeful lack of services specifically set up for the latter group and once someone has decided to detransition they are very likely to feel adrift and unsupported.

Those in the transgender population with psychological or psychoanalytical training could perhaps write similar books to this. They could explore the trauma, psychological state and sexual preferences that they feel perhaps accompany the development of transgender feelings and how their patients can best be helped to deal with their psychological distress wherever it might come from.

Those who have detransitioned could perhaps also write books and continue to form organisations that can help those who are suffering from gender transition regret and are going through the difficult process of detransition.

It is remarkably difficult to write a book on transgender matters without upsetting either "opinion group" of the "transgender argument". The author offers profuse apologies for any offence caused but hopes it can be seen that the theme of the book was purely to be one of caution and safeguarding but also acknowledgement that some people can live their best life through hormonal and surgical gender transition - *treatment decisions just have to be correct*.

As requested in Important Note Number 5 at the beginning of the book perhaps a future book on this subject could be *co-written* by those with pro-gender transition and gender transition-cautionary viewpoints in conjunction with those who have detransitioned. We must all get this right - *particularly for the welfare of the younger age group.*

The author of this book would like to see people of all sexual orientations and gender identity having a life that is as good as possible for them. This will depend on making fully informed decisions having weighed up the medical, psychological and social benefits versus risks of medical gender transition. Getting it wrong can mean a life irreversibly ruined or at the very least made far more difficult.

To an extent, the onus is on the pro-gender transition psychological, medical and surgical practitioners to accurately statistically justify their clinical decisions. Having said that, a transgender life can appear to be the best way for *some* people even though most cisgender people have a lack of understanding of it and therefore cisgender people might benefit from hearing statistically based justifications for the current ever-increasing rush into gender transition.

As was said earlier in the book, ciswomen and cismen may feel uncomfortable in the presence of transgender people in ways in which they cannot understand or put into words. Of course, it is also the other way around as transgender people may feel uncomfortable in a crowd of cisgender people. It is hoped that the more and more that cisgender and transgender people interact, the less mutual discomfort and misunderstanding there will be. Transgender people can help cisgender people to help them. Sometimes it is not possible to be sure of the gender identity of a transgender person and therefore how best to relate. It is all too easy for the wrong pronouns to be accidentally used whether the preferred pronouns are of the traditional type or are of a newer type. The controversy regarding the use of non-standard pronouns is not a matter that can easily be resolved, and no attempt is made to discuss this matter in depth in this small book. Quite understandably, some transgender people use names that are not obviously female or male or could be either. Transgender people can help cisgender people to be appropriately accommodating as the majority of cisgender people will *and should* wish to be polite and accepting. In a transgender social group, there is often a greater readiness to help each other with identity and pronoun matters than when a single transgender person is in a cisgender group. A transgender person may be feeling uncomfortable as may a cisgender person, but all can be helped to be put at ease with a statement of preferences - but with an acknowledgement and understanding that accidents will happen with pronouns. However, a simple and easy solution that might make things easier and more comfortable for transgender and cisgender people regarding pronouns is to simply to use a person's name rather than pronouns, "Robin is over there", "Robin's mobile phone", "Robin is early" etc. rather than struggling to remember whether they preferred she/her, he/him, ze/hir, xe/xem, hy/hym or co/cos and so forth.

Please let's live together in a way that suits us all.

Discussing our different views makes us better able to understand others and even ourselves - this can surely help to make us all more sympathetic and to be able to comfortably coexist. If we can avoid letting our own story get in the way of acknowledging and accommodating each other's preferences, so much the better.

Mutual courtesy, sensitivity, acknowledgement of difficulties and understanding are the key principles to be adopted. As was said at the very start of the book, we would be better off engaging in each other's humanity rather than focusing on our disagreements regarding gender matters. There is much work to be done to ensure mutual respect between transgender and cisgender people. Transgender and cisgender people have the moral and ethical responsibility to protect the future lives of certain very young people who need to be safeguarded.

Thank you for reading this book.

BIBLIOGRAPHY, ACKNOWLEDGMENTS REGARDING CONTENT AND HIGHLY RECOMMENDED READING

Ambrosia, A. (Ed) (2009). *Transvestitism, Transsexualism in the Psychoanalytic Dimension*: Karnac Books.

Bion, W. (1962). *Learning from Experience*: Karnac Books (1984).

Bion, W. (1967). *Second Thoughts*: William Heinemann Medical Books Ltd. Reprinted Wheaton and Co. Ltd., Exeter (1987).

Blanchard, R. (2005). Early History of the Concept of Autogynaephilia. *Archives of Sexual Behaviour, 34*: 439-446.

Brown, J. A. C. (1954). *The Social Psychology of Industry*: Penguin Books.

Celenza, A. (2014). *Erotic Revelations*: Routledge.

Di Ceglie, D. (Ed) (1998). *A Stranger in My Own Body - Atypical Gender Identity Development and Mental Health*: Karnac Books.

Digman, J.M. (1990). Personality Structure: Emergence of the Five Factor Model. *Annual Review of Psychology, 41*: 417-440.

Dyer, C. (2021). Puberty Blockers do not Alleviate Negative Thoughts in Children with Gender Dysphoria, finds study. *British Medical Journal* 2021; 372:n356

Evans, M. & S. (2021). *Gender Dysphoria - A Therapeutic Model for Working with Children, Adolescents and Young Adults*: Phoenix Publishing House.

Fonagy, P., Krause. R. & Leuzinger-Bohleber, M. - (Eds) (2006). *Identity, Gender and Sexuality - 150 Years after Freud*: Karnac.

Freud, S. (1953-74). *The Standard Edition of the Complete Psychological Works of Sigmund Freud.* Trans. Strachey, J. 24 Volumes: Hogarth.

Frederickson, J. (2017). *The Lies We Tell Ourselves - How to Face the Truth, Accept Yourself and Create a Better Life*: Seven Leaves Press.

Gillies, G. E. & McArthur, S. (2010). Estrogen Actions in the Brain and the Basis for Differential Action in Men and Women: A Case for Sex-Specific Medicines Pharmacology Reviews. *American Society for Pharmacology and Experimental Therapeutics, 62* (2): 155-198.

Greenson, R. R. (1978). *Explorations in Psychoanalysis:* International Universities Press.

Heylens, G. et al (February 2014). Psychiatric Characteristics in Transsexual Individuals: Multicentric Study in Four European Countries: *British Journal of Psychiatry, 204*: 156-6.

Holmes, J. (1993). *John Bowlby and Attachment Theory (Makers of Modern Psychotherapy)*: Routledge.

Hutchison, G. L. (2001). *Disorders of Simulation*: Psychosocial Press.

Joyce, H. (2021). *Trans - When Ideology Meets Reality*: Oneworld Publications.

Joshi, R. S. (2022). Look-alike Humans Identified by Facial Recognition Algorithms Show Genetic Similarities: *Cell Reports, 40,* Issue 8, 111257.

Keysers, C., Gazzola, V. (2014). Hebbian Learning and Predictive Mirror Neurones for Actions, Sensations and Emotions. *Philos Trans R Soc Lond Biol Sci. Jun 5; 369* (1644): 20130175: The Royal Society Publishing.

Lemma, A. (2010). *Under the Skin: A Psychoanalytic Study of Body Modification:* Routledge

Malleson, A. (2002). *Whiplash and Other Useful Illnesses:* McGill-Queens University Press.

Malone, W. J., Wright, C. M. & Robertson, J. D., (24 September 2019). "No One Is Born in The Wrong Body": *Quillette.* (The "double curve sexual characteristics" graph was taken from this publication).

Mann, D. (Ed) (2002). *Love and Hate - Psychoanalytic Perspectives*: Brunner-Routledge.

McWilliams, N. (1994). *Psychoanalytic Diagnosis - Understanding Personality Structure in the Clinical Process*: The Guildford Press.

Moore, M., Brunskill-Evans, H. (Editors) (2019). *Inventing Transgender Children and Young People* Cambridge: Scholars Publishing.

Nield, D. (2022). The Cerebellum Has a Function We Didn't Even Know About: (An article based on a paper presented in the Proceedings of the National Academy of Sciences of the United States of America): *Science Alert*.

Perry, F. (2019 and 2020). *How to Have Feminist Sex - Lessons in Life, Love and Self-Confidence*: Particular Books thereafter Penguin Books.

Perry, P. (2019). *The Book You Wish Your Parents Had Read (and Your Children Will be Glad That You Did)*: Penguin Random House UK.

Semple, D. & Smyth, R. (2013). *Oxford Handbook of Psychiatry*: Oxford University Press.

Shrier, A. (2021). *Irreversible Damage Teenage Girls and the Transgender Craze*: Swift Press.

Smith, J., Walsh, K., & Hunter, D. J. (2001). The "Redisorganisation" of the NHS: *BMJ (Clinical research ed.), 323* (7324): 1262-1263.

Soh, D. (2020) *The End of Gender*: Threshold Edition.

Surströmming, H. (2019). *The "Ah, Bullsh*t" Technique. The Way to Improve Your Life - From the Old You to the New You - It's as Simple as ABCDEF*: Grosvenor House Publishing.

Vaillant, G. E. (2000). Adaptive mental mechanisms: Their role in a positive psychology. *American Psychologist, 55* (1): 89–98.

Von Kraft-Ebbing, R. (1894). *Psychopathia Sexualis*: The F. A. Davis Company.

Walsh, M. (2022). *Johnny the Walrus*: DW Books.

Weinstock, L. (2022). *How the World is Making Our Children Mad and What to Do About It*: Penguin Random House UK.

Welldon, E. V. (1988). *Mother, Madonna, Whore - The Idealisation and Denigration of Motherhood*: Free Association Books.

Winnicott, D. W. (1973). *The Child, The Family and The Outside World*: Penguin.

World Health Organisation (2004). *The ICD-10 Classification of Mental and Behavioural Disorders: Clinical Descriptions and Diagnostic Guidelines - Tenth Revision (2nd ed.).* Geneva: World Health Organisation.

www.4thwavenow.com - "A Community of People which Questions the Medicalisation of Gender-Atypical Youth".

www.genderexploratory.com (Gender Exploratory Therapy Association - GETA). - "We are here because those who are exploring gender identity or struggling with their biological sex should have access to therapists who will provide thoughtful care without pushing an ideological or political agenda".

www.genderhq.org (Gender Health Query). - "A resource & community for people concerned about same-sex attracted young people harmed by medical transition for gender dysphoria".

www.genome.gov (For information on the Y chromosome - The Y Chromosome Infographic produced by the National Human Genome Research Institute).

www.genspect.org - "An international alliance of professionals, parent groups, transpeople, detransitioners and others who seek high-quality care for gender distressed young people. We have concerns about the currently popular 'gender affirmative' approach and favour therapeutic approaches that offer a more exploratory approach to gender. Using 20 different organisations in 18 countries. We don't just speak for a few: we speak for thousands".

www.post-trans.com - "Post-Trans is a collection of detransition stories of female detransitioners and desisters. Our goal is to provide a space for female detransitioners to share their experiences as well as giving an alternative narrative to the common discussions on transidentity".

www.sexchangeregret.com - "You are not alone. Up to 20% have regrets about their sex change. Sex change procedures are not effective, say researchers. Ten to fifteen years after surgical reassignment, the suicide rate is 20 times that of comparable peers. Here we reach out to those considering detransitioning".

www.sex-matters.org - "Clarity about sex is crucial for safeguarding everybody's human rights. We are campaigning to establish that sex matters in rules, laws, policies and culture. We aim to: 1. Establish clarity on single sex services. 2. Enable people to speak up. 3. Make debate possible. We lobby for clarity on sex in law and institutions. We publish research, guidance and analysis. We support and mobilise people to speak up. We hold organisations accountable".

www.sebgm (Society for Evidence Based Gender Medicine) - "Our aim is to promote safe, compassionate, ethical and evidence-informed healthcare for children, adolescents and young adults with gender dysphoria".

www.transgendertrend.com - "We are an organisation of parents, professionals and academics based in the UK who are concerned about the current trend to diagnose children as transgender, including the unprecedented number of teenage girls suddenly self-identifying as 'trans'. We are also concerned about legislation which places transgender rights above the right for safety for girls and young women in public lavatories and changing rooms along with fairness for girls in sport". (The originator of Transgender Trend, Stephanie Davies-Arai has been awarded to British Empire Medal for her indefatigable and valuable work in children's welfare).

www.transback.org - "While some decisions taken in life are permanent, some are not. A few of these decisions are life-altering. Allow your TransBack Family to assist you through you next life-changing journey. We are here to encourage you, support you and help you create your own happy identity".

YouTube:

Blaire White. She is a transwoman who has a million subscribers. Her views are generally similar to those in this book and this allows the reader to see that the author's views are agreed with by a highly significant transgender figure. Whether you agree or disagree with the author, please refer and subscribe to Blaire for a very reasonable, mature and balanced viewpoint. Her excellent discussions with Buck Angel a similarly famous transman are illuminating and give an extremely fair and equally balanced viewpoint.

The Offensive Tranny. The name of the broadcaster may in and of itself be offensive. However, the well-meaning and balanced opinions from this transman would be invaluable for parents of transgender children.

BV - #0006 - 060123 - C1 - 229/152/19 - PB - 9781913839925 - Gloss Lamination